Managing Displacement

BORDERLINES

For more books in the series, see p. vi.

Managing Displacement

Refugees and the Politics of Humanitarianism

JENNIFER HYNDMAN

BORDERLINES, VOLUME 16

 University of Minnesota Press

Minneapolis

London

The University of Minnesota Press gratefully acknowledges permission to reprint the following articles. Chapter 2 originally appeared in an earlier form as "Border Crossings," *Antipode* 29, no. 2 (1997): 149–76; copyright 1997 Blackwell Publishers. Chapter 3 originally appeared in an earlier form as "Managing Difference: Gender and Culture in Humanitarian Emergencies," *Gender, Place, and Culture: A Journal of Feminist Geography* 5, no. 3 (1998); published by Carfax Publishing Ltd. and reprinted with permission of the publisher, Carfax Publishing Ltd., P.O. Box 25, Abingdon, Oxfordshire, OX14 3UE, United Kingdom.

Published by the University of Minnesota Press
111 Third Avenue South, Suite 290
Minneapolis, MN 55401-2520
http://www.upress.umn.edu

Library of Congress Cataloging-in-Publication Data

Hyndman, Jennifer.
    Managing displacement : refugees and the politics of humanitarianism / Jennifer Hyndman.
        p.   cm. — (Borderlines ; v. 16)
    Includes bibliographical references and index.
    ISBN 0-8166-3353-3 (hc : acid-free paper) — ISBN 0-8166-3354-1 (pbk. : acid-free paper)
    1. Office of the United Nations High Commissioner for Refugees.
2. Refugees—International cooperation.   3. Humanitarian assistance—Political aspects.   4. Political refugees.   5. Refugee camps.   I. Title.
II. Borderlines (Minneapolis, Minn.) ; v. 16.
HV640.3 .H85 2000
362.87'526—dc21   99-056469

Printed in the United States of America on acid-free paper

The University of Minnesota is an equal-opportunity educator and employer.

11 10 09 08 07 06 05 04 03 02 01 00   10 9 8 7 6 5 4 3 2 1

To Mary and Lou

BORDERLINES

Contents

Acknowledgments

Many people, from very distinct walks of life, have contributed to this work. Thoughtful provocation and suggestions from Dan Hiebert were indispensable to the writing of this book. Gerry Pratt and Wenona Giles each provided valuable insights on earlier drafts of the manuscript. Thanks to Derek Gregory for his theoretical contributions and enthusiasm in the project's early stages. Julie Murphy Erfani, Mike Shapiro, and Bo Viktor Nylund taught me the value of interdisciplinary collaboration and perspectives, while Katharyne Mitchell proved to be a strong and instructive influence within geography. David Ley, Isabel Dyck, and Tamar Mayer provided close readings and constructive comments as well. In particular, I would like to thank Nadine Schuurman for her exhaustive editorial and cartographic contributions, which were exceeded only by her encouragement when the task seemed endless.

I wish to thank my parents, Mary and Lou Hyndman, for their infinite support, patience, and inspiration. Their interest in the book has been genuine, despite unusual detours to sites off their map. The encouragement of Anne Fanning is much appreciated, as is the influence of Lynn Eyton, both of whom have distinctive commitments to social issues. The incisive words of Rose Marie Kennedy were also formative to the project. I benefited daily from the support and mindful provocation of my colleagues at Arizona State University (ASU) West and from the valuable assistance provided by the

Fletcher Library staff. Research assistance from Noel Schaus and Laura Miller was most appreciated.

The research presented examines the workings of a large and dynamic UN organization. I am very grateful for the cooperation of the Office of the UN High Commissioner for Refugees (UNHCR) at so many levels. I would like to thank Mr. Carole Faubert, a former Country Representative for UNHCR in Kenya, for his endorsement of this project from the beginning. In Geneva and Nairobi, other staff members who assisted in organizing everything from interviews to transport and housing include Annette Ludeking, Binod Sijapati, and Nana Mallet. In the camps, I am indebted to Jacinta Goveas, Ann Carlson, and Gunther Scheske, who made my stay in Dadaab both enjoyable and productive. The translation skills and contribution of Magala were crucial to the interviews conducted with Somali refugees in the camps. I thank Koru Mohammed, Fantu Tadesse, and the rest of the UNHCR compound staff for their work and insights during my months in the camps. For reasons of confidentiality, I cannot name but want to thank the senior staff and other professional employees at UNHCR, NGOs, and government offices who took time to meet with me for interviews. I would also like to thank a number of others who made my contact with UNHCR a positive experience: Mrs. Guenet Guebre-Christos, Martin Staunton, Yukiko Haneda, Askali Benti, and Kristina Jonsson. The help of the staffs at CARE in Dadaab and the Red Cross in Mombasa was also much appreciated.

Beyond UNHCR, in other UN agencies, I enlisted the help of Antonio Donini, Nora Niland, and Monika Sandvik-Nylund at the Office for the Coordination of Humanitarian Affairs (OCHA), for which I am grateful. Many thanks to Angela Ravens-Roberts and Philip O'Brien at UNICEF who shared their insights into the shifting landscapes of humanitarian assistance. The usual disclaimer applies: the errors are my own, as are the conclusions drawn.

The geography of research activities was, in this case, far-reaching. In New York, Ann Carlson's apartment was a home away from home. In Geneva, Bernadette Eygendaal was a gracious host throughout my stay. In between stops, the hospitality shown by the Perkins family in Kent was extraordinarily generous. The various flats of Laurence de Sury, now Le Masne, in Paris provided comfortable refuge and great company on more than one occasion. Thanks to all for both putting me up and putting up with me, sometimes for extended periods.

Funders' contributions to research activities presented here made this work possible. The Social Sciences and Humanities Research Council of Canada (SSHRC) generously provided me with a fellowship throughout much of the research process. The Gender Unit of York University's Centre for Refugee Studies contributed a critical research grant to launch the project in 1994. The Canadian-based International Development Research Centre (IDRC) also provided significant funding for the Kenyan component of the project under its Young Canada Researcher Award program. A Scholarly Research and Creative Activities grant from Arizona State University West provided important support for the final phase of research.

Finally, I would like to thank the book's editors, whose interest and attention to detail have been unfaltering. Mike Shapiro and David Campbell provided unqualified support for the project from its inception. And without the interest and hard work of Carrie Mullen at the University of Minnesota Press, you would not be reading this.

Abbreviations

CARE	CARE International in Kenya (Canadian NGO)
CBO	Cross-Border Operation
CIDA	Canadian International Development Agency
DHA	Department of Humanitarian Affairs
FGM	female genital mutilation
FIDA	Federación Internacional de Abogadas (International Federation of Women Lawyers)
GAD	Gender and Development
GOK	government of Kenya
ICRC	International Committee of the Red Cross
IDP	internally displaced person
IFRC	International Federation of the Red Cross
IMF	International Monetary Fund
MSF	Médecins sans Frontières (Doctors without Borders)
NATO	North Atlantic Treaty Organization
NGO	nongovernmental organization
OCHA	Office for the Coordination of Humanitarian Affairs
POP	People-Oriented Planning Process
QIP	quick impact project
SAP	structural adjustment program

SPLA	Sudanese People's Liberation Army
SSEP	Social Services and Education Programme (CARE)
UNHCR	UN High Commissioner for Refugees
UNICEF	UN Children's Emergency Fund
UNITAF	Unified Task Force
UNOSOM	UN Operation in Somalia
WAD	Women and Development
WID	Women in Development
WVV	Women Victims of Violence project

Introduction

Forced to move from their homes to another country, refugees embody a visceral human geography of dislocation. The involuntary migration of bodies across space, however, is neither passive nor apolitical. In the 1990s, humanitarian discourse positions migrants in particular ways, while cultural politics are negotiated by a range of subjects unequally linked within the vast network of the international humanitarian regime. Humanitarianism is the site at which the projects of development and relief are being contested and recast in light of new geopolitical landscapes and neoliberal economies that transgress the boundaries of states.

This book was spawned by three forays into humanitarianism. In Kenya, I worked for a nongovernmental organization (NGO) in Walda refugee camp during a period when its population was growing exponentially because of fighting in the Sidamo region of Ethiopia. In Somalia, I was employed by a UN agency as a field officer in Bardera, a town in the southern part of the country not far from the Kenyan-Somalian border. Finally, I returned to Kenya as a researcher based primarily at the United Nations High Commissioner for Refugees (UNHCR) suboffice for three refugee camps on the other side of this same border. I began mapping the organization of humanitarian aid, interviewing its recipients and providers, and interrogating its practices.

Each of these experiences moved me to query the practices of those administering humanitarian locations and to theorize mobility for people "out of place"—those uprooted from their homes because of fighting, famine, and fear. In 1993, I read a significant amount of feminist, postcolonial, and poststructuralist theory and analyzed the claims in the context of my work in Somalia. These frames of reference, together with my more materialist leanings, rendered intelligible what were often chaotic, frequently ad hoc, and always uneven social and spatial relations of power. At first these links were tentative. Refugees appeared as subaltern subjects.[1] Camps operated akin to Foucauldian youth reform colonies.[2] Despite its (and my) good intentions, I began to see that humanitarian work functioned at times as a colonialism of compassion. Though somewhat crude, these connections attested to the need for more, not less, theory in the ever-practical domain of humanitarian assistance. But one might argue that theoreticians do not get out much. Just as policy makers need to meet their constituents and hear their plaintive anecdotes from time to time, theoreticians of humanitarianism need to see, hear, and analyze life in conflict zones and refugee camps, for such observations provide important insights and fuel the development of fuller, more accountable theory.

My experiences in Somalia led me to believe that the hegemony of the nation-state was in crisis. The relative fiction of the Somali state became clear. Except for its role as a politicized venue for pan-Somali nationalism and as an interlocutor in Cold War agreements on military alliance and aid to Somalia, it was a country precariously sewn together. Not only was its governance historically a regional composite of a different scale,[3] but its borders were edges designed and designated by colonial powers in the nineteenth century. These political borders were defended by colonial authorities in Kenya against the wishes and struggles of Somalis both inside and outside Kenya and were contested by Somali people during the Ogaden War of the 1970s. Borders are cartographies of struggle,[4] and refugees are expressions of such struggle.

Nation-states, borders, and refugees belong to a discourse of conventional geopolitics. Refugees, in the modern sense, are a creation of international law in this century. Though refugees have by no means disappeared, the international refugee regime shows signs of giving way to more complex humanitarian emergencies—distinct modes of multilateral response to human displacement. Conventional geopolitics and neorealist international relations have been carefully and convincingly countered by critical, poststructuralist, feminist, and Foucauldian commentators of international relations and political geography.[5] My aim is to reinforce the importance of such work and to extend it by grounding my analysis in the operations of one UN organization that crosses political borders, raises funds from multiple governments, assists those displaced by conflict, and organizes protection for refugees.

STUDYING UP

Within the realm of assistance to refugees and the displaced, the most powerful UN humanitarian agency is arguably UNHCR. By focusing on the culture, policies, and operations of this organization, my analysis embodies, in part, an ethnographic perspective. It includes an appreciation of realpolitik within the realm of geopolitics, but it also engages with cultural politics and dominant discourses of managing difference. The tendency of refugee studies as a subdiscipline and of area studies in geography has been to reinscribe the importance of specific humanitarian crises and groups of refugees in particular locations. This has occurred at the expense of a sustained examination of practices that cross borders, of policies that manage difference according to organizational and legal standards across space, and of strategies that aim to contain human displacement in highly politicized ways.[6]

Both anthropologists and geographers have issued the call to "study up," to analyze and theorize the institutions, organizations, and bodies that govern human relations rather than to study the governed themselves.[7] This repositioning of the academic gaze may well create its own problems of access, duplicity, and reliance on vision, but it also presents new opportunities for analyzing pervasive issues of gender and cultural politics, racism, and strategic safe spaces. I speak of duplicity because of my positioning both inside and outside the humanitarian project, at once a participant and a critic. I was and remain as concerned about effective planning and provision of assistance as anyone working in good faith for the myriad NGOs and UN agencies on the ground. And yet I cannot comprehend certain assumptions and standard practices in the refugee camps.

Headcounts—the term refers to census-taking procedures in the camps—provide an example of operations that trouble me. That one group of people with certain credentials, political status, and cultural capital could round up another group of people with far less political status and power exploded my sense of what *humanitarian* could mean. To rate cultures and nationalities as cooperative or uncooperative in this process, as was done in Kenya, seems more an exercise in social control than in uniting nations. UNHCR staff have assessed Somali and Sudanese refugees as uncooperative groups, a determination that has had practical and political implications for organizing headcounts.[8] Accurate numbers are a legitimate goal, but the means of achieving them should not undermine it.

Expatriates living in close proximity to refugee camps exacerbate and magnify political, economic, and cultural differences. The social hierarchy of refugees, NGO personnel, and UN staff is spatialized in distinct and segregated spaces. Refugees stay in camps; NGO and UN employees generally reside in the compounds of their respective organizations. Within the UNHCR compound, where I stayed and within which I conducted my research, the hierarchy is replicated on a smaller scale. A select group of refugees worked on "incentive" (about U.S.$2 per day), maintaining the compound, cleaning, cooking, and doing laundry for UN staff. They live in tents along the perimeter of the compound. Kenyan staff working for UNHCR earn competitive wages in their national context but take home a fraction of the salary and benefits that international staff receive. At the time of my visit, the Kenyan staff lived in small rooms with shared bathroom facilities. International staff lived in larger, if modest, duplexes. I was a beneficiary of the privileges afforded international staff, even as an outside researcher, living in a secure compound with the best food and accommodations available. As a former employee, I was generously hosted and my queries tolerated.

UNHCR IN CONTEXT

To state clearly my purpose in this book is critical, given the current crisis and imminent change in the realm of humanitarian operations. I am not interested in simply criticizing UNHCR's staff or its particular actions. Some of these people—like their NGO counterparts—are among the most dedicated of employees in frontline emergency positions. Rather, I am concerned with the conception, organization, and deployment of humanitarian measures within distinct geopolitical and cultural contexts. UNHCR is an obvious focus of inquiry because it is the largest and arguably the most powerful designated humanitarian agency in the world. As states increasingly shirk their legal obligations to those who seek asylum and pare down their respective welfare states, they in a sense reinvent themselves by looking to multilateral organizations, like UNHCR, to take care of the refugee problem.[9] UNHCR is poised to do the job and is paid sizable sums by states to provide humanitarian assistance where donors and UNHCR agree it is needed. The question is not whether UNHCR could do a better job, which it probably can, but whether the context in which it operates enables the organization to take consistent and effective steps in safeguarding displaced people at risk. Should UNHCR be compelled by states to take over responsibilities that formerly belonged to them, and if so, does this shift involve human cost? Theoretically speaking, is the apparent evanescence of state responsibility in humanitarian affairs a productive move away from the problems of an outdated state-centric geopolitics? Or is it simply the galvanization of state interests on a different scale, a scale that dislocates displaced persons further through distancing scripts and geographical segregation administered by a designated UN agency?[10]

The dedication and important work of many humanitarian staff should not be undermined by a sustained and constructive critique of the organizing principles (or lack thereof) of the UN agency that employs them. No amount of goodwill and professional talent in emergency situations can correct foundational assumptions that are outdated, questionable practices that are institutionalized and disseminated by more senior staff, and the absence of a clear, accountable, and current mandate. My own assessment of UNHCR echoes that of Guy Goodwin-Gill, a well-known scholar in international refugee law:

> That UNHCR still has a credible reputation in certain circles is entirely due to the performance, commitment and sacrifice of individuals, in field and headquarters posts, who are able to maintain a protection dialogue with governments and non-governmental organizations, but also somehow survive a system apparently inimical not only to spouses and children, but even to staff themselves.[11]

I have witnessed, and in some cases experienced, the burnout, depression, sickness, and loss of personal relationships that result from UN employees giving everything to their work. Younger staff, in particular, are prey to these conditions, as they are more likely to be working on the front line, in difficult nonfamily duty stations, and under a demanding hierarchy of superiors. Ambition, talent, energy, and commitment characterized most of the junior staff I met, yet almost all of them were on finite and uncertain contracts with the organization. If any one thing characterizes the camps and humanitarian work generally, it is the grinding and constant state of displacement: of staff, of refugees, of local people, and of language. In the words of one commentator, "[m]any of these [humanitarian] agencies do their best under horrific conditions—and sometimes their best is good. But all too often the help they can offer is at best a short-term palliative."[12] This claim forms the basis of the book.

The performance of UNHCR has long been and continues to be monitored either directly or indirectly by a number of credible watchdog organizations, such as Amnesty International, the U.S. Committee for Refugees, and the Lawyers Committee for Human Rights, to name but a few. My concern here is less with monitoring than with analyzing the taken-for-granted practices of ordering disorder and disciplining displacement. Some of these practices occur at roundtables in Geneva, others locally, at the scale of the camps. They challenge the meanings of borders and serve to undermine the notion of discrete states in conflict zones worldwide.

Michael Shapiro distinguishes between strategic and ethnographic perspectives of mapping cultures of war.[13] Whereas strategic perspectives tend to deepen identity attachments and formal boundaries, ethnographic approaches aim to unsettle such attachments by questioning the boundary-making narratives through which they are shaped. Shapiro emphasizes the latter in his own work in an attempt to undo the identity attachments of strategic discourses. This intervention is important, but in the case of humanitarian issues that require practical responses of some kind, it is insufficient. Through ethnographic perspectives, however, embedded identities and strategic ways of seeing conflict and its consequences can be both undone and reconstructed. An examination of humanitarian operations after the Cold War reveals that the deployment of transnational practices that at once undo the taken-for-granted identities produced by nation-states and forge links across axes of difference without effacing them is a viable option.[14] Transnational practices are a necessary, if not sufficient, step toward dis-ordering the conventions of statehood and what is often referred to as neorealist or classical geo-politics. Transnational practices contribute to a feminist geopolitics: "new ways of seeing, theorizing, and practicing the connections be-tween space and politics and between nature and culture."[15] They preclude the simplistic dichotomy of dependency or nationalism within modernity and instead navigate between nations and across space, crosscutting the dominant framing of territorial sovereignty.

A number of other feminist scholars have taken similar ap-proaches, endorsing a disturbance of identities based on formal boundaries and an analysis of transboundary, or transnational, link-ages.[16] The emerging literature on transnationalism, both from post-structuralist and materialist perspectives, attests to the interest and importance of challenging the primacy of the nation-state as *the* venue of human migration.[17] Donna Haraway is concerned with the processes of power that inscribe boundaries, and she notes that "ob-jects are boundary projects."[18] The task of challenging assumed bor-ders, interrogating the categories they designate, and questioning the identities and meanings they engender is a critical project for post-disciplinary discussions of displacement, contemporary geopolitics, and cultural politics.

Feminist politics are vital to my project. I include but do not limit my analysis to the sets of unequal relationships among people based on gender, class, race, sexuality, nationality, and ethnicity. I contend, however, that the defining differences of these categories are insuffi-cient in both exposing the power relations and practices that posi-tion groups of people in hierarchical relations to others and in open-ing up spaces of connection, affinity, and affiliated actions. My research attempts to decipher the processes and criteria that spatially separate distinct groups based on their rank in tacit cultural and po-litical hierarchies. The various modalities of organizing humanitari-an help shape the mobility of displaced people at the finest scale.

Existing criticism of gendered states and masculinist practices within multilateral organizations and of the mutually constitutive processes of militarization and masculinity provide solid feminist analyses at a number of scales. The work of feminist scholars Cyn-thia Enloe, Sandra Whitworth, and Spike Petersen—among others—provides a strong impetus to look beyond gender-blind identity markers of state and citizenship, and their attendant institutions, for links that leak across international borders and connections that grow out of dispersed, or diasporic, notions of nation.[19]

My aim is to locate the reader within moral proximity to refugees and the spaces in which they live—to bridge some of the carefully constructed distance between "us" and "them." Feminist theory and politics expose violent representations and practices; they also call for attempts to invoke change in the face of such violence. Refugees and other displaced persons are most often constructed as "others," and increasingly their identities are territorialized through a discourse of preventive protection, safe havens, and the right to remain at home. Forced migrants are most often represented by others: the international media, humanitarian agencies, and human rights organizations. Though good intentions often fuel these representations, the politics of representation have become, in some cases, more important than humanitarian operations on the ground. Public funding of assistance to displaced persons depends, in large part, on representing need as urgent and deserving. Donor governments tacitly understand that aid has strategic value.

Selected feminist theory is important to my argument because it serves to expose and politicize the deployment of distancing scripts and of distant spaces in which refugees are assisted. Following Judith Butler, certain speech locations are included in representational practices; others are not. Refugees are, I will argue, often relegated to the domain of the excluded, or the "abject," or in Spivak's conceptualization, the "subaltern."[20] Who, in a crisis of mass displacement, is the subject and who is the "abject"? Despite occasional alarming images of displaced people in states of extreme starvation or desperation, these groups are often dematerialized into refugee statistics or homogenized and silenced under the rubric of voiceless refugees.[21] This strange invocation of charitable humanity illustrates a kind of *semio-violence*, a representational practice that purports to speak for others but at the same time effaces their voices. During the Persian Gulf War, warring images began to take the place of warring bodies. These productions are never innocent and almost always "speak for others."[22] Virtual landscapes and dematerialized Iraqi bodies on the TV and video screens were later supplanted by images of underfed and homeless Iraqi Kurds facing an icy winter during the fall of 1991.[23]

The absence of representation can also constitute semio-violence.

The semiotic aporia after several hundred Somali civilians were killed by UN peacekeepers in Mogadishu, the invisibility of Iraqi civilians on CNN maps of Iraqi military installations, and the unimaged and thus unimagined private mourning of thousands of families whose kin were murdered in the so-called UN protected area in Srebrenica, Bosnia-Herzegovina, all attest to a political semiotics of representation. It is no accident that they were edited out of the Western script. My aim, then, is to inject a series of analyses that undoes these dominant representational practices and to pose possibilities for recasting and reconstructing humanitarianism in more accountable ways.

Donna Haraway has argued for situated and partial knowledge claims, an approach that challenges the omniscient, Archimedean view from everywhere at once and nowhere in particular.[24] Her rejection of omniscient Cartesian perspectivalism remains an important springboard for those trying to move beyond a neorealist Cold War geopolitical discourse to more fragmented geographies of displacement.[25]

UN REFORM

Since the appointment of the new UN secretary-general, Kofi Annan, the entire UN system has been undergoing major reform. As the only remaining superpower and the largest UN donor, the United States has had significant influence on this process, including the very selection of Annan, who replaced former Secretary-General Boutros Boutros-Ghali after he had served only one term. The new head of the UN system faces a number of crises as the United Nations marks five decades of existence. Politically, there is less support than ever for requiring governments to fund UN agencies through mandatory financial contributions. The United Nations is perceived to be inefficient and not lean enough for the increasingly neoliberal climate of fiscal restraint, transparency, and accountability. The perceived duplication of functions coupled with the lack of support for any kind of welfare suprastate have rendered UN agencies susceptible to scrutiny by their donor governments.[26]

The political context in which the United Nations operates has also changed dramatically, and this has no doubt contributed to some of the crises mentioned earlier. Born of a liberal humanist agenda after World War II at a time when superpower rivalry was well under way, UN agencies today operate in a vastly different world of civil rather than international wars, many of them outside of Europe. This is arguably the most significant shift in terms of international responses to humanitarian emergencies, peacekeeping, and peacemaking.

The shift from international conflict to intranational war poses a paradox for UN operations. The UN Charter of 1945 is a founding basis of the organization. The United Nations is based on membership by states. The 1948 Universal Declaration of Human Rights, however, enshrines the rights of individuals in a legally nonbinding but increasingly relevant manner. The declaration articles specify protection not for states but for individuals and groups *within* states. Insofar as conflict occurs within states that are considered sovereign, the United Nations cannot normally intervene without permission from the government concerned. This renders the UN Security Council, to take one example, as either increasingly irrelevant or in desperate need of new principles and guidelines for operation. Its ad hoc authorization of recent international interventions has occurred without a clear mandate. At the same time, the UN Security Council was unable to take action in 1999 in Kosovo, where atrocious human rights violations and loss of life ensued, because of the veto power of one of its members. Striking a balance between respect for state sovereignty and protection for particular groups who face persecution within their country becomes increasingly precarious. UNHCR, another example of an agency that must strike a precarious balance, maintains that it "has been transformed from a refugee organization into a more broadly-based humanitarian agency."[27] The agency's focus has broadened to meet the exigencies of current political crises, yet the basis for such changes is not clearly defined:

> The world's most powerful states and the United Nations itself have been placed in a considerable dilemma by the rash of internal conflicts and humanitarian emergencies since the demise of the bipolar state system. While the old rules of the game have evidently changed, the international community has found it extremely difficult to articulate a coherent set of principles and practices which are geared to contemporary circumstances.[28]

To date, a coherent new set of guidelines has yet to be developed. In the absence of any new standards or modes of responding to humanitarian crises, a number of ad hoc and sometimes contradictory measures are being employed to manage the negative effects of conflict, including human displacement. These include the recent use of various so-called safe spaces for civilians threatened by war at home. Part of the emerging humanitarian and geopolitical discourse of preventive protection, these measures aim to protect people in their home countries and to prevent states from having to bear the legal obligations and costs of asylum, as outlined in the 1951 Convention Relating to the Status of Refugees and the 1967 Protocol Relating to the Status of Refugees. The shift in responsibility from individual states to multilateral agencies, particularly to UNHCR, signals a change in the state-centric mapping of the international refugee regime that was conceived after World War II. Though states remain the members of the United Nations, they have proven less inclined to harbor refugees and more inclined to intervene in conflict areas so that the need to provide asylum is prevented if possible. This trend recognizes the limitations of states and illustrates the limits that states place on their obligations to those displaced in and by the new world order.

Contemporary histories of migration attest to the fact that state interests are not necessarily confined to territorial boundaries, nor do they necessarily reflect the desires of particular national, cultural, and gender groupings within a given country. "Even when there is no specific clash on a specific territory, the naturalized equation of territory = state = nation is problematic because states do not always correspond to their territorial borders, and nations very rarely if at all correspond to their territory and state."[29] Few, if any, countries in the world can claim the purity of nation = state = territory, and nowhere have I encountered a convincing explanation of why this should be the case.

The politics of national belonging—based on beliefs in common origins—decisively include and exclude certain groups of people in the nation. Such politics give rise to the possibilities of political mobilization, on the one hand, and the tragic potential of war and murder on the other.[30] "Imagined communities" of belonging may constitute national identities, but they can also create the basis for noncommunities of the excluded.[31] Those who do not belong provide a constitutive outside for the identity formation for the communities of those who do.[32] This book intrudes into these noncommunities, in particular into refugee camps, which house those displaced by conflict in their home countries. The mandate to assist refugees belongs to the UNHCR. This mandate has informally expanded to include other "persons of concern," including internally displaced people, repatriating refugees, and other migrants affected by persecution or violence.[33] Current UN reforms point to UNHCR as an organization central to humanitarian response, if not the lead agency, in emergencies concerning displaced persons.

UNOFFICIAL REFORM: THE CRISIS OF HUMANITARIAN ASSISTANCE

The less visible and perhaps more crucial reform process in humanitarian circles is that generated by events that transpired in the Great Lakes region of Africa, beginning with the genocide of Tutsis and moderate Hutus in Rwanda in April 1994. The absence of UN intervention in this massive yet calculated slaughter of up to one million people has caused much critical reflection.[34] Riding a wave of unprecedented operational capacity at the time, UNHCR accepted much of the responsibility for assisting some two million refugees created in the wake of the genocide in the former Zaire (now the Democratic Republic of Congo), mainly Hutus fleeing Rwanda in fear of reprisal. That the United Nations, including UNHCR, failed to separate the refugees from those who conducted the mass killings in Rwanda has generated even more sober second thought for the organization and the role of humanitarian agencies generally. Militarization of the camps raised one of the most pressing dilemmas for humanitarianism. "The 'refugee camps' in Zaire from 1994 to 1996 were a sick caricature of what asylum is supposed to be. Minimally the term 'refugee camp' connotes safety; in Zaire, it meant intimidation, lawlessness, and violence. This bloody travesty, this human tragedy, cannot be repeated."[35] The camps, in effect, became rebel bases for forces opposing the new Tutsi-led government in Rwanda. If this were not enough, the forced repatriation of those in the camps back to Rwanda, as well as the disappearance and murder of others, testified to UN inability to protect displaced persons in the midst of regional warfare.

Analysis, evaluation, and action since then have been more positive. Perhaps now more than ever, critical questions about the role, means, and efficacy of humanitarian assistance are being asked. The experience of genocide in Rwanda has proven unique: In the aftermath of genocide, the international community did not create a separate, sovereign state for the cultural group attacked as it did for the Armenian people in the early twentieth century, for the Jewish people after the Holocaust, and in effect, for the people of Bosnia-Herzegovina under the Dayton Accord. Instead, the new Rwandan government is attempting to reinvent the state for both Hutus and Tutsis. At another level, external evaluations of UN operations during the Great Lakes crises have been commissioned, and a number of thoughtful, politically astute, and sometimes cutting analyses of UN operations have been written.[36] Serious reconsideration and reinvention of humanitarianism is under way. It is my hope that this book will contribute constructively to the lessons learned from Somalia and Rwanda.

MAPPING THE TERRAIN

The chapters that follow theorize refugee mobility at a number of scales. Chapter 1 introduces UNHCR in its geographical and historical context. Moving quickly to the present, I examine a recent shift in humanitarian practice from allowing people to leave their countries of origin in the face of danger to ensuring their right to remain at home. This trend is analyzed in light of neoliberal policies among national governments and declining support for refugee settlement. The discourse of preventive protection is pivotal in legitimizing this shift.

In chapter 2, I present a close reading of the long contest over the Kenyan-Somali border and argue that discrimination and containment of Somalis in Kenya began with colonial rule and was reinscribed by Cold War alliances. I contend that humanitarian funds cross borders more easily than do displaced people. Relief and assistance often move to crisis locations more quickly than adversely affected populations can move from them. This makes containment and preventive protection possible in some instances and suggests the concept of a transnational politics of mobility.

Chapter 3 traces the construction and use of gender and race within UN circles. The tension of culture as a basis of universal humankind and as a marker of social difference poses several dilemmas in UNHCR policy. Employing the concept of "UN humanism," I argue against the conception of gender and culture as categorical variables and give examples of political projects that manage to avoid this fate. A specific UN initiative, the Women Victims of Violence project, is analyzed within the context of this argument and UNHCR gender policy.

The stories of refugees' daily lives are an important part of this book. Chapter 4 focuses on interviews with Somali refugee women. The research on which this chapter is based is riddled with questions of translation and unequal power relations, but the chapter aims to illustrate in very concrete terms the daily routines of refugees and some of the difficulties they face. On another level, I discuss camp design in the context of logistics and staff security, on the one hand, and refugee needs on the other. The overarching organization of the camps, the coded language administrators employ, and the location of refugees within this discursive network are also analyzed as a way of distinguishing supracitizens from subcitizens.

The term *microphysics of power* refers to the everyday practices that produce desired behaviors in the camps.[37] Power is exercised through both coercive and disciplinary means. The use of particular reporting practices by UNHCR and other agencies are reminiscent of colonial practices that aimed to standardize, control, and order the fields from which they were generated. Humanitarian operations and their subjects are represented in very specific, historically constituted ways. In chapter 5, I examine their administrative practices and representational strategies and assess efforts to counter these protocols.

In chapter 6, I write outside the logic of the camps and examine some of the ways in which refugees deal with displacement beyond official channels. Both in practice and in theoretical terms, I analyze the ways in which displaced persons often defy the spaces, categories, and structures in place to assist and monitor them. Just as refugees are a transgression of statehood, migrant identities are constituted by more than one geographical location and more than one appellation. Building on identity construction based in multiple locations and constrained by political conditions, I discuss alternatives to the dominant narrative of nation.

The final chapter is less a conclusion than a consolidation of findings and a discussion of current directions. UNHCR's mandate is to find and enact permanent solutions for displaced persons. There is some evidence to suggest that UNHCR—heeding the preferences of its major donor states—is reneging on this obligation and managing forced migrations close to their sources in order to avoid meeting the obligations and guaranteeing the minimal rights to which recognized refugees are entitled. The significant decline in refugee admissions and the fortification of borders against refugee claims speak to the refusal of states to extend social responsibility and its costs beyond borders. In the absence of the Cold War, this has become a stark political reality. The role of humanitarian operations is under review. This rethinking of complex emergencies extends far beyond UNHCR alone. The questions it raises are more difficult than any faced since the founding of the United Nations.

As UNHCR's mandate has strengthened and expanded during the 1990s, an analysis of the organization's aims, operations, and practices on the ground is both timely and significant. At a time when UN member states are interested in minimizing their commitments under international legal instruments, UNHCR has proven to be one of the main multilateral organizations that can pick up the slack, operate in emergency situations, and manage—if not always optimally— the outcomes of mass displacement. Between UN-protected areas and refugee camps lie fine but important lines: international political borders. Borders are tacitly reinscribed by the refugees who manage to cross them in an effort to seek safety and claim asylum on the other side. At the same time, UN safe spaces within conflict zones serve to challenge, if not undermine, these sacrosanct signifiers of state sovereignty in the name of humanitarian assistance.

Using analytical approaches to unsettle conventional images and constructions of displaced people, I document different stories of life in the refugee camps and other safe spaces. The book is also grounded by the alarming need to do something in the face of widespread human dislocation, moving between modest developments of theory and its deployment to practical ends. Despite a significant change in the nature of forced migration and the tactics of response, at the end of the day, something must be done. Without speaking for anyone, I animate and proximate the abstract and distanced locations of mass displacement. This book represents a sustained effort to analyze critically the dominant representational and material practices within the realm of humanitarian activity and to engage in salient issues that currently plague the international refugee regime during a period of intense change.

1

Scripting Humanitarianism: A Geography of "Refugee" and the Respatialization of Response

[It is] not whether you are a refugee but where you are. . . . it's all a question of space and distance.

—SENIOR STAFF MEMBER, UNHCR

Doing political and accountable protection work seems no longer the fashion. . . . UNHCR is tempted to engage in the politics of assistance, the politics of solutions, or the politics of prevention.

—GUY GOODWIN-GILL,
"UNITED NATIONS REFORM AND THE
FUTURE OF REFUGEE PROTECTION"

Borders breed uneven geographies of power and status. Crossing them in the name of humanitarian assistance is a political act, one that is more available to the governments of donor countries than to those who receive humanitarian assistance. Since 1991, when the United Nations entered northern Iraq for humanitarian reasons, this disparate power dynamic has been witnessed during numerous multilateral humanitarian interventions into countries at risk of producing refugees, a strategy known as preventive protection. Borders are material locations that embody specific historical, cultural, and political meanings. They are also testimony to dominant geopolitical discourses that generate states that are at once inclusive and exclusive. Political borders designate a constitutive outside, a basis for identity formation against the identity or threat of something else.[1] This function of identity formation nonetheless privileges the nation-state as the venue for political contest and change. In this chapter, I undertake the project of unmaking the state and an analysis of the ways in which its borders position some citizens more equally than others. In turn, I present a critical examination of a relatively new discourse in humanitarian circles, that of "preventive protection," that is, a spatialized strategy of assisting displaced persons within countries at war rather than as refugees in countries nearby. It is less a humanitarian practice than a donor-sponsored effort to contain forced migration and to avoid international legal obligations to would-be refugees.

International responses to human displacement in the 1990s have become increasingly politicized and emphasize managing migration. This chapter traces the emergence of complex humanitarian emergencies and addresses the respatialization of responses to crises of human displacement. Who counts as a refugee varies across world regions and over time, but most definitions include the criterion of crossing an international border. In crossing an international boundary, refugees trade the entitlements of citizenship in their own country for safety on terms decided by international legal instruments, host governments, and humanitarian agencies. Not all of those displaced by conflict and violence, however, are able to cross a border. They too may receive assistance, albeit on different terms and with less political leverage. Displacement—as involuntary movement, cultural dislocation, social disruption, material dispossession, and political disenfranchisement—is a disparate and often desperate condition that connects the experiences of forced migrants. Humanitarian assistance, in contrast, is the relatively centralized, authorized, and increasingly politicized antidote to human displacement.

Donor governments who fund assistance to displaced persons, whether they be refugees who have crossed international borders or people uprooted in their own countries, have increasingly urged UN organizations to assist displaced persons at home, preferably, or in a first country of asylum nearby. Emerging national and ethnic divisions of power in the post–Cold War period have generated strategies of containment that serve to keep refugees and internally displaced people "over there," far from the borders of charitable donor countries in the West. Since 1990, particular strategies have been employed to curb refugee flows through such measures as preventive protection and through the extended use of technically temporary refugee camps. The quotation at the outset of the chapter from a senior staff member from the Office of UNHCR suggests a reappraisal of the fixed category "refugee." He grounds human displacement in a contingent geographical context rather than in a legal definition that emphasizes the responsibilities and borders of states. This approach aims to be more inclusive in terms of who UNHCR assists, but it also has strategic value for the UNHCR, which has become one of the more popular and powerful UN agencies in the realm of humanitarian assistance. Perhaps more importantly, UNHCR is responding to its donor governments, who wish to maintain "space and distance" from the massive numbers of displaced persons. Governments prefer interventions that provide assistance before potential refugees cross a border, as migrants increasingly pose an economic, if not political, threat to traditional refugee resettlement countries in the North.

Complex humanitarian emergencies are more difficult to stabilize and organize than ever before. They often involve the displacement of people within war zones and multilateral interventions to assist them by a number of specialized humanitarian organizations. This chapter moves from an analysis of the uneven geography within the international refugee regime to the respatialization of humanitarian response beyond refugees and across the borders of warring countries that hold captive displaced populations.

HUMANITARIANISM AND ITS CRITICS

The collapse of Communism and the demise of the Cold War has deprived international affairs of an organizing script and a defining drama. . . . Geopolitics produced international politics as theater: Geography was the stage, politics the drama, and geopolitics the detached observation of this representational spectacle.

— GEARÓID Ó TUATHAIL, *CRITICAL GEOPOLITICS*

There is no pure, apolitical humanitarian solution to the politically charged events of mass human displacement. Humanitarianism is an increasingly well-funded and politicized process of balancing the needs of refugees and other displaced persons against the interests of states. Many critics argue that humanitarianism should not be political, nor should it involve compromises of refugee protection because of state interests. But it is and it does. The rise in humanitarian efforts can be correlated with a decline in conventional protection, or asylum, for people forcibly displaced and in a reduction in official development assistance.[2] Médecins sans Frontières/Doctors without Borders argues that the idea of humanitarianism has been inflated:

> The most obvious and most telling recent example has been Bosnia. The West never defined a political objective for the former Yugoslavia. Humanitarianism was used as a cloak for this failure. The badly named UN Protection Force, UNPROFOR, was established not to protect the citizens of the former Yugoslavia but [to help] the humanitarian relief programmes run (efficiently) by the UNHCR. UNPROFOR undoubtedly saved lives and alleviated much misery. But its other effect was—as with so many relief operations—to reinforce the war parties and extend the war.[3]

Humanitarian assistance at the end of the millennium is synonymous with neither protection, in the legal sense, nor solutions to displacement. In the absence of "an organizing script and a defining drama" for post–Cold War geopolitics, aid for refugees and other displaced people is an ad hoc political tool inspired primarily by the donor governments of this aid. Humanitarian law, which includes the 1949 Geneva Conventions and their Additional Protocols, expounds standards of conduct in war, including the prohibition of war crimes and codes of civilian treatment in conflict zones.[4] Humanitarian assistance, which has come to mean much more than the protections guaranteed by the conventions, is appropriately named because increasingly it is delivered in war zones. Refugees still represent a sizable recipient group for international assistance, but their political significance has waned considerably since the end of Cold War conflict.

International refugee law is comprised mainly of the 1951 Convention Relating to the Status of Refugees, the 1967 Protocol Relating to the Status of Refugees, and the 1969 Organization for African Unity (OAU) Convention Governing the Specific Aspects of Refugee Problems in Africa. It institutionalizes and enforces the UN Declaration for Human Rights, which declares that a person has "the right to leave" and return to her or his own country and "the right to asylum."[5] Humanitarian law and refugee law draw clear distinctions between the rights and entitlements of internally displaced persons (IDPs) and those of refugees. These categories are, however, being challenged because only marginal differences of time and space may distinguish an IDP from a refugee. Some UNHCR policy makers maintain that refugees and IDPs are often qualitatively part of the same group, divided artificially by a political border.[6] The question of whether IDPs should be included or excluded from an operational definition of refugee remains an issue of contentious debate.

As humanitarian assistance in the form of material assistance and temporary protection by UN bodies supplants the legal protection of international refugee law, responses to displacement become increasingly politicized. As UNHCR has absorbed much of the responsibility for meeting this increasing demand for humanitarian assistance, it has become a much more powerful organization and a highly political one. Despite its officially apolitical mandate, UNHCR is funded primarily on a voluntary basis by donor governments, which often designate the use and location of their donations. Funding patterns thus provide some direction for humanitarian action, but operating principles and consistent consultation processes prior to response remain ill defined. UNHCR has acknowledged both the adaptation of its operations to meet the exigencies of current political crises and the dilemma in which it finds itself given the tremendous shift in geopolitics after the demise of the bipolar state system.[7]

The ethics of humanitarian encounter are currently in question precisely because there are no defined and agreed-upon standards of practice. This is not to say that UNHCR is operating without a mandate or without authorization, but, rather, that the organization has become increasingly powerful in its size and scope and that there has been little corresponding increase in cooperation and collaboration with other UN agencies and non-UN bodies working toward the same ends.[8]

The following section provides a brief geography of asylum over the past fifty years and traces the meaning of refugee in international law. It exposes an uneven geography of refugee definitions and entitlement and presents a short sketch of UNHCR in current context. Moving to the present, it discusses the declining relevance of international refugee law in the face of preventive measures by UN bodies.

STATING HUMAN DISPLACEMENT

Themes of containment and exclusion with respect to migration are not new. Aristide Zolberg organizes economic and political migrations into three epochs, the first spanning the sixteenth to eighteenth centuries in Europe; the debut of the second corresponding to the industrial, democratic, and demographic revolutions of the late eighteenth century; and the last emerging in the final decades of the nineteenth century: "The emergence of powerful European states in the 15th century inaugurated a distinctive era in the history of human migrations: the conquest by the Europeans of the New World."[9] The French Huguenots are generally considered the first group of modern refugees, but legal formulations of refugee status are a product of more recent Western history. Before the twentieth century, little attention was paid to the precise definition of a refugee, since most of those who chose not to move to the so-called New World were willingly received by rulers in Europe and elsewhere. The freedom of international movement for persons broadly defined as refugees was adversely impacted by the adoption of instrumentalist immigration policies in Western states during the early twentieth century.[10] This final period has been marked by the development of a gap between a small number of wealthy, technologically advanced, and militarily powerful countries and a larger number of poorer states. Zolberg's analysis is appropriate in the late twentieth century, as a small number of wealthy donor countries consolidate their power by exerting their influence directly within a number of poorer and less stable countries through a relatively new measure: the multilateral humanitarian intervention.

Zolberg notes that improved communication has also rendered information about world conditions more available and that human mobility has increased through various technological advances. This enhanced mobility has given rise to perceived threats of invasion by multitudes of poor strangers, providing a strong impetus for exclusionary measures and stricter border controls. Humanitarian assistance, in the form of multilateral interventions to aid IDPs or as refugee camps, is predicated on the greater speed of capital transfers to assist the needy as compared to their ability to move from adverse conditions of conflict to more hospitable locations.

Despite regional conventions and international protocols to protect refugees, the nation-state remains the main unit of international law and the primary site of enforcement in relation to regional and international agreements and civilian protection. "States are the subjects of international law; individuals are only its objects."[11] With European empire building long over and with the end of the Cold War, some states have become balkanized, on the one hand, and borders and regional blocs have been formalized, on the other. The porosity of borders is historically and geographically contingent: "The reaction among the receiving nations of the North . . . has been . . . to attempt to contain or 'regionalize' refugee problems; that is, to keep those in need of protection and solutions with their regions of origin."[12] Hyndman

The modern institution of asylum is rooted in political geographies of displaced populations during World War II. Denial of asylum and strategies to contain forced migrants were part and parcel of this institution. Camps were the rule, not the exception, for dislocated groups in Europe. "[I]f the Nazis put a person in a concentration camp and if he made a successful escape, say, to Holland, the Dutch would put him in an internment camp . . . under the pretext of national security."[13] Displaced within or beyond the borders of one's country, residence in camps signaled statelessness: "The stateless person, without right to residence and without the right to work, had of course to transgress the law . . . . neither physical safety—being fed by some state or private welfare agency—nor freedom of opinion changes in the least their [refugees'] fundamental situation of rightlessness."[14] Arendt's clairvoyant reasoning points to some of the problems and dilemmas of humanitarian assistance in the international refugee regime today. Most refugees in camps today are prohibited from seeking employment or establishing livelihoods independent of the international assistance provided in camps.

The mobility of refugees and displaced persons remains constrained by borders of the nation-state. Asylum requires, by definition, the crossing of an international border. If successful in their crossing, refugees become wards of an international refugee regime that relies on the endorsement, financial support, and refugee determination processes of individual nation-states. The primacy of the nation-state, both as the subject of international law and as a context for citizenship, has as its corollary the imagined global community—the perceived relationship among states and peoples of the world.

The Changing Geography of Refugees

Once geographers accept that space is not a backdrop to political and social action but is, instead, a product of such action, the role of law becomes central to the analysis of space.
—NICHOLAS BLOMLEY AND JOEL BAKAN, "SPACING OUT"

Articles 1, 55, and 56 of the United Nations Charter outline the provision of political and legal protection to refugees, displaced persons, and other vulnerable groups. UNHCR is one of the international organizations charged with this responsibility.[15] Formally established after World War II in Europe, the Office of the UNHCR was a response to the many displaced and stateless people who required legal protection and material assistance. It replaced the International Refugee Organization (IRO), which had been established immediately after the war. The Office of UNHCR was to complement international law, which provided potentially permanent protection for refugees under the 1951 Convention Relating to the Status of Refugees.

Despite the fact that in 1995, 125 states were party to the 1951 Convention, it remains both explicitly and implicitly Eurocentric. From its conception, the convention clearly demarcated geographical and historical limits. It was designed to apply to refugees in Europe displaced by events that occurred prior to 1951. The convention is characterized by its strategic conceptualization of "refugee" and is spatially coded as European.[16] Substantively, its emphasis on persecution based on civil and political status as grounds for refugee status expresses the particular ideological debates of postwar European politics, particularly the perceived threats of communism and another Holocaust. In emphasizing civil and political rights, the convention had the effect of minimizing the importance of socioeconomic human rights: "Unlike the victims of civil and political oppression, . . . persons denied even such basic rights as food, health care, or education are excluded from the international refugee regime (unless that deprivation stems from civil or political status.)"[17] These features of the convention, its European geographical focus and emphasis on civil and political rights, have generated an uneven geography of refugee asylum that, today, is the source of contentious debate.

The convention mandate includes anyone who

as a result of events occurring before 1 January 1951 and owing to well-founded fear of being persecuted for reasons of race, religion, nationality, membership of a particular social group or political opinion, is outside the country of his nationality and is unable or, owing to such fear, is unwilling to avail himself of the protection of that country; or who, not having a nationality and being outside the country of his former habitual residence as a result of such events, is unable or, owing to such fear, is unwilling to return to it.[18]

The definition implicitly promulgated a hierarchy of rights, privileging political and civil rights of protection from *persecution* over economic, cultural, and social rights and scales of violence broader than individual persecution.[19] The definition was also an expression of a particular geopolitics: "The strategic dimension of the definition comes from successful efforts of Western states to give priority in protection matters to persons whose flight was motivated by pro-Western political values."[20] The convention's refugee definition was based on an ideologically divided world, grounded in relational identities of East and West. The 1951 convention was designed to facilitate the sharing of the European refugee burden:

Notwithstanding the vigorous objections of several delegates from developing countries faced with responsibility for their own refugee populations, the Eurocentric goal of the Western states was achieved by limiting the scope of mandatory international protection under the Convention to refugees whose flight was prompted by a pre-1951 event within Europe. While states might opt to extend protection to refugees from other parts of the world, the definition adopted was intended to distribute the European refugee burden without any binding obligation to reciprocate by way of the establishment of rights for, or the provision of assistance to, non-European refugees.[21]

Assistance to non-European refugees was optional. Solutions to the displacement of Europeans after World War II were the focus of the convention.

Complementing this emerging state-based regime of international law, the role of UNHCR is outlined legally in the Statute of UNHCR (1950). The statute defines UNHCR's mandate as one of protecting refugees, as defined by the convention, and of seeking permanent solutions for refugees in cooperation with governments through their voluntary repatriation or assimilation within new national communities. Also, "the work of the High Commissioner shall be of an entirely non-political character."[22] In contrast to the convention, the statute emphasizes that the work of UNHCR will relate to groups and categories of refugees, not individuals.[23] From the outset, then, UNHCR faced the practical difficulty of a definition of refugees based on individual determination, yet the statute outlined responsibilities for "groups and categories of refugees." This disjuncture has been identified by international legal scholars, one of whom notes the increasing slippage between UNHCR and state responsibilities:

> The disjuncture between the obligations of States and the institutional responsibilities of UNHCR is broadest and most clearly apparent in respect of refugees, other than those with a well-founded fear of persecution or falling within regional arrangements. . . . it was during this period (the early 1980s) that States' reservations as to a general widening of the "refugee definition" began to confirm the resulting disjuncture between the functional responsibilities of UNHCR and the legal obligations of States.[24]

The vehicle used to bridge the discrepancy between the statute and the convention mandates was the good offices of UNHCR, first employed in assisting Chinese people fleeing to Hong Kong in 1957 and then made applicable to all potential situations of displacement not envisaged at the time the original mandate was established. UNHCR's good offices were created by Resolution 1673 (XVI) of the UN General Assembly on December 18, 1961. The resolution provided a basis for action that aimed to be flexible, responsive, and meaningful in emerging refugee situations, and it allowed the high commissioner to define groups as prima facie refugees without normal determinations procedures.[25] Prima facie refugees were a new category of displaced person, a category subordinate to the convention definition and more likely to be applicable to crises outside of Europe.

Historian Louise Holborn describes the deployment of UNHCR's good offices in Africa as a just-in-time measure. But she points out that the deployment was qualified: (1) The good offices would provide only material assistance; legal protection was not seen to be required; (2) refugees on this continent were considered too numerous, dispersed, and poor to make individual assessments necessary for convention refugee designation; and (3) Europeans considered it too difficult to establish a well-founded fear of persecution in Africa, compared to Europe.[26] Many of these qualifications are, of course, Eurocentric, Orientalist, even racist constructions of African peoples and politics. They point to the hierarchy of cultures and continents that UNHCR and other humanitarian organizations must be vigilant of, even today. The drawback of the good offices provision of material assistance is that it can only occur where and for as long as governments *invite* UNHCR to assist.[27] Also, because of the poverty of many African countries, material needs have been provided to refugees, arguably at the expense of legal status and protection.[28] This institutional framework speaks from and to a period when African states were beginning to agitate for and gain independence. It created the basis for a hierarchy of refugee definitions later in the century. The convention amplified the legitimacy of asylum from persecution related to Nazism and communism:

> [T]he definition of the term "refugee" . . . was based on the assumption of a divided world. . . . The problem of refugees could not be considered in the abstract, but on the contrary, must be considered in light of historical facts. In laying down the definition of the term "refugee," account had hitherto always been taken of the fact that the refugees involved had always been from a certain part of the world; thus, such a definition was based on historical facts. *Any attempt to impart a universal character to the text would be tantamount to making it an "Open Sesame."*[29]

The convention's definition was never intended, despite claims to the contrary, to be universal. In making the definition of "refugee" geographically exclusive, it underplayed violence and material deprivation linked to colonialism and imperialism by including affected populations only with the discretionary, ad hoc efforts of UNHCR's good offices.

The 1967 Protocol Relating to the Status of Refugees amended the 1951 convention. Though it rescinded the spatial and temporal restrictions of the convention by lifting the Europe-based, pre-1951 stipulations, it merely created equal access for all member nations to a legal instrument that remained substantively Eurocentric in focus. Emphasis on the abrogation of individual civil and political rights, based on the outcomes of World War II, remains central to the convention definition of "refugee" that is employed today. Technically, the 1967 protocol made the definition geographically inclusive, yet the imagined geopolitical landscape on which the basic premises of asylum were founded remained geographically exclusive and Eurocentric.[30] Drawing on the work of Simon Dalby and Gearóid Ó Tuathail, the repetition of particular geopolitical tropes conditioned the political imaginary as European, though in principle the definition was applicable elsewhere.[31]

Increasingly, a smaller and smaller proportion of refugees meet the formal Eurocentric post–World War II requirements. The legacy of this discrepancy between convention and other refugees has generated a geographically unequal system of refugee protection and assistance. The convention definition is increasingly irrelevant to the majority of refugees, who today face violence on a broader scale and for different reasons than those of postwar Europe. Civil wars often involve state militaries pitted against other cultural and political groups. For no legal reason, political and civil rights have been underscored at the expense of economic, social, and cultural rights: "[T]hose impacted by national calamities, weak economies, civil unrest, war and even generalized failure to adhere to basic standards of human rights are not, therefore, entitled to refugee status on that basis alone."[32] The definition continues to emphasize the importance of civil and political rights based on "fear of persecution," a concept based on ideological divisions of East and West in Europe, far more than the material conditions or cultural and political differences in other world regions. In Africa, the perceived inadequacy of this pair of legal instruments resulted in the drafting of a legally binding regional policy by the OAU. The 1969 OAU Convention Governing the Specific Aspects of Refugee Problems in Africa not only broadened but also reformulated the definition of refugees. It included the 1951 convention definition, but added, in Article 1.2, the provision that "the term refugee shall also apply to every person who, owing to external aggression, occupation, foreign domination or events seriously disturbing public order in either part or the whole of his country of origin or nationality, is compelled to leave his place of habitual residence in order to seek refuge in another place outside his country of origin or nationality." The OAU definition thus incorporated generalized violence associated with colonialism and other kinds of aggression, including flight resulting from the serious disruption of public order "in either part or the whole" of one's country of origin, as grounds for seeking asylum.[33]

> This . . . represents a departure from past practice in which it was generally assumed that a person compelled to flight should make reasonable efforts to seek protection within a safe part of her own country (if one exists) before looking for refuge abroad. There are at least three reasons why this shift is contextually sensible. First, issues of distance or the unavailability of escape routes may foreclose travel to a safe region of the refugee's own state. Underdeveloped infrastructure and inadequate personal financial resources may reinforce the choice of a more easily reachable foreign destination. Second, the political instability of many developing states may mean that what is a "safe" region today may be dangerous tomorrow. . . . Finally, *the artificiality of the colonially imposed boundaries in Africa has frequently meant that kinship and other natural ties stretch across national frontiers. Hence, persons in danger may see the natural safe haven to be with family or members of their own ethnic group in an adjacent state.*[34]

The OAU definition recognized that protection is inscribed with cultural politics, as well as, and potentially in conflict with, geopolitical ones. This revised geography of asylum was then codified in the OAU convention. The OAU definition translated the initial meaning of refugee status into the economic, cultural, political, and social realities of the so-called Third World.[35] The definition also recognized in law the concept of group disenfranchisement and the legitimacy of flight in situations of generalized danger not limited to individual persecution.

In 1984, the Cartagena Declaration on Refugees was adopted by ten Latin American states. Written to address the forced migration of people fleeing generalized violence and oppression in Central America, it too represents a regional approach to recognizing and improving upon the inadequacy of the 1951 convention definition. The definition derived from the Cartagena declaration goes further than that of the convention, including claims based on internal conflicts and massive violations of human rights and the idea of group designation. It does not extend as far as the OAU convention, however, to protect people fleeing disturbances of public order that affect only one part of a given country. Whereas the OAU convention is legally binding, the

Cartagena declaration—which provides the basis for the Organization of American States (OAS) definition—is not.[36]

The establishment of regional instruments points to an uneven geography of refugee definitions in international law. The 1951 convention and 1967 protocol definition speaks to the experience and prevailing conflict in Europe after World War II. The OAU convention broke new ground by extending refugee status to groups affected by less-discriminate violence and public disorder in Africa. Though not legally binding on member states, the Cartagena declaration addressed the distinct regional politics and related human displacement in Central America. On a more modest scale, the Council of Europe has also extended the definition to include de facto refugees, that is, "persons who either have not been formally recognized as Convention refugees (although they meet the Convention's criteria) or who are 'unable or unwilling for . . . other valid reasons to return to their countries of origin.'"[37] The 1951 convention and 1967 protocol, together with these regional instruments, constitute the major bases of refugee protection in international law.[38] Nonetheless, a sizable class of refugees remains outside the scope of this legal codification. Though most of these refugees are recognized as having legitimate protection needs, legal scholars have generated considerable debate over whether the international practice of granting protection has become part of customary international law or is simply an institutional practice of UNHCR that is not binding on states. The current politics and funding of humanitarian activities suggest that protection and assistance afforded those who fall outside the scope of international law is institutional and not part of customary law. In the 1990s, assistance to displaced persons had less and less to do with international refugee law and more to do with UN-endorsed humanitarian interventions in countries experiencing conflict where displaced populations were helped at home.

One Organization Geographically Distributed: UNHCR

Twenty years ago, the Office of the United Nations High Commissioner for Refugees consisted of some lawyers in Geneva revising and amending the international conventions concerning refugees. Now it is a global rapid-reaction force capable of putting fifty thousand tents into an airfield anywhere within twenty-four hours, or feeding a million refugees in Zaire. . . .

The United Nations has become the West's mercy mission to the flotsam of failed states left behind by the ebb tide of empire.

— MICHAEL IGNATIEFF,
"ALONE WITH THE SECRETARY-GENERAL"

The UNHCR operates today on a scale unimaginable at its conception. Its initial temporary mandate of three years, from 1951 to 1954, has been extended at five-year intervals since that time. It is responsible for more people today than any other period since World War II.[39] Annual expenditures of US$8 million in 1970 increased to almost US$1,167 million in 1994, reflecting intense growth. Most of this expansion has occurred in the post–Cold War period.[40] In 1990, the agency had a budget of US$544 million and a staff of 2,400. By 1996, the budget had grown to about US$1.3 billion and the staff to 5,000.[41] Despite a more recent decline in funding, the organization maintains an impressive global reach. As of October 1994, UNHCR employed more than 5,000 people at its headquarters in Geneva and overseas in more than 100 countries. The advent of post–Cold War displacement and the responses it has generated have contributed to this transformation. In the decade following the end of the Cold War, Western governments (or those of the North, to be oriented more geographically) have demonstrated unprecedented generosity in funding UNHCR's efforts, which occur on a more massive scale than ever before. The displaced people these governments support, however, are located elsewhere. There is virtually no overlap between donor countries and refugee/IDP countries.

Recent changes within UNHCR are expressions of transformations on a broader scale, as the post–Cold War lack of order is fashioned. The neoliberal tendencies of Western governments were also galvanized, at least during the 1990s, into a trend affecting even the United Nations. The Office of UNHCR has a mandate to assist and protect refugees and to arrange permanent solutions to their displacement. This mandate has evolved over time and space. Once limited to assisting refugees in Europe displaced by the events of World War II, UNHCR now works worldwide to assist not only refugees but other displaced groups. In the post–Cold War period of fiscal austerity, the organization has moved from operating exclusively in safe countries of asylum to operating in war zones. Where it once cooperated with development agencies, it now collaborates with peacekeepers in places like northern Iraq and Bosnia-Herzegovina. As the UN reform process and cost cutting continue, UNHCR promises to maintain its high profile during complex humanitarian emergencies.

As a measure of the new alliance between peacekeeping and humanitarian operations, the United Nations launched thirteen peacekeeping missions during the first four decades of its operations; between 1988 and 1995, it authorized twenty-five.[42] Save for the tragic lack of peacekeeping action during the Rwanda genocide in 1994, the contemporaneous deployment of humanitarian staff and peacekeeping forces in the same place—for example, in Bosnia and Somalia—was a distinct feature of humanitarianism in the 1990s. A more startling aspect of this transformation is the significant amount of money targeted for military peacekeeping operations compared to the relatively paltry funds earmarked for humanitarian assistance or social and economic development. In September 1993, *Harper's Index* reported that the ratio of UN monies spent in 1992 on peacekeeping as compared to economic development was 5:2.[43] Since 1995, however, there has been a dramatic decline in the number of peacekeepers in the field, from a peak of approximately 70,000 to 21,000 in 1997.[44] The peacekeeping experience in Somalia, discussed in chapter 2, combined with difficulties in Bosnia-Herzegovina, directly contributed to this decline.

Increasingly, UNHCR is faced with economic and political pressures to rethink its terms of reference and operational mandate. The U.S. government, in particular, has wielded its power as the UN's largest funder by refusing to pay its UN bills, lobbying for its own choice of appointment for the position of UN secretary-general, and demanding UN reform. The more interventionist geopolitical landscape of the post–Cold War period and the rise of neoliberalism and New Right politics in many industrialized nations signal shifts both within UNHCR as an organization and within the internationally funded realm of humanitarian assistance. Though the Persian Gulf War reminded governments that *inter*national conflict has not disappeared in the absence of superpower rivalry, the vast majority of refugee-producing conflicts today are civil wars, or internal.[45]

Individual states increasingly rely on multilateral agencies, such as UNHCR, to deal with humanitarian crises.[46] This shift outsources responsibilities formerly belonging to the state to UN and other multilateral agencies, but with the interests and survival of the state in mind. Part of this shift toward multilateral responsibility lies in the trend toward downsizing the welfare state in many industrialized countries. On the one hand, resettling refugees represents an unwanted burden on the welfare states of traditional UNHCR resettlement countries. On the other, the international refugee regime is a supranational welfare system, funded by these same governments, which faces pressure to reduce its expenditures and the number of its wards on a different scale. UNHCR has moved from interpreting legal obligations and encouraging humanitarian response on the part of member states to managing crises of displacement on the ground.

Strategies of Containment:
Preventing Protection, Negotiating Borders

Whereas the older paradigm can be described as reactive, exile-oriented and refugee-specific, the one which has started to emerge over the past few years can be characterized as pro-active, homeland-oriented and holistic. . . . in contrast to the traditional paradigm, which placed primary emphasis on the right to leave one's own country and to seek asylum elsewhere, the newer perspective focuses equal attention on the right to return to one's homeland and on a notion which has become known as the "right to remain."

—UNHCR, *THE STATE OF THE WORLD'S REFUGEES*

The word "protection" has become something of a term of art. . . . The word "refugee" is also a term of art in international law.

—GUY GOODWIN-GILL, "THE LANGUAGE OF PROTECTION"

Preventive protection is a term that describes a recent trend in managing forced migration. Increasingly UNHCR has become involved in operations within countries in which people are displaced, often in conflict zones. Preventive protection is part of a paradigm shift in refugee policy that occurred in the early 1990s.[47] It belongs to a discourse that emphasizes the right to remain in one's home country over the former dominant discourse of the right to leave. The right to remain was endorsed by UN High Commissioner Sadako Ogata in the early 1990s. UNHCR originally defined "preventive protection" as

> the establishment or undertaking of specific activities inside the country of origin so that people no longer feel compelled to cross borders in search of protection and assistance. In this sense, for instance, action on behalf of the internally displaced can be defined as preventive

protection, although the primary motive may be to address a genuine gap in protection rather than to avert outflow. Preventive protection in this sense may also include the establishment of "safety zones" or "safe areas" inside the country of origin where protection may be sought. It relates therefore to the protection of nationals in their own country.[48]

A politicized discourse of border crossings and safe areas sometimes replaces the term "preventive protection," but not the basic concept. This entire discourse is interesting because it gives rise to *a new set of political spaces* and management practices for forcibly displaced people. Safe havens for Iraqi Kurds, zones of tranquillity for returning Afghan refugees, open relief centers for would-be Sri Lankan refugees, and safe corridors to Muslim enclaves in Bosnia are all examples of this current trend and expressions of a post–Cold War, neoliberal discourse.

In 1991, the Kurds in northern Iraq would neither formally nor in normal practice have been UNHCR's responsibility, but the agency was called upon because of its "response ability." "The Iraqi Kurds were internally displaced but not refugees; UNHCR could do the job so we were given the go ahead."[49] The intervention to assist Iraqi Kurds in the fall of 1991, a mission known in UN circles as Operation Provide Comfort, followed the Gulf War. It was possible for UN relief workers (mostly UNHCR staff) and UN peacekeepers to operate in the northern part of the country because it was impossible for Saddam Hussein to deny them access after losing the war.

Many consider Operation Provide Comfort as the turning point in the management of displaced persons. This new development has continued within UNHCR with respect to its role in the former Yugoslavia: "[L]ook at the mix of people . . . nobody really sat down to say 'refugees,' 'displaced persons,' 'war victims'; it doesn't matter. . . . they need protection and assistance. UNHCR is there; they're equipped to do it."[50] The definition of refugees at UNHCR is no longer predicated on the crossing of an international border. Increasingly, UNHCR's job has become to assist people in order to avoid such crossings.

To justify its involvement in war zones, UNHCR has adopted a seemingly practical approach that emphasizes action and downplays the importance of its formal mandate as well as the political meaning of borders. In reference to the former Yugoslavia, one senior staff member at UNHCR commented on Croatian borders and the confusion that recognition of such borders bred:

> [T]here were a lot of people displaced within these borders, and then persons displaced across borders that nobody recognized; and then you had persons displaced *within* borders that nobody recognized; and then you had persons who weren't displaced at all, but were sitting being shelled to death in Sarajevo, and all of these people fell under the action of UNHCR, and nobody really cared. It's a big change from these years of the 1980s.[51]

Thus, one rationale—albeit functionalist—justifying UNHCR's role in assisting during emergency situations is that it is able to do so.[52]

A more cynical rationale is that UNHCR responds if donor governments are willing to pay. Most of UNHCR's budget is generated through voluntary contributions on a project-by-project or crisis-by-crisis basis. Donor hegemony can occur where funds are earmarked for particular refugee relief efforts. UNHCR has extended its scope to operate *within* countries at war because funders are willing to pay the organization to do the work. In the face of cuts and calls for rationalization within all UN agencies, UNHCR has so far been successful in customizing its competencies—emergency and protection roles in particular—to ensure continued financial viability.

The legitimacy of international borders is a related and current question among organizations managing displacement. In the foreword to a UNHCR document addressing the plight of internally displaced persons, the former director of international protection notes that people who are internally displaced, on the "other" side of the border

> have been called "refugees in all but name." . . . Because they have not crossed an international boundary, the internally displaced have no access to the international protection mechanisms designed for refugees. . . . UNHCR finds it operationally untenable—as well as morally objectionable—to consider only the more visible facet of a situation of coerced displacement. . . . No two humanitarian crises are ever the same, and a global approach to such complex situations requires, if anything, finer tools of analysis and a larger arsenal of flexible responses.[53]

Except for the unnecessarily militarized language of "arsenal," this is a compelling and sympathetic plea for inclusion on the part of the former head of the protection division. It represents not a new idea, but a timely one.[54] UNHCR has admitted, however, that repeatedly crossing an international border to assist displaced people in their own country—for instance in Iraq—may have unintended political consequences. Such a strategy may undermine the concept of the state, state authority, and most alarmingly, the obligation of the state itself to provide protection if an international agency will do it instead. Providing protection and assistance in safe spaces may also prove ineffective, as fatal attacks on UN protected areas, such as Srebrenica during the summer of 1995, illustrated. Thousands of unarmed civilians lost their lives when Bosnian Serb forces besieged the city, kidnapping 30 of 439 Dutch peacekeepers. The remaining troops and some 30,000 Bosnian Muslims fled the city the evening of July 11, 1995, when it became clear that peacekeepers could not guarantee their protection.[55]

Though UNHCR recognizes this risk, it continues to expand its clientele to include internally displaced people in selected cases. Space, distance, and context may be increasingly important to UNHCR interventions, but they are also part of an emerging discourse that legitimizes strategies that are flexible, financially viable, and politically popular with donors. Interventions predicated on the popularity of the cause risk politicizing need. Legal arguments of protection and assistance are navigated, and in some cases avoided, through the introduction of a more politicized and exigent set of humanitarian practices.

Human displacement does not occur in neutral spaces, reducible to particular places and void of political meaning.[56] Histories of conflict and antagonistic but spatially contingent relations of power are often what force people to move from their homes in the first place. Equally, histories of domination and uneven geographies of power and influence shape the directions in which displaced people move. "Places constituted in political discourse need not be stable to be politically useful."[57] The example of Iraq after its defeat in the Persian Gulf War provides a telling example: The United Nations was in an advantageous position to demand from President Hussein's government the required "consent" to intervene in order to assist the Kurds.

By framing human displacement within specific geographical contexts, UNHCR questions the utility of its own abstract, admittedly outdated operational definitions and proposes a potentially more situated and inclusive approach:

> [C]oerced displacement, whether within or across national borders, should be seen as the consequence and symptom of a broader problem involving the absence or failure of national protection, a problem which should be addressed globally rather than piecemeal. . . . Where called upon to provide assistance and protection to groups . . . it accordingly seeks to respond to the relevant needs of *all* members of the community, making distinctions, where appropriate, on the basis of actual need rather than status.[58]

It does so, however, by employing a set of safe spaces, such as UN protected areas and preventive zones, that may be less than safe.

THE SOMALIA-KENYA CONNECTION: PREVENTIVE ZONES AND REFUGEE CAMPS

The events that transpired in Somalia and their outcomes illustrate the idea of preventive protection in Africa. Containment strategies similar to those in Iraq and Bosnia-Herzegovina have been tested in the Horn of Africa. In southern Somalia, UNHCR created a preventive zone along the Kenyan border in order to slow the flow of potential refugees into Kenya and to encourage Somali refugees in Kenyan camps to return home (see figure 1.1). This Cross-Border Operation (CBO), launched in 1992, was also a strategy to empty the Kenyan camps after the government of Kenya signaled its intention to forcibly return Somali refugees. At the same time, the U.S.-led Operation Restore Hope was also initiated. It sent tens of thousands of troops to Somalia on a humanitarian mission to assist the starving civilian population in December 1992. In May 1993, peacekeepers from the Second UN Operation in Somalia (UNOSOM II) replaced the Unified Task Force (UNITAF) of Operation Restore Hope. UNHCR believed that the presence of these forces would represent security to refugees living in Kenya and attract them back to Somalia. Some refugees did return home, but other Somali nationals left their war-torn country for Kenya during the same period. In the short term, the Cross-Border Operation did not meet its objectives, despite generous initial funding from donors.

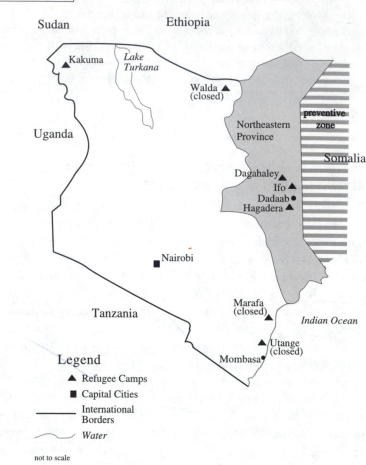

Sudan

Ethiopia

Kakuma

Lake Turkana

Walda (closed)

preventive zone

Northeastern Province

Somalia

Uganda

Dagahaley

Ifo

Dadaab

Hagadera

Nairobi

Tanzania

Marafa (closed)

Indian Ocean

Utange (closed)

Mombasa

Legend

▲ Refugee Camps
■ Capital Cities
── International Borders
∿ *Water*

not to scale

Figure 1.1. Map of Kenyan-Somalian border and preventive zone. Credit: Nadine Schuurman.

Safe havens and preventive zones are expressions of an emerging geopolitical discourse and are strategic spaces to contain would-be refugees in their home countries. This strategy is endorsed by Western governments, which fund UNHCR to execute the necessary emergency relief operations. While compromising the sovereignty of others, donor governments consolidate their own countries by gaining support at home. UNHCR is revising its own traditional category of refugee, recasting its protection mandate, and extending its reach inside the borders of countries at war where displaced people require assistance and safekeeping. The efficacy and safety of these efforts are still in question after the U.S./UN intervention in Somalia. The massacre of civilians in Srebrenica in July 1995 and the killing of several thousand refugees in Kibeho camp in Rwanda in April 1995 also cast doubt on them.

Refugee camps constitute another strategy of containment with assistance. Though camps are arguably a useful and acceptable short-term emergency measure, the second-rate status accorded to refugees in these "temporary cities" is problematic. In Kenya, the vast majority of refugees are Somalian nationals. At the height of displacement in 1992, more than 400,000 refugees were living in Kenya. By the end of 1996, approximately 185,000 refugees remained; 150,000 of these were Somali refugees. Smaller numbers of Sudanese and Ethiopian refugees were also counted. UNHCR is responsible for refugees based on its statute and in conjunction with the 1951 convention and 1967 protocol, which oblige signatory states to assist forcibly displaced migrants who meet specific criteria. Despite being a signatory to the 1951 convention and 1967 protocol, the Kenyan government is currently not considering asylum seekers for full convention refugee status. Accordingly, UNHCR has been called upon through its good offices to assist refugees who cannot be processed under convention or statutory definitions but who require protection. This residual group is generally granted prima facie refugee status.

Prima facie designation is usually made on a group basis rather than by the individual determination procedures that are the norm for determining convention status. It is conceptually linked to preventive protection in that it is a temporary measure that tends to provide assistance in a contained area to a displaced group of persons. Prima facie refugees, however, are distinguished from internally displaced persons by the obvious fact that they are outside their country of origin, generally in a country of first asylum.

In Kenya the vast majority of displaced Somalis and Sudanese fall into this ad hoc category of refugees. Though this status does entitle them to basic food, shelter, and health and social services in the camps, it precludes the possibility of their generating a more independent livelihood elsewhere. Employment is prohibited, and mobility beyond the borders of the isolated camps is restricted. All prima facie refugees are required by the Kenyan government to live in camps located in arid and semiarid border areas.[59]

These authorized spaces for the displaced have been described as "bleak and insecure holding camps along the Kenyan-Somali border."[60] UNHCR is careful not to make the camps too attractive to potential refugees or other migrants by maintaining minimum educational and other facilities, an approach that has been called "humane deterrence."[61] The Kenyan camps illustrate how protection and assistance are inextricably linked to refugee containment and immobility. A historical geography of politics along the Kenyan-Somalian border area is discussed in the next chapter. It speaks to the hotbed of protest and repression from the time of Kenyan independence, in 1963, until 1967, when the Republic of Somalia renounced its goal of annexing Kenya's Northern Frontier District, known also as Kenyan Somaliland. From independence until 1991, this region was under "emergency rule" by the government of Kenya. Many Kenyans of Somali ethnicity have faced arbitrary arrest, harassment, and discrimination. Banditry and general insecurity continue to prevail in this region today.

Both UN and NGO relief staff working in the camps make the best of difficult situations with the interests of refugees in mind. The formal administrative practices employed, however, attest to authoritative structures and a quasi-military mode of operations that may detract from this goodwill and hard work. Administration of the camps in this region involves a number of surveillance practices through which refugees are continually mapped, marked, and monitored. Though these are certainly not the only techniques employed, the primacy of monitoring in the camps is revealed in the opening paragraph of the UNHCR's Country Operations Plan for 1995:

> The reconciliation of data on the refugee population in Kenya has become a priority exercise of the Kenya programme during 1994. The Branch Office has addressed the intractable problem of discrepancies between feeding figures, registered numbers, and total populations, by camp site as well as by overall caseload and nationality, through physical headcounts and registration of refugees in the camps. These discrepancies are due to acts of refugee sabotage; double registration

within camps and between camps; and inflation of the number of dependants on ration cards in a bid to maximize their entitlements to food and other relief assistance distributed in the camps.[62]

is it elsewhere in document

The counting and coding of refugees in this particular passage is unsettling. Nowhere is refugee assessment or need mentioned. Rather, displaced people are converted into suspicious subject populations, figures, and numbers. Though not all or even most of UNHCR's reporting sees people as mere numbers, this sample of humanitarian discourse echoes other "imperial encounters" by producing an untrustworthy and inferior other, which, in turn, legitimizes a full complement of surveillance and disciplinary practices (see chapter 5).[63]

Because the vast majority of refugees in Kenya have prima facie status, they are entitled to assistance through the good offices of UNHCR, but they remain, in a practical sense, second-rate refugees. Their containment in camps renders them wholly dependent on international humanitarian assistance. They are given temporary safety and protection from *refoulement*—forcible return to the country from which they fled—but the price they pay for this safety is high. Though refugees are officially prohibited from moving outside the camps, some are able to move to more strategic locations. This unauthorized movement of Somali refugees, in particular, annoys the government of Kenya (GOK), which then complains to UNHCR. Yet it is also a political statement that these authorities cannot simply contain the refugee problem. Nonetheless, the movement of displaced people, whether they are in safe havens or refugee camps, is highly restricted, and their safety is spatially circumscribed. The placement in displacement matters. Mobility is political.

So far a number of parallel trends in the management of displacement have been identified. First, there is increasingly a two-tier refugee system in which fewer and fewer refugees meet the criteria for full convention refugee status. Convention status has been displaced, in the Kenyan case, by the discretionary group designation of prima facie refugees, whose movements and entitlements are much more restricted. In Kenya, prima facie refugees are involuntary migrants contained in refugee camps far from the borders of donor states. Related to this trend is a shift in the locus of responsibility for displaced people—whether they are refugees or not—from individual states to international UN agencies, in particular to UNHCR, which is funded by the very states that have traditionally received refugees in their countries. In 1995, the senior staff member of a U.S. agency based in the Kenyan camps said, "[T]he donors are willing to pay them [UN agencies] off. . . . Africa is a sinkhole. 'You [UN agencies] take care of it; here's the money' will eventually turn to 'you [UN agencies] take care of it; we're not paying anymore.' Now we are in a grazing period where there is big money to be made [working in the aid industry]."[64] In large part, her prediction has been correct. Donor governments and related UN agencies hesitated at becoming involved in Rwanda during the 1994 genocide, with horrifying consequences. When they finally stepped in with relief for refugees and murderers fleeing the scene (figure 1.2), donors and UN organizations were paralyzed by the realization that their support caused as much harm as good in the absence of an effective sorting process to weed out perpetrators of the genocide from genuine refugees in the camps. Meanwhile, the perpetrators planned their next move from (then) Zaire with the material and tacit political aid of UN agencies. This series of events and responses has generated serious soul-searching among donors and humanitarian organizations alike. The virtual absence of UN peacekeeping forces and humani-

Figure 1.2. Refugees from Rwanda/Ngara, Kagera region (UNHCR). Courtesy UNHCR/24067/04.1994/P. Moumtzis.

tarian agencies in the Democratic Republic of Congo (formerly Zaire), despite threats to the civilan population, is also telling.

The popularity of and sympathy for displaced peoples on the part of Western governments lies precisely in their location "over there." As they approach "our" borders, they become "immigrants," "foreigners," and "bogus refugees" who face a less enthusiastic reception. The distance is a discursive and geographical one: As long as there is no need to engage in face-to-face conversations with these unfortunate people whose plight is witnessed on television or through other media, their situation remains a tragedy.

UNSTATING THE CASE

Borders breed politics and uneven geographies of power and status. They can generate marginalization, racism, and other unequal relations of power. Convention refugees are those who have crossed international borders, especially in Europe, and are recognized as such. They have the right to work, to move freely within the country that hosts them, and to participate in civil society to some degree. Prima facie refugees are also designated by a border crossing, though their status is more tentative. In the Kenyan context, they are given temporary sanctuary *as a group* in a specified and contained location, and they are precluded from holding employment or moving from that location. Internationally displaced persons assisted through the strategy of preventive protection have not crossed an international border. Rather, multilateral peacekeeping and humanitarian assistance come to them within their own country in designated safe havens or protected areas. Border crossings are prevented where possible, and entitlements are minimized when refugees do make their way to another country. Increasingly, multilateral agencies cross borders and would-be refugees wait.

Borderlands and boundaries have been widely discussed by geographers, feminists, and cultural theorists in many contexts.[65] They are at once locations and testimony to dominant geopolitical discourse that create both conflict and violent representations, designating those who do and do not belong. This process of identity formation nonetheless privileges the nation-state as the venue for political contest and change. Preventive protection is at least as much about states' interests as it is about assisting displaced persons in need. As such, it consolidates state power among the countries that pay for humanitarian intervention and destabilizes states in which intervention occurs. Preventive protection is an expression of the more powerful states' desire to avoid the legal obligations of refugees and to save nonrefugee taxpayers' money in their home territories. It speaks to a desire for a multilateral, or UN, solution to displacement in order to avoid incurring the perceived expense of refugees, both economically and politically, within the precarious and declining welfare states of donor governments.

In practice, the state-based system of administering international refugee law is unraveling. Just as assistance to non-European refugees was optional when the 1951 convention was written, so too is international assistance for internally displaced nonrefugees optional today. Governments are working to prevent the seeking of asylum where feasible, and UNHCR is working to assure standards of practice that apply to internally displaced persons. The recent debut of preventive protection and safe areas, as geopolitical discourse, is both politically and theoretically significant. It produces a legitimacy for multilateral interventions into sovereign states––a mode of unmaking the state—but at the same time embodies the interests of donor states, which favor certain modes of managing displacement at arm's length. There is at once a disparate weakening and strengthening of states vis-à-vis the international humanitarian regime. State power is at once obfuscated and transformed by multilateral operations on geographically uneven terms. What follows is an effort to simultaneously theorize mobility and ground it in a historically contingent political geography within the Horn of Africa.

2

Border Crossings: The Politics of Mobility

Theorizing mobility begins with people's stories and histories of migration. In Xavier Koller's 1990 film, *Journey of Hope,* a poor peasant family sells its meager farm assets in rural Turkey, banking on swift passage to the utopic Switzerland that it has seen on a postcard sent by a relative. Of their many children, the parents take only one, their youngest son, who is to be the bearer of the family's name and the agent of its future fortunes. Their journey is arranged by a contact whose trade and trafficking in illegal migrants is a lucrative business. In the company of a sympathetic German truck driver, the family fails in its first attempt to gain entry and is turned backed to Italy. There the trio finds another agent, who assures them he can help if they can pay. The business of trafficking in migrants is increasingly depicted as unsavory as the Turkish family approaches the mountainous Swiss-Italian border. The family, now part of a larger group of migrating clients, is transported to the frontier in the back of a van and instructed to pose as political refugees as soon as they cross the border. Unprepared for a snowstorm and the struggle over the Alps before them, some members of the group, many near death, are discovered by Swiss border patrols when they finally arrive at the border. The *journey of hope,* embodied by the young boy, whose linguistic dexterity enables the migrants to cross cultural boundaries and whose winning spirit with strangers renders new lands less daunting, culminates in his death, the imprisonment of his father, and the grief of his mother. At the same time, many along the way have been enriched by the failed journey. Borders breed loss and conflict, but they also breed profit.

In this chapter, I employ the notion of a "geopolitics of mobility" to argue that international borders are more porous to capital than to displaced bodies. The mobility of international humanitarian aid is juxtaposed with the relative immobility of migrants, specifically refugees, generating two distinct but related geographies. The significantly large global economy in refugee relief activities and humanitarian interventions operates in a localized manner, usually in close proximity to sources of human displacement and crisis. This economy is historically constituted by colonial practices, Cold War interests, and cultural politics that operate at several geographical scales.

This chapter draws attention to the organizations whose money makes the status of refugee possible. I trace the locations and destinations of funds provided by powerful humanitarian organizations, and I argue that the tensions that humanitarian assistance aims to ease are historically and spatially specific. The regime of international humanitarian assistance—the refugee industry—concentrates power at specific sites but operates across political borders and between groups of unequal positioning. In presenting a critical examination of the power relations that structure global humanitarian flows, I contend that core/periphery and center/margin binaries are inadequate tools for theorizing mobility. The dynamics of forced migration combined with voluntary donations produce nuanced, contradictory patterns that defy overarching narratives of humanism, development, and unitary subjects. The transnational politics of mobility introduced in this chapter attempts to move beyond the binary geopolitical divisions of North and South, West and East, as well as the problematic categories of First, Second, and Third Worlds. It aims to theorize unequal power relations in a context that pays attention to identities formed within, beyond, and in spite of nation-states, that is to say, in a transnational context. Transnational flows of refugees and donor funds are juxtaposed to accentuate their culturally marked, politically unequal positions, as well as their differential mobility across sites of humanitarian activity.

This chapter focuses on an analysis of organizations, networks, and brokers of power rather than on the powerless. To ignore the organizations that embody this power is to mistake the object of inquiry. Though critics have argued that any object of inquiry is an invention in itself,[1] this chapter focuses on UNHCR and its operations in two locations, Switzerland and the Horn of Africa. The analysis draws on the political histories and cultural politics of each location to illustrate how connections between them have been unevenly constructed and why humanitarian funds are more mobile than displaced peoples.

Changing geopolitical relations of power and the economic resources they command shape mobility and access in material ways. Attention to these political constellations of power is vital to any analysis of humanitarian operations. Just as cultural geographies cannot simply be privileged over political ones, geopolitical theories, ranging from the postmodern to the neorealist, are not foregrounded at the expense of cultural politics. Theories of migrant subjectivity and identity are important tools for teaching us to think outside the conventional box of the nation-state. They do not, however, account for the political trade-offs of money for displaced bodies. Approaches attentive to the hypermobility of capital in relation to the markedly restricted movement of members from the displaced diaspora pose a stark contrast, and yet a complementary materiality, to the incisive analyses of theorists more focused on cultural issues. My theoretical aim is neither to weigh nor to assess the merits of these two literatures in relation to one another but, rather, to bring them together in some kind of dialogue that speaks to the hierarchies of humanitarian spaces and the people who occupy them. On a more grounded level, the mobility of financiers of refugee relief is compared with and connected to that of forced migrants, who rarely share the same location as their patrons. In what follows, I present a short vignette of humanitarian flows in and out of Switzerland, and then introduce a historical and contemporary case study from the Horn of Africa. In so doing, I illustrate two kinds of spatially coded border crossings: one financial and predominantly European; the other corporeal and African.

BORDER CROSSINGS AND THE POLITICS OF MOBILITY

Although segregation can be temporarily imposed as a sociopolitical arrangement, it can never be absolute, especially on the level of culture. All utterances inescapably take place against the background of the possible responses of other social and ethnic points of view.

— ELLA SHOHAT AND ROBERT STAM, *UNTHINKING EUROCENTRISM: MULTICULTURALISM AND THE MEDIA*

We can redraw borders; we recognize that different types of boundaries operate at different scales.

— GERALDINE PRATT, "COMMENTARY"

How human displacement is defined and managed depends on historically specific configurations of geopolitics as well as on cultural and economic relations of power. The politics of mobility is a useful tool for analyzing migration, specifically because it recognizes the variable movement of refugees and other disenfranchised groups. With reference to the relations of power and resources that bear on people's movement, Doreen Massey has raised the idea of a politics of mobility and access, arguing that different groups of people have distinct relationships to mobility: "[S]ome are more in charge of it than others; some initiate flows and movement, others don't; some are more on the receiving end of it than others; some are effectively imprisoned by it."[2] Though Massey's "power-geometry" notes differential mobility among distinct groups of people, she does not delve far enough into the economies of power that regulate and facilitate their movement. In the case of refugees and other displaced persons, the "geo-politics of money"[3] is as important as the geopolitics of the crisis that precipitates forced migration. Without international funding, few refugee camps would exist, expensive international interventions in Somalia and the former Yugoslavia would not have taken place, and refugee-receiving countries would not host as many asylum seekers as they currently do. Even the Turkish family in *Journey of Hope* could not embark on its migrant journey without liquidating its land to pay for passage. A transnational geopolitics of mobility must be attentive to "money, power and space"[4] and to cultural theories of displacement and travel to be an effective tool for analyzing forced migration. Just as "feminists need detailed, historicized maps of the circuits of power,"[5] geographers and other scholars require better analytical tools to examine critically the connections between migrant subjects, the geopolitics of money, and the borders—political and cultural—they cross.

"As free-trade zones proliferate and tariffs are dismantled, mobility, flexibility, and speed have become the watchwords of both the traders and the theorists in metropolitan cultures."[6] In the case of refugees and other displaced peoples, movement is shaped not only by global geopolitics of money but also by displacement caused by violent conflict and disparate social conditions of wealth and opportunity. Forced migration today constitutes a sizable segment of transnational movements. In 1995, more than 27 million refugees and other "persons of concern" were counted by the Office of UNHCR.[7] Diasporic distributions are not, however, based on an equality of mobility and access among all groups. Opportunities to cross borders and move within a country, whether made voluntarily or involuntarily, depend on prevailing politics, economic resources, gendered access to jobs, and other key positionings.

Approaching the geopolitics of mobility as a network of unequal and uneven links between displaced bodies within the global economy of humanitarian assistance risks undermining more conventional political struggles between "us" and "them." Nonetheless, such a transnational analysis can contest accepted readings of border meanings and, in this chapter, border crossings. At one level, the geopolitics of mobility is a tool for contesting master narratives of humanism, humanitarianism, and statehood itself. At another, it serves as a link for materialist accountability to the unimpeded traveling cultures and diasporic populations heralded by some theorists.[8]

Arjun Appadurai introduces the idea of "ethnoscape" as a "landscape of persons who make up the shifting world in which we live."[9] These include tourists, business executives, exiles, immigrants, guest workers, refugees, and members of other mobile groups. He argues that any analysis of "ethno-" without a spatial referent, or "-scape," is aspatial. Though an ethnoscape may descriptively ground the mobility of particular ethnic groups, the concept does not account for the differential power and resources of distinctive migrant groups— for example, women as compared to men—nor does it examine politics of location and ethnonationalism for people who do not move. Just as cultural relationships and identities produce and position subjects, economies of money, space, and power shape their mobility unevenly within and across migrant groups.

In his more recent work, Appadurai has written about the slippage and change in the relationship between state and territory, which were generally assumed to be synonymous. He notes that "global competition for allegiances now involves all sorts of non-state actors and organizations and various forms of diasporic or multilocal allegiance."[10] This observation is important in that it recognizes new and multiple forms of subjectivity linked across axes of political, economic, cultural, and social power. Appadurai develops the term "translocalities" to describe places largely divorced from their national contexts, characterized by cultural heterogeneity, and often straddling formal political borders. To the extent that this idea encourages us to think beyond the customary formulation of the nation-state, in a transnational context, it is useful as both a theoretical and a political tool. As in his discussion of ethnoscapes, however, the author lumps together free-trade zones, existing political borders (such as the U.S.-Mexican frontier), tourist areas, world cities, ghettos, refugee camps, concentration camps, and reservations under the rubric of translocalities. As such, the term loses its strength as a political tool that might otherwise examine links between these historically distinct and unequal sites of transnational migration.

In calling for reflexive ethnographic practices in Third World locations, James Clifford maintains that "[t]here is no longer any place of overview (mountain top) from which to map human ways of life, no Archimedian point from which to represent the world." Rather, "[h]uman ways of life increasingly influence, dominate, parody, translate, and subvert one another."[11] Though the omniscient universal subject or narrator has no doubt given way to partial truths and more-limited ways of seeing, and at the same time interconnections among cultures have multiplied, the relations of *domination* Clifford hints at remain undeveloped. "Traveling culture" might better be described as a relationship of power that is inherently political because it is predicated upon a hierarchy of cultures that articulate unequal positions of authority and mobility. By textualizing the ethnographic experience, Clifford constructively problematizes culture, but the cultural encounter nonetheless occurs in a space void of the geopolitics of money, identity documents, and funding that enable traveling culture to occur.

Clifford makes a distinction that captures the point I underscore throughout this book. He describes diaspora as connecting multiple communities of a dispersed population. Diasporas presuppose longer distances and a separation more akin to exile than do the populations with which border theorists are concerned: "These [border] approaches share a good deal with diaspora paradigms. But borderlands are distinct in that they presuppose a territory defined by a geopolitical line: two sides arbitrarily separated and policed, but also jointed by legal and illegal practices of crossing and communication."[12] My argument acknowledges that these theoretical orientations are indeed distinct but claims that their particular modes of tracing and mapping displacement overlap on the ground and are both vital to any analysis of humanitarianism.

Theories of traveling culture and postmodern ethnography provide sustained and convincing criticism of central epistemological locations, prevailing political rationalities, and the structures that propagate them. Yet in the cases just noted, such theories have yet to alter these relations of power. Humanist sensibilities and humanitarian agencies have been and continue to be formative in the organization and reorganization of power among sedentary and migrant groups, especially in formerly colonized locations: "[W]hat now becomes important is not a 'decentering' of Europe as such, but in fact a critical interrogation of the practices, modalities, and projects through which *the varied forms of Europe's insertion* into the lives of the colonized were constructed and organized."[13] Analyzing Europe's insertion into the postindependence, or postcolonial, lives of the presently displaced and formerly colonized is an important step toward developing a transnational geopolitics of mobility.

The feminist and arguably postcolonial criticism of Trinh Minh-ha engages with the politics of mobility, albeit in a different register. She focuses on subjectivity in the context of inequitable power relations and traces movement as a basis of identity formation. Her writing, like her films, at once subverts linear Western representations of space and engages in a politicized critique of their material effects. Nonetheless, she retains a unitary, if non-Western, self that belies an arguably anticolonial sensibility rather than a postcolonial one. An excerpt from her recent work illustrates this well:

> To travel can consist in operating a profoundly unsettling inversion of one's identity: I become me via an other. . . . Travelling allows one to see things differently from what they are, differently from how one has seen them, and differently from what one is. These three supplementary identities gained via alterity are in fact still (undeveloped or unrealized) gestures of the "self"—the energy system that defines (albeit in a shifting and contingent mode) what and who each seer is. The voyage out of the (known) self and back into the (unknown) self sometimes takes the wanderer far away to a motley place where everything

is safe and sound seems to waver while the essence of language is placed in doubt and profoundly destabilized. Travelling can thus turn out to be a process whereby the self loses its fixed boundaries—a disturbing yet potentially empowering practice of difference.[14]

Trinh Minh-ha displaces the Western gaze, the universal subject, and the pretense of order in the world by theorizing the unsettling experience of travel constitutive of migrant subjectivity. She qualifies her comments about traveling theory: "Dispossessed not only of their material belongings but also of the social heritage, refugees lead a provisional life, drifting from camp to camp, disturbing local people's habits, and destabilizing the latter's lifestyle. . . . On the one hand, migrant settlements can turn out to be 'centers of hopelessness' which soon become 'centers of discontent.'"[15] Trinh Minh-ha contributes a feminist critique to investigations of human mobility, but she maintains a center/margin dichotomy and does not account for the economies of power that govern the movement of refugees and the international capital earmarked for their assistance. At the expense of geopolitical considerations, she focuses on the relationship between cultural politics and mobility. If "[t]he war of borders is a war waged by the West on a global scale to preserve its values,"[16] as she contends, then any theoretical and political framework that aims to address these relations of power must incorporate the Western funders of this war, which operates between and across First and Third Worlds, across borders, cultures, and historical contexts. Her transnational analysis of cultural politics and refugee identity calls for a complementary transnational analysis of mobility attentive to geopolitics and economies of refugee aid.

Combined with the increased mobility of space-time compression, questions of travel, identity formation, and displacement represent a major tour de force in the social sciences and humanities. Caren Kaplan provides a detailed feminist analysis and account of the development of cultural studies and feminist theory in relation to travel and displacement.[17] Her genuinely postdisciplinary contribution argues, among other things, that "contemporary theories of exile must delineate the material conditions of displacement that generate subject positions."[18] Though her own analysis is located almost exclusively within a poststructuralist theoretical domain, Kaplan cites important works that do forge materialist links and asks the poignant question, "Can colonial spaces be recoded or reterritorialized without producing neocolonialisms?"[19] This question is central to the chapter.

What many cultural theorists do not focus upon is the way in which the accelerated movement of people across the globe parallels that of money: Those with money can take advantage of space-time compression.[20] Those who are uprooted from their homes and forced to flee their country with few resources experience migration in a very different way. After a discussion of Geneva as the historical if contradictory heartland of humanitarian aid, a detailed analysis follows in which the identities and spaces of Somali people during the colonial and Cold War periods are linked to the contemporary positionings of Somali refugees vis-à-vis the international humanitarian regime. This conflation of cultural and political power relations aims to disrupt the nation-state, as common territory and time. The remainder of this chapter tracks a transnational imaginary, one that comprises "the *as-yet-unfigured* horizon of contemporary cultural production by which national spaces/identities of political allegiance and economic regulation are being undone and imagined communities of modernity are being reshaped at the macropolitical (global) and micropolitical (cultural) levels of everyday existence."[21] A genuinely transnational geopolitics of mobility calls for a critical analysis of both political and cultural networks, which focuses on the negotiating and financing of particular humanitarian sites by the international refugee regime.

This story of mobility begins first in Europe and then moves to the Horn of Africa, a region in which Europe invested heavily during the colonial era and in which Soviet and U.S. superpowers exerted control through alliances for strategic purposes during the Cold War. The geography of finance for humanitarian crises that follows, I contend, is linked to the geography of human displacement in the Horn of Africa. The borders that produce refugees and circumscribe their movement in the Horn of Africa today, I contend, are predicated on colonial and Cold War political geographies, cultural politics, and economic alliances. The formation of borders during colonial partition was reinscribed by infusions of arms and other investments during the period of superpower rivalry. Today these borders continue to be reinforced by the large, and no less political, flows of humanitarian assistance. The flow of resources to the Horn continues today, albeit from different locations and to serve ostensibly humanitarian rather than colonial or superpower interests. The relative immobility of refugees in the region is contrasted with the hypermobility of capital to the region, both of which have historical antecedents.

Of the 27.4 million refugees and other persons of concern counted at the end of 1994, 11.8 million lived in Africa alone.[22] The huge
flow of humanitarian capital into Africa during the 1990s in the
form of peacekeeping and refugee relief has been far more impressive
than the number of refugees and displaced persons who have been
allowed to leave.[23]

GENEVA: NODE OF HUMANITARIAN FLOWS

Switzerland hosts a large number of international banks and humanitarian organizations. Geneva, in particular, is both an international

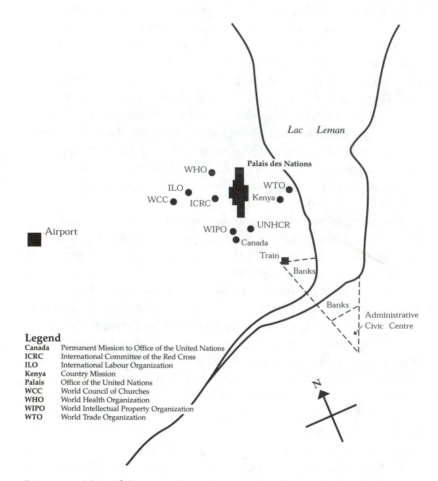

*Figure 2.1. Map of Geneva's Humanitarian City Center. Credit: Nadine
Schuurman.*

banking capital and a seat of power for the United Nations and other international agencies whose mandates include humanitarian and development assistance. Northwest of the commercial city center, an entire neighborhood of these organizations exists in which the UN Palais des Nations forms a kind of humanitarian city center (see figure 2.1). The concentration of international organizations forms a kind of global locale that serves as the financial district and administrative center of humanitarian assistance. Various countries have permanent missions to the Office of the United Nations, and most vie for a space close to the Palais. The World Health Organization, the International Labor Organization, the World Trade Organization, the World Intellectual Property Organization, and the UNHCR, among others, share the neighborhood with bilateral missions from individual governments and a range of international NGOs (see figure 2.2). The proximity and sociability of these organizations to one another, and especially to the Office of the United Nations, is critical to the politics of humanitarian funding that take place in Geneva.[24] As an international financial center for private and public capital, the city has both symbolic and practical value. It is the place of emerging news, expert views, and key meetings determining the direction of financial decisions.

Figure 2.2. UNHCR Headquarters, Geneva. Author's photograph.

Among the humanitarian organizations in Geneva is the International Committee of the Red Cross (ICRC), one of the most reputable nonpolitical organizations, whose location in Switzerland is deliberate. Until recently, only Swiss citizens could work for this humanitarian organization, visiting political prisoners and entering into discussions with governments holding such prisoners in efforts to secure their release. Since 1815, Switzerland has remained politically neutral. It does not belong to the European Union or NATO, nor has it signed many of the human rights instruments and international legal conventions that would oblige it to act according to external international standards. Key concepts of independence and neutrality have been constant since the first Geneva Convention of 1864. It is no accident that the Geneva Conventions of 1949, outlining minimum standards for the treatment of civilians in countries at war, were written in Switzerland.

Banking in Switzerland is also predicated on this reputation of neutrality. Geneva has an advantage over Luxembourg—where banking space is cheaper and situated within the European Union—because of Swiss neutrality. Bankers in Geneva are "discreet." They carry two business cards: one with the standard information, that is, name of the employee and bank, full telephone number, and address; the other with only the banker's name and a local phone number without any country or area codes. The first is for people who are not crossing borders or who have no need to be concerned about such crossings; the second is for investors and people who want to bring money into Switzerland without being recorded. (A French citizen, for example, can bring only 50,000 French francs—approximately U.S.$10,000—into Switzerland; any amount beyond that will be taxed.) There is no information on the second card through which to trace the location of the person named. Bankers answer the phone at their offices with a familiar salutation and give no identifying information. Most banks offer named accounts and numbered accounts, which, like the two types of business cards, are used for different reasons, but both can be coded for increased privacy and can be declared or undeclared for tax purposes. All accounts are protected by the banking secrecy act, *La Loi Féderal sur les Banques et les Caisses d'Epargne*. Bank business cards and accounts disguise locations and identities in order to render the Swiss border fluid and friendly to incoming capital.

The situation for bodies wanting to locate in Switzerland is considerably more restricted. Though Switzerland is one of only ten UN member states to announce annual resettlement quotas for refugees—quotas that are shrinking in the major resettlement countries—asylum seekers who arrive at the airport in Geneva are required to stay in an "international zone"; they are not considered to have entered the country until officials assess the validity of their claims and accept or deport them accordingly. Switzerland accepts comparatively few refugees for permanent resettlement, but it offers temporary protection to some and provisional status to others in refugee-like circumstances through "special action programs." In 1994, a bill was passed giving the Swiss Federal Office for Refugees (FOR) the right to detain, for up to twelve months, any asylum seeker over the age of fifteen who does not have proof of identity or legal residence, regardless of whether she or he has committed a crime.[25] A complex hierarchy of designations and entitlements exists, and these are available to some non-Swiss residents, though work permits and permission for long-term stays are difficult to obtain. *Journey of Hope* presents rather starkly the unlikely scenario that many of the outsiders who arrive at the border will be allowed entry into the orderly Swiss state.

Two of Switzerland's specialties—banking and humanitarianism—have recently come face-to-face, creating somewhat of a crisis in both sectors. Switzerland's reputation as a place of refuge and humanitarian assistance has been tarnished by fresh evidence that prior to and during the Holocaust, Jewish money was welcomed but Jewish refugees were not. Heirs of Holocaust victims demanded access to Swiss bank accounts set up by their ancestors, some of whom were refused entry into Switzerland and were unable to escape the Nazi executions. "Swiss banks had insisted heirs produce account numbers and death certificates, which were never issued by the Nazis."[26] The Swiss Bankers Association responded to pressure from Holocaust survivors and the World Jewish Congress by setting up a central registry to track dormant accounts. In 1996, the Swiss Bankers Association reported the existence of some 775 dormant accounts, worth about U.S.$32 million excluding interest. In July 1997, Swiss banks waived their tradition of secrecy and published in newspapers around the world a list of approximately 2,000 dormant accounts from the World War II period. The accounts are thought to contain the assets of Holocaust victims.[27]

On June 19, 1998, the three biggest Swiss commercial banks offered U.S.$600 million to settle a class-action suit brought by 31,000 Holocaust survivors and family members, who maintain that the banks stole their assets during World War II. This offer was called "humiliating" and "insulting" by Jewish leaders and the lawyers representing the Holocaust survivors, who about a week later proposed a U.S.$1.5 billion settlement.[28] In August 1998, representatives of Swiss banks and Holocaust survivors finally reached a settlement in which the banks agreed to pay U.S.$1.25 billion in reparations to those who lost assets during World War II.[29] Archives in Eastern Europe, which were inaccessible during the Cold War, have come under scrutiny and point to pre–World War II transfers to Swiss banks of money and gold looted by the Nazis. Recent research suggests that at least 10,000 Jewish refugees were turned away from the Swiss border and that records of their exclusion were destroyed by the Swiss government just after the war. Fifty years later, the Swiss government has formally apologized for destroying the record of refugee applications.

Switzerland hosts international centers for banks and humanitarian organizations. Even though Geneva champions itself as a "city of refuge," the Swiss government is in fact extremely careful as to whom it lets in. For investors, borders are blurred by discreet business practices and Swiss laws protecting privacy; capital is welcome.

THE HORN OF AFRICA: REINSCRIBING BORDERS

My analysis principally concerns Somali peoples in the Horn of Africa and their displacement across and within borders that were drawn during the colonial period and reinscribed at the time of independence. In particular, the imagined pan-Somali nation has never corresponded to the colonial or postcolonial borders of the country (see figure 2.3).[30] The difference between the imagined Somali nation and the Somalian nation-state has been the basis of a nationalist project and a major source of geopolitical conflict in the region throughout the colonial, Cold War, and contemporary periods. Each period is marked by political and economic global influences as well as regional tensions that have together shaped Somali displacement. Though not all Somali people in the postcolonial context are Somalian nationals, Somalis on all sides of political borders in the Horn of

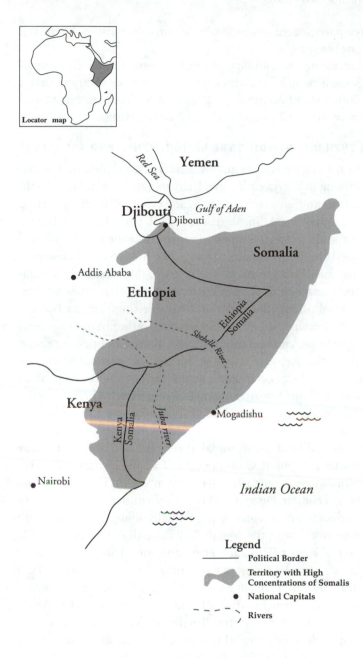

Figure 2.3. *Map of territory of ethnic Somali concentration. Credit: Nadine Schuurman.*

Africa have participated in economies of corporeal displacement and transnational capital.

In underscoring the mobility of capital versus the relative immobility of Somali people over three historical periods, I argue that a former colonialism of derision along this border has been reinscribed in the current context as a colonialism of compassion.

DRAWING THE LINE, DIVIDING THE NATION: KENYA AND SOMALIA

The government of Kenya has not hidden its disdain for either Somali refugees living in Kenya or its own Kenyan nationals of Somali ethnicity. Racism and discrimination against Somalis are practiced today just as they were during the colonial period, when Britain ruled Kenya and northern Somalia, France controlled Djibouti, and Italy occupied southern Somalia. Though the first colonial powers in the Horn exercised only a maritime presence, the "scramble for empire" among European nations in the late nineteenth century accelerated the process of colonial partition. Unsurprisingly, many borders in Africa were drawn with European interests rather than indigenous settlement patterns, class relations, or precolonial politics in mind.[31] Conflict over the Kenyan-Somalian border, in particular, can be traced back to colonial occupation at the turn of the century, when Britain exerted control over the semiarid region now known as the Northeast Province of Kenya. The British colonial administration wanted to establish a buffer zone between its borders with Ethiopia and Italian Somaliland (now Somalia) on one side and its railway and white settler population on the other (see figure 2.4).[32] Accordingly, administrative boundaries were drawn within Kenya, creating the Northern Frontier District (NFD). The frontier in the district's name was elucidated in 1909 when Somalis living in Kenya were prohibited from crossing the Somali-Galla line that divided the NFD from the rest of Kenya. This early effort to contain Somalis in northeast Kenya led to strategies by subsequent governments to curtail the mobility of Somali Kenyans in relation to other Kenyan nationals.

The 1909 policy generated significant resistance to colonial rule among Somalis. In response, the British administration enacted a legal ordinance declaring the NFD a closed district in 1926, a move that afforded it broad powers to sweep, in its terms, the "Somali problem" behind the line, as it were, using whatever force was necessary. In the face of sustained political organization among Somalis, a

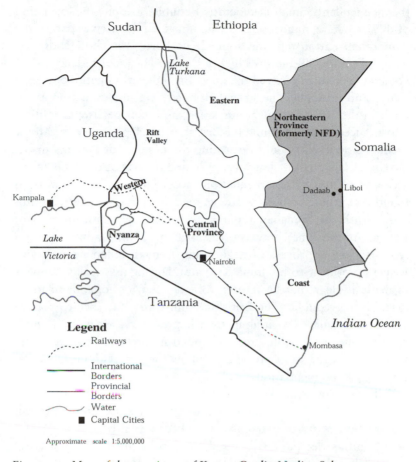

Figure 2.4. Map of the provinces of Kenya. Credit: Nadine Schuurman.

subsequent legal ordinance designated the NFD a Special District and required its Somali inhabitants to carry passes or seek approval from authorities to enter other districts. Predictably, the colonial administration made little attempt to promote social or economic activities in the district or to integrate it politically with the rest of Kenya. This geographical and socioeconomic segregation was continued after Kenya achieved independence. Even today, this Special District remains distinctly poorer and less politically powerful than the rest of Kenya.

In 1960, British Somaliland, located in the northern part of the emerging country, united with Italian Somaliland in the south to form the independent Somali Democratic Republic. Despite the formation of this new state, many Somalis who imagined themselves part of the pan-Somali nation remained outside its borders in the Ogaden region of Ethiopia and in the NFD of Kenya. The independence of the Somalian republic renewed the quest for unification with Somalis in Kenya and Ethiopia. The struggle for self-determination among Somalis in the NFD of Kenya intensified, and their persistent political efforts succeeded in pushing the British colonial secretary to call for a commission that would determine the opinion of Somalis in the district. A UN commission was appointed to consult residents of the area and to make recommendations accordingly.[33] The commission found that ethnic Somalis in Kenya overwhelmingly preferred unification with the Somalian republic to remaining politically part of Kenya. At the time, however, the British colonial administration was also in the process of negotiating Kenyan independence with Kenya's president-to-be, Jomo Kenyatta. During these talks, Kenyatta made it clear that he refused to cede Kenyan Somaliland to its neighboring republic. The British administration decided to placate Kenyatta by quickly writing its own *Report of the Regional Boundaries Commission,* which recommended its preferred course of action, and reneged on its promise to follow through with the UN commission's recommendations.

When this decision was announced, the government of the Somalian republic severed its diplomatic ties with Britain and mounted an insurrection in northeast Kenya that became known as the Shifta War.[34] Shiftas were, and still are, defined as bandits. (Bandit activity is exacerbated by the systematic economic marginalization of ethnic Somalis living in this region of Kenya, the Northeast Province of Kenya being one of the poorest regions in the country.)[35] By relegating resistance in the area to mere regional "banditry," the British administration tried to undermine the political legitimacy of Somali actions. In efforts to counter resistance, the colonial administration of the day declared a state of emergency in the district in March 1963. Immediately after Kenya's independence in December 1963, the newly independent Kenyan government also declared a state of emergency in the Northeastern Province and held the Somalian government responsible for rebel activity in the region.[36] Surveillance of Somalis continued despite the change in government. Once again, mobility was curtailed and due legal process suspended. The late-nineteenth-century colonial partitioning was reinscribed as the Somalian-Kenyan border at the moment of Kenyan independence with the help of the British administration. Patterns of government discrimination against Somalis in the Northeast Province of Kenya continued, contributing to the ongoing economic marginalization of the area.

After Kenyan independence, the political struggle for the unification of a Somali nation continued at regional and continental levels. The Somalian government looked for support from the OAU, founded in 1963, but found none. Though the OAU admitted that the borders of postindependence African states were artificial, it was committed to territorial integrity and the survival of these borders as a practical compromise to achieve peace among African states. Between 1964 and 1967, reports suggest that some 2,000 Somalis were killed by Kenyan security forces.[37] The pressure for unification continued, however, and at the OAU Summit in Mogadishu in 1974, a memorandum was circulated to delegates demanding the return of the disputed territory to Somalia. Attorney General Charles Njonjo of Kenya, who was attending the summit, declared that "Kenya could never agree to surrender part of her territory. Kenyans, be they Borans or Somalis, who did not support Kenya 'should pack their camels and go to Somalia.'"[38] The position of the government of Kenya, which vowed not to cede any ground to Somalia, had very material implications for Kenyan Somalis. In the struggle to gain independence from colonialism, the new Kenyan government was complicit and reinscribed the colonization of the Northern Frontier District. Soon after, expelling inhabitants of the area became a means of addressing Somali resistance and rectifying the "Somali problem." Although Somalia formally renounced its claim on the Northeast Province in 1967, the state of emergency policy remained in effect in the region until 1991, and the surveillance and expulsion of Somalis—Kenyan or Somalian—by the Kenyan government remains current practice.

COLD WAR PROXIES AND REFUGEES

During the Cold War, Somalia's strategic location near the oil-rich Middle East was perceived to be of great value to the U.S. and Soviet superpowers. The border tensions generated by the pan-Somali project shifted in the late 1970s because of Cold War rivalries in which

Somalia and Ethiopia both became proxies in the periphery. Ethiopia had benefited from huge amounts of U.S. military assistance since the 1950s, and the United States had a well-established base in what is present-day Eritrea. When Somalia signed a friendship treaty with the Soviet Union in 1974, the tension between superpowers in the region intensified, and the Somalian government used this alliance as a lever for obtaining substantial economic and military assistance. By 1976, the U.S.S.R. had almost 4,000 military and civilian advisers in Somalia,[39] and Somalia had one of the largest and best-equipped armed forces in sub-Saharan Africa. Then President Siad Barre sought arms to increase control on the domestic front and "in pursuit of expansionist goals, with a view to annexing part of Ethiopia and Kenya."[40] Superpower influence could not be separated from regional tensions in the Horn, particularly between Somalia and Ethiopia over the Somali-occupied Ethiopian Ogaden territory. While Ethiopia struggled with internal crises, Somalian forces prepared to attack the country, against Moscow's advice. In 1977, they invaded the Ogaden region of Ethiopia in a move to annex it. In a complicated changing of client states during the same year, the United States withdrew from Ethiopia; Ethiopia then invited Soviet assistance, which it received. The Somalian government, angered by the Soviet betrayal, forced the U.S.S.R. to leave its military base at Berbera in northern Somalia; the base was taken over by the United States, which was still keen to retain an influence in the region. Whereas colonial interests had shaped geopolitics in the Horn of Africa only a decade earlier, superpower rivalries in these strategic postcolonial proxy states had become the major external influence, both politically and economically, in the region by the late 1970s.

The Somalian government lost its bid to take over the Ogaden region from Ethiopia. With one of the largest armament airlifts in African history, the Soviet Union and Cuba enabled Ethiopia to defeat the Somalian military in 1978. After the Ogaden War ended that year, the avowedly anticommunist President Daniel Arap Moi of Kenya sided with ardent Marxist President Haile Mengistu Mariam of Ethiopia against the perceived threat that Somalia posed. Cold War ideological bases of opposition were subsumed by regional geopolitics and a common enemy, testimony to the tenacity of the pan-Somali project of unification despite colonial and superpower influence. While Ethiopian and Kenyan governments gladly accepted investments of aid from anticommunist First World nations, they exercised direct control where possible over the ambitions of the Somalian state and Somalis outside its borders. Both global and regional in terms of political scope, "[t]his long history of conflict and tension has created a distorted and hostile image of the Somalis as 'enemies' of the Kenyan state."[41]

The legacies of Cold War rivalry in the Horn were basically twofold: Large quantities of armaments were transferred to the region, on the one hand, and a significant number of refugees were generated along the Somalian-Ethiopian border, on the other. The presence of internationally recognized refugees inside Somalia proved profitable. The Office of UNHCR—in conjunction with other international aid organizations—supplied large quantities of food to Somalia throughout the 1980s, though not all of it went to feed the hundreds of thousands of refugees. In 1988, UNHCR officials were denied access to refugee camps in northern Somalia by Somalian government officials; one census revealed that the population in a given camp was 39,000—less than half the Somalian claim of 82,000.[42] The presence of large numbers of refugees in Somalia nonetheless precipitated infusions of First World capital to support the anticommunist cause. Though Cold War strategies treated Somalia as little more than a surface on which to exercise superpower influence, the economic and military gains from such alliances provided ammunition for pan-Somali nationalism and for Somalia's regional ambitions.

AFTER THE COLD WAR :
GLOBAL DISINTEREST AND KENYAN CRACKDOWNS

Postcolonial, or postindependence,[43] geopolitics along the Kenyan-Somalian border are historically contingent expressions of colonial and Cold War investments combined with regional ambitions of a pan-Somali state. The Mau Mau Rebellion and other anticolonial pressures led to Kenyan independence in 1963 under the leadership of Jomo Kenyatta. Kenyatta was a member of Kenya's largest ethnic group, the Gikuyu; his positioning within the ruling party introduced a different dynamic in the cultural politics of the country.[44] Kenyatta was replaced by President Daniel Arap Moi, a Kalenjin, and by the 1980s, border confrontations and general insecurity had provoked severe military repression and many civilian deaths in the former Northern Frontier District. Arguing that Somalians were infiltrating the country, the government began screening all ethnic Somalis in Kenya in 1989. At the same time, it forcibly removed some 3,000 Somalis to Somalia.[45] Some Kenyan nationals were among the 500 Somalis sent across the border to Somalia in December 1989.[46] Kenyan Somalis who had never been to Somalia were "returned" to Mogadishu if they did not have proper identification when stopped by police. The politics of mobility for Kenyan Somali citizens remains precarious. One test used by Kenyan authorities to distinguish "authentic" Kenyan Somalis from Somalians is language-based: If a Somali can speak English and Kiswhahili, Kenya's two national languages—one being a legacy of colonialism—she or he is more likely to be Kenyan, despite the fact that Somali is spoken on both sides of the official political border.

The program of the Kenyan government in the late 1980s made life grim for Somalis from either side of the border. State of emergency laws in the area allowed for up to fifty-six days' detention without trial, and harassment, beatings, and torture of Somalis were reported.[47] Africa Watch noted:

> The Kenyan authorities are also using the influx of Somalis seeking sanctuary to impose a discriminatory and repressive screening process on its own ethnic Somali community, which has suffered a history of persecution. . . . The arrival of the refugees is being used as an opportunity to impose compulsory screening on all Kenyan-Somalis, in order to identify "illegal aliens."[48]

The screening process, combined with the strategies of keeping Somalians in camps and of involuntary repatriation, forms an unstated policy of refugee deterrence.[49] On June 16, 1991, hundreds of Somalis were rounded up by Kenyan authorities for screening; a subsequent report noted that

> [o]n the weekend of August 15/16, the police burst into the temporary homes of 2,000 Somali and Ethiopian refugees in Nairobi and Mombasa, rounded them up, forced them to board lorries at gun point after which they were driven to refugee camps. Families were separated and many small children left abandoned. The police were apparently in search of any "Somali-looking person" in areas with large groups, such as Eastleigh (a Nairobi suburb), South C and Koma Rock.[50]

It is ironic, given this situation, that the word "asylum"—which comes from the Greek *asylon,* inviolate—means "something not subject to seizure" or "freedom from seizure."[51] Many Somali asylum seekers did not find sanctuary in Kenya; instead, they were the targets of racist raids and random removal to a country to which some had never been. Again in August 1992, August 1993, and July 1997, Kenyan authorities rounded up refugees living in urban areas and purposefully transferred them to remote camps and border sites located in the Northeastern Province.[52] The government refused to allow UNHCR to house any refugees in central Kenya, protecting this area (as the British administration before it had) from a Somali "invasion."[53]

Despite deterrence measures and government roundups, several hundred thousand refugees from Somalia began pouring over the border into Kenya as civil conflict in southern Somalia mounted early in 1992. Widespread famine and the collapse of the Somalian state exacerbated this situation, in which an estimated 500,000 Somali citizens died. Well over a million Somalians were internally displaced, and some 600,000 fled the country, most of them seeking asylum in nearby Kenya. Though they were not warmly welcomed, the Kenyan government was obliged to tolerate them, partly because of its commitment in international law to the UN Convention and Protocol Relating to the Status of Refugees and to the OAU Convention, and partly because it continued to need the foreign aid of donor countries, many of which had suspended funds to Kenya at that time. While donor countries were awaiting a satisfactory outcome of the country's first multiparty elections before reconsidering their aid commitment to Kenya, President Daniel Arap Moi grudgingly allowed Somali refugees into Kenya on the condition that they reside in the border camps. Continued capital flows of development aid from Europe and North America to Kenya were conditional upon a proven commitment to democratic process and on the country's acceptance of Somalis in need of humanitarian assistance, some of which would no doubt benefit Kenya. In 1992 and 1993, UNHCR spent U.S.$40 million to establish refugee camps and border sites in Kenya.

Less than a week after President Moi won the Kenyan election in December 1992, he announced that refugees would be sent back to

Somalia immediately.[54] Having expressed this sentiment earlier, in August 1992, he now had the diplomatic and political power to withdraw his support for Somali refugees in the country. Meanwhile, at the request of the UN secretary-general, UNHCR initiated the Cross-Border Operation (CBO) inside Somalia in order to stem the flow of refugees from Somalia to Kenya and to entice those refugees already in Kenya to come home. Without President Moi's support, UNHCR could not operate on the same scale within Kenya, and so sustained efforts to fund CBO ensued. The idea was to invest in community rehabilitation in southern Somalia to encourage refugee repatriation to Somalia and thus resolve the problem. The UNHCR headquarters in Geneva established the Special Emergency Fund for the Horn of Africa (SEFHA) and began fund-raising among donor countries to finance CBO. To cover the anticipated costs of repatriation, U.S.$5.5 million was requested; UNHCR appealed for another U.S.$13 million for CBO.

UNHCR established four outposts in southern Somalia as part of CBO. The distance between the Kenyan-Somalian border and the outposts located a few hundred kilometers inland along the Juba River circumscribed the preventive zone, an area strategically planned to stem potential refugee flows. The buffer zones of the colonial and postindependence periods were effectively transposed to the Somalian side of the border, where prevention, rather than containment in Kenya's Northeastern Province, was thought to be an effective means of managing the mobility of Somalis. Considerable sums of money were required to maintain the preventive zone. More than twenty NGOs were hired by UNHCR as partners in the CBO initiative, which included quick impact projects (QIPs) to regenerate local towns and villages. These projects, which aimed to help communities resume a normal life after the devastation of war, normally had a funding ceiling of U.S.$50,000 per project. In 1993, 320 QIPs were recorded as part of CBO.[55]

By June 1993, some 30,000 Somali refugees had returned home, 12,000 of them with the help of UNHCR.[56] Unfortunately, the material incentives to return to Somalia were sufficiently lucrative—usually a three-month food supply for each person—to encourage some refugees to return more than once. A Dutch evaluation of aid to Somalia reported that some refugees returned as many as eight times with the help of international humanitarian assistance provided through CBO. The 285,000 refugees remaining in the camps at that time were considered potential returnees until peacekeeping operations in Somalia, also being carried out in the name of humanitarian assistance, went seriously awry.

As civil war continued to ravage large parts of Somalia in 1992, observers outside the country watched the politically induced famine take its toll on much of the civilian population and declared Somalia a country in anarchy, unable to rule its own affairs. This thinking gave rise to UN Security Council Resolution 794, which authorized sending thousands of UNITAF peacekeeping troops to Somalia to ensure the delivery of relief supplies. Operation Restore Hope, as the mission was called, was the first peacekeeping operation to intervene in a sovereign member state that was not presenting a military threat to its neighbors.[57] Reports that more journalists than soldiers took part in the amphibious landing of U.S. Marines just before Christmas 1992 speak to the popularity of the Somalian cause and international awareness of the humanitarian tragedy it represented. Operation Restore Hope was an experiment in post–Cold War humanitarian intervention on a global scale. "It [the West] denounces Somalia as unfit to govern itself, but says nothing of superpower rivalries in nourishing armed conflict there,"[58] nor does the West like to account for the investments during its own colonial occupations.

The U.S. Marines were replaced by a UN peacekeeping force— UNOSOM II—in May 1993. The UNOSOM II operation cost sponsoring governments U.S.$1.5 billion during its first year of operation. On the nonmilitary side of humanitarian intervention, UN agencies proposed a ten-month budget for relief and rehabilitation in 1993, to the tune of U.S.$166 million. More than fifty international NGOs, funded principally by the United Nations, operated in Somalia during that year. However, in June 1993 the popularity of Somalia as destination for millions of dollars in humanitarian assistance began to decline. A faction leader, Mohammed Farah Aideed, ambushed and murdered fourteen Pakistani UN peacekeepers in retaliation for a UNOSOM II weapons sweep in the Mogadishu neighborhood he controlled. A UNOSOM II air attack in Mogadishu was launched to bring Aideed to justice; unfortunately it also killed a number of Somali civilians, which severely damaged UNOSOM II's reputation in Somalia as a humanitarian peacekeeping force. The death of eighteen U.S. soldiers later in 1993 adversely affected the popularity of the Somali cause abroad. *Time* magazine ran a photograph of one dead U.S. soldier being paraded around the streets of Mogadishu by anti-UN Somalian protesters. Before long, funding for humanitarian projects in Somalia began to drop dramatically, and in March 1995 UNOSOM II withdrew from Somalia.

Civil conflict in Somalia continues, fueled in part by the huge quantities of arms provided to Somalia during the Cold War, when it was being courted by both superpowers. In 1995, continued support to Somali refugees across the border in camps remained fairly constant, given the perceived and real problems within Somalia that precluded refugee repatriation in several areas. Approximately 160,000 Somali refugees were living in Kenyan refugee camps in 1995; 100,000 were living in three camps located in the Northeastern Province (see figure 2.5). Some refugees accept confinement in the camps, and another 20,000–100,000 are estimated to reside illicitly in the country's two major cities, Nairobi and Mombasa.

In the Northeastern Province, economic and social underdevelopment are abated only by the relative economic boom provided by refugee relief operations in the area. Foodstuffs are distributed every fifteen days in the camps, and international NGOs provide social, health, and other community services. After the Ogaden War, the large number of Ethiopian Somali refugees remaining in Somalia provided an important source of foreign capital to the economy; President Barre used them to obtain external aid easily. Now the Kenyan government profits from its tolerance of refugees. Not only does it receive financial incentives from UNHCR and other international organizations, but in a backhanded and perhaps ironic way, the refugee situation in Kenya's Northeastern Province has stimulated economic and social development—in the form of jobs, commodities, primary education, and medical services offered in the camps—in this systematically deprived area.

REFUGEE RESETTLEMENT OUT OF AFRICA

Compared to the unfettered flows of humanitarian assistance into the Horn of Africa, refugee movement in the opposite direction is unremarkable. Refugee resettlement abroad is one permanent solution for refugees living in temporary camps, but access to resettlement opportunities is becoming increasingly difficult as the number

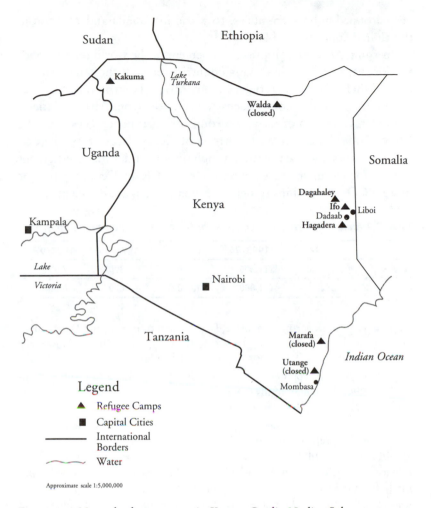

Figure 2.5. Map of refugee camps in Kenya. Credit: Nadine Schuurman.

of government-sponsored refugees accepted by some of the major
host countries declines. At the same time as general resettlement targets are decreasing, the allotment of refugee places for Africa remains a small proportion of the declining total. During 1992/93,
Canada and the United States had overall targets of 13,000 and
142,000 government-sponsored refugees, respectively. Projections for
government-sponsored refugees to be resettled in the 1994/95 fiscal

year dropped in both countries, to 7,300 in Canada and 110,000 in the United States (see table 2.1).

In 1994, Africans comprised 36 percent of the world refugee population, yet no refugee-receiving countries set aside the same proportion of their places for refugees from Africa. For 1994/95, Australia offered 800 of 13,000 places for refugees from Africa. Canada offered 1,520 spots of its 7,300 total for African refugees, and the United States had a ceiling for Africa of 7,000 places of its 110,000 total for this same fiscal year. Though opportunities for resettlement out of Africa are increasingly slim, UNHCR in Geneva pays for more NGO partnerships to deliver humanitarian assistance in Africa

Table 2.1 Annual Resettlement Ceilings for Government-Sponsored Refugees

	1992/93	1993/94	1994/95	1995/96	1996/97
Canada	13,000	11,000	7,300	7,300*	7,300
USA	142,000	121,000	110,000	90,000	78,000**

Sources: U.S. Department of State, Department of Justice, and Department of Health and Human Services, "Report to the Congress on Proposed Refugee Admissions for Fiscal Year 1996" (July 1995, prepublication copy); "Report to the Congress on Proposed Refugee Admissions for Fiscal Year 1995" (September 1994). Canadian totals are announced every November 1; they come from Citizenship and Immigration Canada and were confirmed for the purpose of this table by the Immigrant Services Society of British Columbia.

* Canada's refugee numbers have actually fallen in comparison to 1994/95 targets. In 1994/95, special programs for a category of "3–9" refugees from the former Yugoslavia and Afghanistan were counted separately from the CR-1 (government-sponsored) refugees listed above. For the year 1995/96, these 3-9 refugees have been reclassified as CR-1 refugees and included in the 7,300 total. Through this decrease is invisible in official statistics, the total number of refugees *other than* members of these particular groups has dropped.

In 1995, the Canadian Council for Refugees (CCR) provided statistics showing that the number of refugee landings had decreased, both as a percentage of total immigration and in absolute numbers, each year since 1989. The CCR said that the reduction in the number of government-sponsored refugees could be partly explained by the reduction in resources allocated to overseas resettlement.

** This statistic was taken off the U.S. State Department homepage at <http://www.state.gov/www/global/prm/table02.html>.

than in any other continental region. In 1992, 125 NGOs were hired by UNHCR to work in Africa; this represents 35 percent of the NGO total.[59] In the same year, UNHCR spent 27 percent (U.S.$298 million) of its total budget on refugee relief operations in African countries, down from 34 percent in 1991.

Screening activities for refugee resettlement in Africa are also geographically concentrated. Most of this activity was and is based in Nairobi, where the U.S. Immigration and Naturalization Service (INS) has its only office in sub-Saharan Africa.[60] Other governments that actively process refugee resettlement applications in situ, namely the Australians and Canadians, also have their largest offices here. In addition to these immigration services, UNHCR maintains a high profile and large international staff for both Kenyan and regional operations in Nairobi. This concentration of resettlement services is somewhat surprising, given that refugees are officially required to remain in the rural camps. The INS set up its Nairobi office in 1987, initially to deal with refugees coming out of Ethiopia and the Sudan.[61] It contracts a U.S. church-based organization, the Joint Voluntary Agency (JVA), to travel to refugee locations where JVA staff members assess refugee eligibility for resettlement. This approach is unique among resettlement countries screening applicants in Kenya, and Africa generally. Only the United States has its own screening agency, and in Kenya, the JVA staff works in the camps where refugees are required to stay. Nonetheless, resettlement places remain few. Just as organizations, like UNHCR, make the status of refugee possible, individual host governments determine the flow, or rather the trickle, of refugee resettlement.

The relative containment and immobility of Somali refugees could not provide a more vivid contrast to the hypermobility of humanitarian dollars from donor countries abroad. Responsibility for refugees is expressed in two geographically distinct ways: on a minor scale as an issue of resettlement among a few individual states, and on a major scale as an issue of funding relief activities in countries that both create and receive refugees. On the one hand, refugees are a concern of international politics; on the other, they are the basis of a huge global economy in humanitarian relief. In 1994, more than 95 percent of UNHCR's donations for humanitarian assistance came from fourteen governments of industrialized countries and the European Commission.[62]

Whether a financial crisis is looming in the global economy that funds responses to humanitarian crises remains to be seen. What is clear is that the availability and mobility of money corresponds inversely to the relative poverty and confinement of refugees in Kenya. Those without money, in fact, become less mobile as humanitarian aid is able to cross borders more quickly. The geopolitics of mobility points to the importance of the international humanitarian machinery, which has the power to mobilize vast amounts of money on a global scale. The effects of these power relations are felt by refugees and other displaced persons whose own mobility is shaped by this economy of assistance.

TOWARD A TRANSNATIONAL GEOPOLITICS OF MOBILITY

Freedom of movement is the rule under international law and restrictions should be the exception, though some restrictions—such as the location of refugees away from the border—respond to protection concerns.
— UNHCR, "RESETTLEMENT HANDBOOK,
UPDATE, APRIL 1998"

During the colonial period, Somalis were divided by borders demarcating Kenyan, Ethiopian, and Somalian territories. In what became Kenya's Northeast Province, the will of the majority of Somali people to join the Somalian republic was disregarded by the ruling British colonial administration, and the existing border was reinscribed by the nascent Kenyan government. Somalia mounted the Shifta War to take the Northeast Province from Kenya but succeeded only in reinforcing the marginal economic and social position of Somalis within Kenya. During the period of superpower influence and investment in the Horn, Somalia attempted to extend control over Somalis living in the Ogaden region of eastern Ethiopia. Again, the effort was unsuccessful, though indirectly Somalia profited by harboring large numbers of refugees. This, in turn, provided funds from the coffers of First World international humanitarian assistance to this Third World proxy and ally; Somalia became one of the most heavily armed countries in sub-Saharan Africa. Despite ambiguous Cold War posturing, superpower interests were often used as levers to win financing for regional geopolitical strategies.

The coup d'état in Somalia in 1991 and the ensuing famine generated human displacement on a massive scale; this forced migration, combined with severe malnutrition, precipitated the arrival of hundreds of millions of dollars, which flowed freely into Somalia and Kenya to fund rehabilitation and refugee relief activities. These two distinct geographies of mobility point to the variable porosity of borders at regional and international scales. They testify to the fact that humanitarian capital crosses borders much more easily than refugees can traverse the same frontiers. Because all Somali refugees in Kenya are required to live in one of three camps located in the Northeast Province, the contemporary geopolitics of mobility for Somalis has been linked to the same politics in earlier periods, especially to strategies of containment practiced by the British colonial administration and the Kenyan government, which maintained the province's designated state of emergency status until 1991. The geopolitics of mobility points to the imbrication of humanitarian funds and refugee status. Without donor funding and support, ad hoc recognition of and support for Somali refugees in Kenya would not have been possible.

The treatment of Somalis during each of these periods is distinctive and indicative of a particular geopolitics of mobility underscored by a First World–Third World geography of managing the Somali people. In the first instance, colonial partition divided the Somali nation, an act that was reinscribed at Kenyan independence. Somalis were not allowed to leave the newly forming Kenyan state, though they remained marginal along the Kenyan-Somalian border. Later, many were literally "sent home" to Somalia, a country that some had never even visited. Finally, Somalians fleeing internal strife crossed the border into Kenya, where, due to international obligations and the need for international aid on the part of the Kenyan government, they were reluctantly accepted. The transnational politics analyzed here point to historically contingent sites of contest, geopolitics, and related international investments in the Horn of Africa. The geopolitics of mobility is a tool for analyzing the economic and corporeal power invested in managing migration.

Given the failure of the international intervention in Somalia, the implementation of humanitarian programs in war zones is perhaps a predicament of culture. The refugees who flee such violence, however, are part not of a traveling culture but of a relatively immobile institutionalized culture of containment in camps. Responses to forced migration are governed by the geopolitics of international relations and financed by the brokers of humanitarian assistance. Geneva remains the main international financial and administrative site where the geopolitics of money are negotiated and humanitarian dollars are solicited. The managers and funders of the international refugee regime, in Switzerland and elsewhere, have their own priorities. Increasingly, opportunities for refugee resettlement in industrialized countries are declining. The decline in political will to accept large numbers of refugees is, arguably, an expression of neoliberal politics in many countries in Europe and North America combined with the absence of Cold War rivalries.[63]

I have argued for a transnational geopolitics of mobility that is attentive to material and historical locations of struggle. Borders are more porous to humanitarian aid flowing from Europe to Africa than to the displaced people for whom such aid is intended. The Horn of Africa is the site of several geographies of mobility marked by historical layers of overlapping tension, conflict, and investment. Though Somalia and Kenya remain nominally postcolonial states, the geopolitics of mobility for Somali refugees today is informed largely by a colonialism of compassion.

There is no single project of human development or of emancipation from oppressions brought on by poverty, displacement, colonialism, or conflict. Rather, the fighting and forced migration these unequal power relations generate are historically and geographically contingent. "The global and the universal are not pre-existing empirical qualities; they are deeply fraught, dangerous, and inescapable inventions."[64] Though they may be inescapable, the global and the universal are negotiable, just as the dichotomies of North/South, modern/traditional can be contested by forging transnational connections, and even affinities, across borders. Transnational practices that attend to the mobility of bodies, of money, of power as well as the colors, flags, and performances that mark them provide tools for challenging existing "inventions." Such a transnational politics of mobility generates potentially strategic constellations of power to unsettle the existing operations of humanitarian assistance in the Horn of Africa.

3

Managing Difference: Gender and Culture in Humanitarian Emergencies

Responding to humanitarian emergencies is fraught with difficulties from the outset. Human displacement created by conflict, ethnic cleansing, or politically induced famine often emerges unannounced, rendering it difficult to plan for. No world region is immune to humanitarian crises and the implications of forced migration. In 1997, more than 22 million people were affected by displacement, both within and beyond the borders of their home countries. Humanitarian responses invariably involve communication among speakers of several languages, interpretation across more than one cultural divide, and the negotiation of political agreements at every step. Increasingly, assistance is being provided in war zones, where the conditions of work are far from ideal. Yet something has to be done. The shortcomings of humanitarian aid and its delivery in particular situations are generally outweighed by a political consensus that action must be taken.

This chapter sets out to "navigate the pitfalls of universalizing talk which mute critical aspects of diversity and difference"[1] among people of different genders and cultural locations, without authenticating a particular approach or set of categories that fix identities in the context of humanitarian crises. The ways in which difference is used, managed, and theorized both fuel conflict and potentially open up other less violent and less hierarchical spaces. Notions of belonging

61

based on constructions of common ethnicity or nation exacerbate differences between "us" and "them," often in strategic ways. During the Quebec referendum on separation in 1996, a minority of ethnic nationalists called for a French (that is, nonimmigrant) Quebec based on the exclusionary concept of *pure laine* (Quebecois with ethnic French heritage). The racist connotations of this position were not well tolerated by federalists or by the majority of separatists. Nonetheless, it was used as a strategy to fuel the separatist cause vis-à-vis ethnic nationalism. Elsewhere such language has been used to exacerbate differences and mobilize people to engage in hateful, violent acts, including ethnic cleansing and rape. At the same time, however, containing difference within a dominant discourse of unity—despite the historically and geographically contingent experiences and identities of particular groups—is equally problematic. Human rights instruments, which espouse the legal entitlements of universal subjects, and international laws pertaining to refugees, for example, may on paper apply equally to all countries that are signatories, but the outcome of such measures is uneven because individual nations and groups of people within them are unequally positioned in relation to one another. Differences defined through hierarchical relations of power and unequal subjects within webs of humanitarian action have the potential for both conflict and affinity. How, then, in the context of humanitarian assistance can one practically avoid the consequences of constructing subjects as universal—a move that effectively subsumes differences of gender, ethnicity, and nationality—without essentializing identities and reifying these same categories?

Many of the ideas for this chapter stem from discussions held at the first meeting of the Women in Conflict Zones Network in November 1996. The network is a collection of feminist scholars, community organizers, and representatives of UN agencies and human rights organizations. A number of feminist scholars participating in the network collaborate with groups of women organizing against conflict in ways that cultivate affinity and advance work toward resolution where conflict prevails. As feminists, we aim to take responsibility for the implications of our research and put the welfare of the researched group and its members before that of the research objectives. Other members are activists *and* scholars whose work is as political on the ground as it is in theory. Still others are working in war zones and refugee camps as feminist researchers to analyze the gendered outcomes of conflict and the strategies employed to govern these spaces: how disorder is ordered. No one approach is sufficient to advance the challenges posed by mass displacement, ethnic-based violence, and conflict. At the same time, linking these various projects and people without subscribing to categories of increasingly institutionalized difference is a vital part of feminist politics. Toward the end of this chapter, I advance the meanings and political implications of these connections.

I am concerned principally with the human impact of conflict and responses to it. In particular, I focus on how the United Nations manages displacement and asylum, the ways in which these are gendered, and the cultural politics they entail in the context of refugee camps. How can institutions with global mandates conceptualize issues that differ across cultural and other contexts? And how can they act without systematically privileging certain gender identities over others? Modes of managing diversity and UN approaches to difference are discussed first, as a framework for subsequent analyses. A short discussion of UNHCR gender policies follows, underscoring the liberal tendency to subject gender difference to mainstreaming and integration. This creates a context for discussion of a particular, and somewhat puzzling, UN initiative called the Women Victims of Violence project, an initiative launched in the Kenyan camps for Somali refugees. The project highlights the dangers of subscribing to or unintentionally reproducing categories of difference, without attending to their practical implications. Finally, these approaches are analyzed in terms of their theoretical and on-the-ground implications.

THE PERILS OF PERFECT PLURALISM

The research that provides the basis of this analysis does not focus exclusively on the conditions of Somali women in the camps and the antecedent civil war in Somalia that had displaced them but, rather, looks at the organization that has managed this crisis of forced migration. UNHCR does important work, and the scale of its operations have increased dramatically in the 1990s. The ways in which it manages difference among groups of displaced people thus warrants careful examination and consideration. The agency's outlook, history, and geography still espouse a universal humanism—albeit a subtle one that recognizes certain bases of difference. Its treatment of gender and cultural differences provides a case in point. UNHCR maintains that its mandate is a preventive one: "to manage ethnic diversity in a way that promotes tolerance within and beyond national borders."[2] Despite the groundbreaking work of feminists and other scholars in development circles to deconstruct dominant discourses and recover the voiceless subjects of these discourses,[3] the still-universal humanist subjects of a multicultural United Nations remain intact.

The UN "family of man," "family of nations," and "international community" are unavoidable concepts for feminists concerned with deconstructing the universal subject and its attendant constellations of social power. Each term is an expression of the overarching narratives of statehood and humanism. Liisa Malkki explains how ritualized evocations of common humanity are constructed and celebrated as an egalitarian diversity among peoples and nations. In particular, she identifies the "family of nations" and the "international community" as discursive practices that serve "to reproduce, naturalize, legitimate and even generate 'the nation form' all over the world."[4] Her main point is that terms like "international community" obfuscate the unequal power relations among states, especially the hegemony of European nations. Differences among countries are constructed as plural and are valued as a part of a diverse whole. In Malkki's analysis, difference is domesticated and contained within a liberal-humanist discourse of "cultural diversity." Two processes often occur together: "a *creation* of cultural diversity and a *containment* of cultural difference."[5] There are at least 5,000 ethnic groups organized within roughly 200 independent states globally. Just as cultural and political differences among states are balanced within a contained order, so too are differences within such large organizations as the United Nations. Akin to criticisms of multiculturalism, Malkki's argument challenges the idea of cultural containment within a hegemonic, overarching framework of power in which the North dominates the South.

The tension between culture as a basis for universal human experience and culture as the primary basis of difference has important social and political implications for humanitarian practices. As an organizational culture, UNHCR is an expression of this tension today, embodying an antagonism between the acceptance of plural cultures and the standards of international law and universal human rights. In one of UNHCR's most recent public relations posters, issued ostensibly to promote tolerance of refugees, dozens of different toy LEGO people are pictured, conveniently all in yellow; the text states, "You see, refugees are just like you and me. Except for one thing. Everything they once had has been left behind. . . . we are asking that you keep an open mind. And a smile of welcome." This plea for acceptance and understanding of difference on the basis of a shared humanity speaks to and is constructed as part of a European cultural dominant. Though its intentions are laudable, its politics are predicated on minimizing differences to engender tolerance and even acceptance. UNHCR nuances this effort to promote sameness with the T-shirts it sells that read, "Einstein was a refugee." Bell hooks makes a parallel argument:

> Their [white people's] amazement that black people watch white people with a critical "ethnographic" gaze, is itself an expression of racism. Often their rage erupts because they believe that all ways of looking that highlight difference subvert the liberal conviction that it is the assertion of universal subjectivity (we are all just people) that will make racism disappear. They have a deep emotional investment in the myth of "sameness."[6]

Difference can be framed not as "almost-the-sameness" or as the object of a benevolent act of accommodation but as a basis for connection. Its valence can be positive, and its meaning is not simply an obstacle to overcome in organizing people. Connecting across difference, however, does not lend itself easily to posters or T-shirts.

Transnational practices require analyzing dominant constructions of difference and acting to change them in relationally grounded ways. In Belfast, coordinators from Irish women's centers on both sides of the Protestant-unionist–Catholic-nationalist battle have organized the Women's Support Network.[7] The network is consciously cross-communal, although it exists more as a vehicle for social change than as a symbolic gesture. Women from its member groups work to address the poverty and violence in working-class areas of the city in which the centers are based. Linking these women, the network works for political visibility and conveys knowledge and experience among its members. The women of the network defy the difference that underpins much of the ethnic violence in Belfast, and in so doing, they create an unusual coalition. During conflict in the former Yugoslavia, Women in Black, representing various ethnic backgrounds, silently protested the mobilization of ethnic nationalism to legitimate war in Belgrade, at once mourning for those lost to the conflict and creating cause for reflection and potential change among those who took notice. A similar antiwar Women in Black organization exists in London. Drawing their own transnational links, a group of feminists in Toronto recently formed a Women in Black group—albeit to address loss of entirely different scope—to protest and mourn the demise of the welfare state and its most basic provisions in Ontario, Canada.

One of the most accomplished analyses of political organizing across lines of gender, nationalism, and conflict is Cynthia Cockburn's book *The Space between Us*. Nowhere is the transnational practice of politics across difference better illustrated. Cockburn documents the work of women's groups whose members straddle divides in their home countries of Northern Ireland, Israel/Palestine, and Bosnia-Herzegovina. The women's efforts to make peace in contexts of intense, ongoing conflict and nationalism are literally and figuratively given a human face. Working across deeply embedded and geographically segregated lines that divide their communities, Cockburn conducts her research as a participant observer, exploring the ways in which these groups reject violence and notions of nationalism without denying or denigrating differences. Her book and the groups of women she carefully represents are testimony to the possible politics and workable frames of reference that do not efface difference but, rather, develop a common agenda for change in spite of them.[8]

In a more economic context, transnational feminist and labor lobbies concerned with the impact of the North American Free Trade Agreement (NAFTA) make connections, based on shared political goals, across borders, languages, and industrial sectors.[9] Transnational economic connections have been forged where shared interests are identified. In a more political context, the diffusion of national diasporas in various geographical directions generates the possibilities of connecting cultural groups dispersed across space and of forging connections across cultural and geographical locations where people have similar political objectives. People displaced from Burma, also known as Myanmar, offer a case in point. Student and minority groups, as well as a government in exile, have generated an impressive geography of resistance—from the Thai-Burmese border to Washington, D.C.—to protest the repressive rule of the State Peace and Development Council (formerly the State Law and Order Restoration Council, or SLORC) that governs Burma. The history of conflict among ethnic groups represented by these activists, cultivated in part by colonialism in Burma, created deep divisions, but ultimately a coalition front against SLORC has proven more viable politically.

The question remains, however, as to how UNHCR might approach difference on a global scale as an apolitical organization whose mandate is to deliver humanitarian assistance, not to engage in the politics of the conflicts that precipitate displacement. It begs for a more transnational approach to broaching difference. If one approaches relationships among cultural groups and the spaces they occupy not as harmonized "us" and "thems" living together but as a series of unequal and uneven links between different subjects, then the question itself changes. Difference is not a question of accommodation but of connection.

CULTURE: SHARED HUMANITY OR THE BASIS OF DIFFERENCE?

This section begins by examining some of the ways in which the categories of race and woman have been constructed in subordination within a discourse of UN humanism. Historically, racial equality preceded concerns for gender equality within the UN framework emerging after World War II. The universal subject, the UN family of nations, and international human rights were part of this discourse of humanism that emerged from the aftermath of the war. Despite the political, intellectual, and cultural changes since that time, they remain the basis of much international law and UN institutional practice almost fifty years later. In order to create international declarations, instruments, and laws protecting human rights, a common bearer of these rights—the universal subject—was born. The universal has always been qualified by the particular, distinguished by culture, national integrity, and most recently, concern for gender equity. UNHCR has been forced to face the issues of gender and cultural politics head on. The pervasive and in some ways persuasive discourse of human rights and universal standards of humanitarian assistance in the face of displacement remain, however, deeply embedded in the structures, policy, and practice of the organization today.

I recognize that many feminists and other scholars eschew the "vulgar" strand of humanism broached here, for "it is now widely accepted that the autonomous, neutered and sovereign subject at its core was a fiction, implicated in an ideology of humanism which suppressed the multiple ways in which subjects were constructed in order to promote a white, masculine, bourgeois subject as the norm, from which others were to be seen as departures or deviants."[10] Furthermore, development theorists have exposed an economy of discourse and unequal power relations encoded in the charitable gestures of aid and assistance.[11] 'UN humanism' might be considered an ideological construct or discourse which is past its prime. Nonetheless, remnants of it are alive and well in locations of conflict and displacement.

THE BIRTH OF THE UN FAMILY

Culture never stands alone but always participates in a conflictual economy acting out the tension between sameness and difference, comparison and differentiation, unity and diversity, cohesion and dispersion, containment and subversion.

—ROBERT YOUNG, *COLONIAL DESIRE*

The legal and organizational protocols of UNHCR are an expression of the larger liberal discourse of UN humanism. This brief account of the birth of UN humanism elucidates constructions of race and gender within UN discourse more generally, followed later by UNHCR gender policies in particular. Robert Young chronicles contests over race in the nineteenth century and suggests that though culture has replaced race in twentieth-century debates, the debates remain otherwise much the same: "Culture has always marked cultural difference by producing the other; it has always been comparative, and racism has always been an integral part of it. . . . Race has always been culturally constructed. Culture has always been racially constructed."[12] Young usefully documents arguments about racial difference and superiority in the nineteenth century, despite the tautology of his argumentation about the mutual construction of race and culture. Monogenists believed that all human beings belonged to one race because they were the creation of a divine god, whereas polygenists (the progenitors of the notion of miscegenation) maintained that there were distinct races hierarchically positioned in relation to one another.[13] Throughout the nineteenth century, whites, the interlocutors in these debates, were considered the "naturally" superior race by the polygenists. This period gave rise to racial tests, such as the measurement of the human cranium as an indicator of intelligence. "[F]or two hundred years culture has carried within it an antagonism between culture as a universal and as cultural difference, forming a resistance to Western culture within Western culture itself."[14] UNHCR embodies this antagonism and embraces both humanism's universal subject and the concept of cultural difference as a means of accommodating difference. Though culture may have supplanted race in measuring difference, the politics and distance it generates remain the same.

In 1948 the Universal Declaration of Human Rights was proclaimed, a declaration in which "universal man" replaced "international man" in a final amendment. René Cassin, who lobbied for this change, argued that "'universal' man is more easily extracted from the complications of history."[15] He did not consider the ramifications of these "complications," namely, the importance of cultural and political geographies among nation-states and implications of gender for "universal man." Before long, the abstract, race-neutral, gender-blind concept of humanity encountered its own limitations. In 1950 and 1951, the United Nations Educational, Scientific, and Cultural Organization (UNESCO) published statements on the supposed scientific nature of race and racial differences. Donna Haraway spells out the connections between these statements and the construction of universal man after World War II:

> [T]he authority of the architects of the modern evolutionary synthesis was crucial to the birth of post–W.W.II universal man, biologically certified for equality and rights to full citizenship. Before W.W.II, versions of Darwinism, as well as other doctrines in evolutionary biology, had been deeply implicated in producing racist science as normal, authoritative practice. It was therefore not sufficient for social science, set across an ideological and disciplinary border from nature and natural science, to produce anti- or non-racist doctrines of human equality and environmental causation. The body itself had to be reinscribed, reauthorized, by the chief discipline historically empowered to produce the potent marks of race—Darwinian evolutionary biology. For this task, "behavior" would be the mediating instrument.[16]

Authorized by science, the birth of a universal subject was timely. Poised between the victory over fascism and the horror of the Holocaust, the politically significant emergence of the "united family of man" was legitimized by evolutionary biology and physical anthropology. The rallying point for humanists was that the scientific differences among individuals of the same so-called race were greater than those among different races, the political corollary of which was the birth of UN humanism and the attendant declarations, legislation, and human rights instruments that shape the humanitarian terrain today.

This UN discourse was implicitly and explicitly gendered. Concerned mainly with erasing racial difference, gender was a secondary consideration at best. The statements of the 1950s spoke of universal brotherhood, a language of androcentrism if not exclusion. The gender blindness of UN humanism generated the Man-the-Hunter image produced and institutionalized by scientific meetings such as the 1955 Pan-African Congress in physical anthropology held in Nairobi. Discussion of racial politics and of natural tendencies to cooperate was itself gendered: "Man the Hunter's and UNESCO man's unmarked gender were part of the solution to one kind of racism at the inherited cost of unexaminable, unintentional, and therefore particularly powerful, scientific sexism."[17] In addition to the displaced notion of difference ushered in by the UNESCO Statement on Race, the cost of this solution was a kind of scientific sexism within the UN family.

The gendered dimension of these race politics was perhaps less obvious to UN humanists than was the exclusion of woman from the ranks of universal brotherhood. Although the United Nations established the Commission on the Status of Women (CSW) as early as 1947, a world women's conference proposed in 1946 did not materialize until the declaration of International Women's Year in 1975.[18] A culmination of women's activism and issues inspired the UN Decade for Women between 1975 and 1985.[19] The decade was punctuated by the 1985 UN Conference on Women in, somewhat ironically, Nairobi, the site of the 1955 scientific meetings that ratified the Man-the-Hunter image. "The UN had to respond to the manifestations of the revolution in gender that is occurring all over the planet in very inhomogeneous, contradictory, and internally contentious ways."[20] The 1995 World Conference on Women in Beijing and the NGO Forum held in Hairou, China, marked another decade of UN efforts to incorporate a gender analysis. For the first time, the UN conference's Platform of Action outlined the strategic importance of protection, assistance, and training for refugee and internally dis-placed women.[21] This represents a victory for UNHCR, whose aim has largely been to integrate gender and the situation of refugee women into mainstream agendas. All of these UN conferences chal-lenged assumptions of a universal brotherhood and created a plat-form for further action at the end of each conference. Even so, the legacy of universal man remains evident in the ways in which UN agencies deal with difference today.

GENDER POLICY AT UNHCR

Though vast improvements have occurred, the implementation of UNHCR policies and projects aimed at promoting women in the 1990s remains problematic. If one takes culture as both universal and a basis of difference, then the development of policies and prac-tices applicable, in theory, to a vast number of geographical regions and cultural groups is made particularly difficult. After a cursory overview and analysis of UNHCR's gender policy on paper, I offer a case study of one UNHCR project aimed at promoting women in practice. The close reading of this project illustrates some of the con-tradictions between and complications of policy and practice. The Women Victims of Violence Project, an initiative to protect refugees from sexual violence, raises questions of gender policy versus gen-dered practice in UNHCR-sponsored refugee camps.

The advent of gender equity policies at UNHCR occurred in the late 1980s. On paper, UNHCR's gender-based initiatives are an im-pressive collation of feminist analyses and recommended action.[22] They include liberal and other feminist sensibilities that address is-sues of discrimination, violence, and systemic material inequality af-fecting women.[23] On one hand, the frequent use of the category "woman" by UNHCR as a primary organizing concept essentializes and reinforces the primacy of female difference over ethnic, clan, and other axes of identification.[24] On the other, this usage seems con-trary to the basic liberal feminist principle articulated in UNHCR policy, namely, "mainstreaming and integration." While certain groups of women refugees are listed as vulnerable and as requiring special assistance in the camps, other planning documents insist that women be equal partners in decision-making processes and that they should have equitable access to services and resources.[25]

These two approaches to women and gender are not necessarily mutually exclusive. For example, the same Somali refugee woman may find herself separated from her family as she flees conflict at home and later, upon arrival in a refugee camp, may emerge as a leader and decision maker, say as a health professional. In the first scenario, she is justifiably vulnerable because her family—an accepted cultural form of protection—is absent. Conflict and displacement have historically often destabilized social relations, and it is possible that this person could well be at risk. In the second scenario, however, the skills and experience she brings to the camp make it equally possible that she will become part of the decision-making apparatus in the health sector. Though they appear contradictory, concepts of women as equal partners and as part of a vulnerable population can coexist. The appropriateness of either approach must, however, be analyzed in the contingent historical and geographical context of a particular humanitarian situation. Women refugees are not vulnerable in any essential way, nor are they all equal participants in the daily governance of a refugee camp. Their locations are at once designated by UNHCR's policies and contingent upon the history and place in which they find themselves.

UNHCR's approach to women refugees cannot be viewed as coherent, unitary, or internally consistent. Nor should it. The main purpose of UNHCR policies to promote women is to encourage and create change within the organization, so that operations on the ground are also positively affected. The barriers to such organizational change, however, are significant. One NGO representative based in Geneva noted some of these organizational obstacles to developing gender policy expressive of a feminist politics at UNHCR:

> [Those promoting gender equity at UNHCR don't] want to use feminism or these terms. . . . the culture just refuses to deal with anything of the sort. . . . and even though [UNHCR is] calling it "people-oriented," [it is] getting the backlash. . . . it's not easy. It's easy to critique a person's efforts, but once you're in it's not easy. Like here, I haven't yet said openly that I'm a feminist—I have with the women and certain groups, but there is an image of feminism, people don't recognize that there are *feminisms*.[26]

Taking gender equity and the provision of refugee assistance grounded in a sustained analysis of gender to mean "feminist" at UNHCR, sustained efforts to integrate feminist policies are, in fact, struggles that demand support from inside and outside the organization.[27] Support for the visibility of gender relations and issues within the organization appears to be in some jeopardy. On June 15, 1998, when the senior coordinator for refugee women left her post, no effort was made to replace her. This post at one time had high visibility and reported directly to the deputy high commissioner. Now it is at risk of being demoted to the technical support unit within UNHCR.

Promoted by the office of the UNHCR senior coordinator for women refugees, the euphemistically titled People-Oriented Planning Process, or POP, as it is called, trains workers in gender analysis and culturally sensitive community planning.[28] Both POP and the "Guidelines on the Protection of Refugee Women" identify the physical spaces in which refugee women live as important to ensure safety and equitable access to basic services and supplies. UNHCR recognizes that women refugees are often more susceptible in camp situations because family protection and traditional authority structures break down and economic support is less available.[29] Camp design, layout, and location produce specific social relations in the camps.

Historical context, regional geopolitics, and cultural and gender differences, however, are left for field workers to fill in once placed in the refugee camps. In development circles, feminists have long challenged many of the assumptions that aid organizations make with respect to gender and the roles of women in development. Several feminist scholars have noted that approaches to "women" and "gender" in development are predicated upon assumptions that subsume, segregate, and essentialize the locations of women.[30] From Women in Development (WID) to Women and Development (WAD) to Gender and Development (GAD) approaches, development discourses fix gender in particular ways.[31] Arturo Escobar has referred to development discourse as the "bureaucratization of knowledge about the Third World," an important concept to which I will return.[32] Some development approaches treat women as subjects excluded from the development process. Women are considered partners in decision making who should be integrated fully into existing political, economic, and social structures. Others cast women as poor and vulnerable mothers with special needs that must be recognized and tended to by aid organizations; they are explicitly included, but their agency is limited. Some projects are conceived by women for women and bypass the dominant circuits of power and authority that the other two approaches rely upon. All represent what Mitu Hirshman calls "the be-all and the end-all of the humanist project: the improvement of the human condition."[33] Like Hirshman, I do not simply dismiss these approaches because of their humanist assumptions but, rather, aim to expose some of the limitations these assumptions pose.

People-oriented planning fixes gender relations and cultural identities by the very schemata and structuring procedures embedded in UNHCR's routine work practices. This institutional production of social reality works because it is represented and thus preserved through a series of textual and documentary forms: "[T]exts are invariably detached from the local historical context of the reality that they supposedly represent."[34] Following the feminist sociologist Dorothy Smith, facts are an aspect of social organization, a practice of knowing that employs categories familiar to the knower but not necessarily to the one "known." It is a practice that constructs an object or person as external to the one inside the organization:

> For bureaucracy is *par excellence* that mode of governing that separates the performance of ruling from particular individuals, and makes organizations independent of particular persons and local settings. . . . Today, large-scale organization inscribes its processes into documentary modes as a continuous feature of its functioning. . . . This [produces] a form of social consciousness that is the property of organizations rather than of the meeting of individuals in local historical settings.[35]

In such situations, it follows, the culture of the institution—in this case UNHCR—produces a profile of the external culture from its own perspective. "The various agencies of social control," writes Smith, "have institutionalized procedures for assembling, processing, and testing information about the behavior of individuals so that it can be matched against the paradigms."[36] The UNHCR guidelines and POP approaches are, then, part of an institutional bureaucracy that attempts to create a grid of intelligibility for the agency without necessarily linking the complications of local histories, cultures, and conflicts to their considerations.[37] POP may well have the potential to change some practices within UNHCR's organizational culture, but it is unlikely to capture the cultural and political complexity of social relations in a context of specific humanitarian emergencies.

The POP framework advocates a three-step approach to camp planning: preparation of a refugee population profile to analyze context, analysis of previous and existing patterns of activities among refugees, such as the gender divisions of social and economic responsibilities, and a comparative analysis of what resources refugees controlled and used before they arrived and what they control and use in the current context. These analyses, grounded in local conditions and cultures, are to be applied to the organization of food distribution, physical layout of camps, and medical assistance for refugees. The POP framework has much in common with gender and development approaches to planning; however, at UNHCR, it is a tool that emphasizes gender sensitivity without naming it, and one that is unaware of the role it has in constituting gender as a knowable set of relationships in humanitarian situations.

An alternative to POP might mitigate the ethnocentrism of this particular humanitarian approach by connecting the social, political, economic, and cultural locations of people who have been displaced through "the meeting of individuals in local historical settings," as Smith puts it. UNHCR has taken partial steps in this direction by, for example, offering POP training to African women who are community workers and encouraging them to interpret the planning framework within their own cultural contexts. Though this is a positive development, it nonetheless attests to the adaptation of an approach without rethinking the epistemological issues of whose knowledge or planning approaches prevail and their practical implications. An alternative approach might also recognize that humanitarian assistance does not have the same meaning in all places, does not include all groups, and may not have equivalent outcomes, despite similar policy and application. The POP initiative does attempt to include the specific dynamics of people and place, but it needs to go much further. Cultural politics, prejudice, and the historical layers of conflict and coalition in a given place cannot simply be *added* to such a framework. Cultural workers within the humanitarian bureaucracy and interlocutors on the outside are sorely needed to create bases for communication and exchange, even if this occurs between participants with unequal access to power.

Traceable to UN humanism, UNHCR policies pertaining to refugee women and to refugees of other cultures fail to recognize the ways in which "women" and "culture" are constructed in subordination. Inderpal Grewal has argued that international institutions like the World Bank and the International Monetary Fund (IMF) contribute to the interpellation of female subjects in varied ways in many parts of the world:

> While the term "woman," as a political category, cannot be dismissed so easily, what needs to be remembered is not only Simone de Beauvoir's notion that "woman" is a social construct, but that first, women are constructed differently within different social categories such as class, caste, and so on. . . . even while it is important to critique an ahistorical category of "woman," it is just as problematic to seek authentic versions of women's locations within societies.[38]

Faced with crises of displacement that require practical responses to assist refugees regardless of gender or culture, UNHCR is also confronted with the need for transnational practices that do not fix gender identities. A multicultural framework incorporates differences of gender and culture as plural expressions of diversity, without necessarily examining power relations among distinct groups.[39] Multiculturalism *includes* differences but does not allow them to alter the master plan or narrative of which it is a part. The deconstruction of dominant narratives of power and the reconstruction of other subject locations comprise a strategy by which UNHCR can resist inserting "woman" and "culture" within a Western economy of difference. Transnational practices can break down authoritative power relations by making connections across cultural and gender differences rather than within planning frameworks based on Western notions of community development. Engagement, translation, communication, and action determined by parties on all sides of the humanitarian situation constitute some of these practices.

Transnational practices would involve ongoing meetings with refugees and their involvement at all levels of humanitarian response, not simply consultations with them regarding pregiven models of refugee planning and management.

> The concept of intervention then needs *deconstructing* so that it is seen for what it is—an ongoing, socially constructed and negotiated process, not simply the execution of an already-specified plan of action with expected outcomes. One should also not assume a top-down process, since initiatives may come from "below" as much as from "above." . . . Using the notion of intervention *practices* allows one to focus on the emergent forms of interaction, procedures, practical strategies, and types of discourse and cultural categories present in specific contexts.[40]

Refugees and other displaced persons have to become part of the implicit "we" in the "us"/"them" dichotomy in order to take apart the paternalist narratives, frameworks, and planning policies that organize their difference. This is not to say that they are the *same* as nonrefugee humanitarian workers, nor do they necessarily have comparable resources and social power. They are, however, likely to be among the best local and historical interpreters and strategists of crisis situations. As it stands, refugees remain the objects—rather than the subjects—of humanitarian planning, despite long-standing agreement on this point. Though the challenges of implementing gender-based policy within UNHCR's organizational culture are significant, the challenges of humanitarian practice in conditions of displacement are at least as difficult, if not more so.

WOMEN VICTIMS OF VIOLENCE (WVV) PROJECT: COMBATING SEXUAL VIOLENCE

Sexual coercion, torture, and rape are relatively common occurrences in conflict zones. Despite being recognized places of asylum for people fleeing persecution, refugee camps can also be unstable environments where residents are susceptible to sexual and physical violence. In the Northeast Province of Kenya, where a history of systematic economic marginalization includes banditry, widespread insecurity has only been exacerbated by the arrival and temporary settlement of tens of thousands of refugees. Those who leave the camps for hours at a time in search of firewood with which to cook, predominantly women and girls, are vulnerable to bandit attacks. After nightfall, unarmed households, especially those known to be headed by women, have been the easy targets of bandits from within the camp itself. During my stay, several attacks of rape, defilement, and spousal assault were reported and documented.

From its inception, the Women Victims of Violence project was an immensely fundable contradiction in UNHCR policy. In October 1992, the U.S.-based human rights monitoring group Africa Watch documented sexual violence against Somali refugee women in the Dadaab camps. This report fueled international concern about rape against refugee women in the area. In the same month, UNHCR hired a consultant to investigate the allegations further. Seven months in the making, her report documented 192 specific cases of rape among Somali woman, noting that these were "only the tip of the iceberg."[41] She proposed a comprehensive response to this sexual violence which became the Refugee Women Victims of Violence special project. The project outlined four specific objectives, including (1) the provision of counseling, therapy, and medical services for those affected by sexual violence; (2) improved physical security in and around the refugee camps to prevent future violence; (3) material assistance and skills training to enhance the livelihood of victims; and (4) increased awareness of the problem among law enforcement personnel, staff, and the general public.

Based on these objectives, WVV was a *special* project. It focused initially on women refugees rather than all refugees affected by physical assault and sexual violence in and near the camps, and it aimed to assist those affected by rape but not by other types of trauma. By focusing on vulnerable women, a senior manager in Geneva admitted that WVV contravened UNHCR's own integrationist policy on refugee women.[42] The project was subject to some of the same critiques made of development literature relating to women: "Much of the WID [Women In Development] and Gender and Development (GAD) literature represents Third World women as benighted, overburdened beasts, helplessly entangled in the tentacles of regressive Third World patriarchy."[43] In the case of WVV, the Western funders of the project could "save," or at least assist, vulnerable Somali women from the chaos and calamity of the camps.

The WVV project provided specified services and potential material assistance to those refugees who could demonstrate that they had been raped, creating a dilemma for many women. The problematic denotation of women as "victims" in the project's title was a minor issue next to the inscription of shame and of violence on the bodies of the Somali women who were "found out" and often consequently disowned by their families.[44] In the case of rape, a woman's body can be thought of as the site of a double inscription: of sexual violence and of institutionalized therapies to treat the affected body. Naming practices matter, and the project's designation "victims of violence" introduced yet another layer of problematic power relations to the incident of rape.

> Through traveling to other people's worlds we discover that there are worlds in which those who are the victims of arrogant perception are really subjects . . . even though in the mainstream construction they

are animated only by the arrogant perceiver and are pliable, foldable, file-awayable, classifiable.[45]

The WVV project posed a number of related problems from the start.[46] On the one hand, if a refugee woman sought assistance through a WVV counselor, she could easily become stigmatized as a rape victim and ostracized by her family or community. On the other hand, if a woman could access the resources or opportunities available through the UNHCR-sponsored WVV project—such as a transfer to one of the better coastal refugee camps, or even a chance at resettlement abroad through the Canadian or Australian Women-at-Risk programs—she might maintain family approval. This kind of speculation led to a number of what were thought to be false claims of rape on the part of Somali women refugees.[47]

In order to be prosecuted, incidents of rape in Kenya must be reported to police within twenty-four hours of their occurrence. A medical certificate, based on a physical examination conducted by a physician to verify clinically that rape occurred, is also required. These legal and medical procedures at once legitimize and invariably publicize acts of rape. They seek to institutionalize women's assaulted bodies at a number of levels. Legal testimony, medical examinations, and the provision of therapy for women victims of violence are all constitutive of power relations that tend to create institutionalized subjects. Whereas the rule of law and the enforcement of human rights are usually the articulated *reasons* for projects such as WVV, the microphysics of power that manage the politics of the body occur on a more local scale. The legal, medical, and therapeutic practices that name, authorize, and organize the treatment of sexual violence are the transfer points of power in the camps.

In Somali culture, the stigma of rape for a women is severe. A system of blood money, or *diya*, is often invoked when accepted codes of behavior among Somalis are violated, as in the case of rape. The family of a woman who is raped, for example, might seek compensation from the family of the culprit in the form of cash or other assets, such as livestock. Although such agreements are often negotiated in the Dadaab camps, UNHCR staff and Kenyan legal counsel provided by the Federacion Internacional de Abogadas (FIDA, International Federation of Women Lawyers) make every effort to utilize official channels so that prosecution in court remains possible. Universal codes of human rights and national provisions in criminal law come face-to-face with Somali codes of justice. Depending on the extent to which women refugees and their families perceive that they can gain material benefits from the project as compensation for the rape, they may approach UNHCR and report the crime. Conflicts between the human rights and international law approach of UNHCR and the socially accepted, culturally specific laws of the Somali refugees in the camps continues to be a problem for the WVV project.

Though the lawyers and medical staff working in the camps have the authority to define rape in official terms, Somali refugees often circumvent these legal and institutional circuits of power and invoke their own system of justice, including material exchange. Nancy Fraser's analysis of the politics of needs interpretation suggests that contests among discourses occur at the site of "the social."[48] Proponents of the UN, Kenyan, legal, medical, and Somali discourses seek discursive hegemony. International and Kenyan law prescribes public punishment for rape. Evidence suggests, however, that many of the Somalis affected would prefer to settle these matters out of public view, through more discreet agreements of compensation, usually between the men in the families affected by the woman's rape.[49] WVV staff publicize the laws against sexual violence and seek prosecution in cases of rape and related crimes.

Nancy Fraser's approach would describe UNHCR, the WVV project, together with the legal and medical authorities in place, as *oppositional* and *expert* discourses in a struggle for rights-based relations of power and justice. For Fraser, oppositional discourses force relations of power that have been sequestered in the realm of the private to become public and in turn more politicized. Though Fraser does not purport to analyze power relations across cultures and nations outside the West, her poststructuralist approach can be transposed to a transnational scale. Her "site of the social"—the public location for politics and contests among discourses—is also the site of a powerful lobby to reprivatize notions of punishment and compensation, in this case, back to the more private family realm. Expert discourses add weight to either side; in the context of UN-sponsored refugee camps, legal, medical, and other experts tend to back those who pay their salaries and whose dominant culture they share. Refugee, local, and UN cultural practices come together to vie for power and efficacy at the site of the refugee camp.

During my fieldwork in the camps, the aftermath of sexual violence posed other questions of discursive politics imbued with contested markings of gender and culture. Genital mutilation, or female circumcision (depending on the discourse one employs), became the focus of complex cultural politics after a young refugee woman was raped in Dagahaley camp. While accompanying the WVV counselor during a follow-up visit, I met the girl who had been raped and her mother. Her mother had not allowed the girl to stay in the hospital after the attack. A local UNHCR employee at the scene, a Somali herself, explained the situation: "She has to be stitched up; the wound is healing. They will do it the traditional way; it is more dangerous." The act of rape tore the flesh sewn together during circumcision/genital mutilation. Her family and community discouraged her from becoming involved with UNHCR and other agencies unless she could get some personal, material benefit. Accordingly, the genital wound was to be treated by a woman trained in circumcision rather than a Médecins sans Frontières (MSF) doctor. Though MSF flatly opposes the practice of genital mutilation (as does UNHCR), its staff is usually prepared to perform the surgery required for women who have been raped. Their rationale is that women who have been raped are less likely to risk infection if the recircumcision/mutilation is performed in the hospital rather than in the community.

One's choice of words is intensely political: Does one employ a discourse of cultural autonomy or of universal human rights? Is protest of practices of female genital mutilation (FGM), or circumcision, a morally coded cultural imperialism, or a bid for justice? It is not surprising that agreement on the issue across cultures in refugee camps is elusive. The tension between culture as universal and culture as particular is clear.

PERFECTING PRACTICE: TOWARD TRANSNATIONAL PRACTICE

We have to transform the field of social institutions into a vast experimental field, in such a way as to decide which taps need turning, which bolts need to be loosened here or there, to get the desired change; bearing in mind that a whole institutional complex, at present very fragile, will probably have to undergo a restructuring from top to bottom.

—MICHEL FOUCAULT, "SOCIAL SECURITY"

Rather than simply criticizing UNHCR's gender policies and the WVV project as imperfect approaches to solving the problems of unequal power relations, I have analyzed some of their implications as responses predicated upon certain assumptions and constructed within a framework of UN humanism. UN humanism and its approach to managing ethnic diversity emphasize integration within a family of nations. Yet it is precisely this notion of family that requires interrogation. Difference is acceptable insofar as it subscribes to the structures and relations of family. At a finer scale, violence against refugee women in and around the Dadaab camps has historical and political meanings that exceed the policies and practical efforts made to assist refugee women. This is not to condemn current efforts within UNHCR to recognize difference and do something but, rather, to point out some of their limitations in humanitarian situations on the ground. Work to create conversations, strategies, and agreement among various parties at a cultural level, a level that is sensitive to other axes of difference, including gender, is as important as the humanitarian functions that UNHCR fulfills.

UNHCR is an organization that responds to both the protection needs and the practical needs of displaced people. It does so within an institutional and legal framework that situates the people it aims to assist in specific ways. Gender policy, then, is subject to the discipline of these schema and cannot wholly represent the range of possible responses that might be worked out in the field. Differences in culture and gender cannot simply be added to an overarching framework of humanitarian assistance, nor can the development of a single set of gender policies be applicable to all humanitarian situations. Spaces to negotiate both the meanings and modes of humanitarian intervention can be opened up, however, without losing sight of UNHCR's organizational goals. UNHCR can "unframe" fixed notions of gender and cultural difference by taking such variables much more seriously.

At the outset of this chapter, I outlined some of the dangers of essentializing "woman" as well as the risks associated with a liberal framework of multicultural UN humanism. By tracing some of the contradictions and assumptions of selected UNHCR gender policy, I have tried to expose the cultural assumptions of people-oriented planning, despite its good intentions and the reluctant institutional context in which it is disseminated. The integration and mainstreaming of gender as an agenda item of the humanitarian mandate is important. Specifying how gender and culture should be incorporated into refugee planning from what is an ahistorical and aspatial perspective, however, is less viable. I recall the quandary I faced as a field officer in southern Somalia, charged with the responsibility of distributing agricultural tools and seed to people in a number of outlying villages decimated by civil war. The very idea that I could independently consult with the women concerned, as the POP framework would suggest, was culturally inappropriate for the context in which I found myself. The male elders were still the recognized leaders within the war-torn society, though their authority had been somewhat undermined by the instability of economic and political relations. They asked that I leave the goods with them for distribution, an idea not popular with the women who heard their request. The question then became, do I act as though I am part of the cultural context in which I find myself; that is, do I give the seed, tools, and food to the male elders to allot at their discretion? Or do I act within my own culturally defined perceptions of what is fair, in this case, what I perceived to be the interests of the much larger number of adversely affected women? Discussing this problem with Somalian UNHCR staff members from the area, two observations arose that shaped my decision: First, Somali men can have more than one wife and maintain more than one household; and second, women generally do most of the seeding and weeding in agricultural work. We decided to give every adult woman an equal portion of what was available, knowing that this plan would not be popular with the indigenous leadership. This scenario illustrates the ongoing negotiation and mutation of humanitarian practice.

The WVV project's own categories of clients generated an intense cultural politics of its own. Though UNHCR gender policy contradicted the manner in which the project was conceived and delivered, the international discourse of human rights politicized the violence against refugee women in northeast Kenya, and the project went ahead. The WVV project is not the only UNHCR initiative that aims to identify vulnerable segments of the refugee population. It is standard practice in all areas of UNHCR competency to identify such groups and ensure adequate provision and protection.[50] Again, the inclusion of vulnerable groups—which invariably refer to some women—as an item on the humanitarian agenda is important. Designating a priori what these groups are and how they should be incorporated into refugee planning is more problematic.

What might replace this additive model of integration in which gender difference and cultural diversity represent deviance from invisible but culturally dominant practices? Inderpal Grewal and Caren Kaplan's work provides a partial answer: what they have called "transnational feminist practices."[51] These practices comprised strategies that conceive of differences as linked, if unequal, and that upset commonplace markers of social, cultural, and political identity. Transnationalism has been broadly defined as an analytical perspective that focuses on the accelerating circulation of goods, people, money, information, ideas, culture, and, I would add, politics.[52] As a theoretical approach, transnationalism emerged out of postmodernist and Marxist-inspired critiques of global capitalism and flexible accumulation. In one sense, transnational practices challenge a purely locational politics of global/local or center/periphery positioning in favor of messier links of historical and geographical contingency. They are strategies that engage and connect rather than distinguish and distance people of different locations—social, political, cultural, or otherwise. Such practices are at once materialist and discursive. They aim to blur the divide between discourse and practice, between people of the West and the rest, and to subvert reified categories such as "Third World woman," "Serb," "Kurd," and "other." Between the universal subjects of UN humanism and essentialist concepts of "refugee woman" are people of various, often unequal locations whose work is to connect with others, persuade others of their projects, and invoke positive change.[53] Such deconstructive impulses have powerful political potential on one level, but their materialist impact is less convincing.[54]

Within UNHCR, practical changes are necessary both in emphasis and approach. In situations of humanitarian response, logistics and health and social services all depend upon cultural work, namely, negotiation, translation, and interpretation. To some extent this work is already being done, primarily by NGOs, and should be expanded by drawing on the geographically diverse and culturally attuned experience of NGO staff. At UNHCR, better practices might include ongoing discussions *with* refugees—women in particular—not simply *of* them, in an effort to bridge some of the social, cultural, and political difference and discursive distance that is reproduced and managed under the rubric of UN humanism. This may seem too simple, and some agency staff members would argue that this is already being done. But as neoliberal thinking shifts political support from development budgets to more defined and finite humanitarian emergencies, there is also decreasing support for such "nonessentials": "[T]he long-established notion that refugees should be active participants in the management of their camps and assistance programmes is quietly being set aside. Increasingly, donor states assess humanitarian organizations in terms of their capacity to deliver emergency relief, rather than their ability to empower marginalized populations and to bring a degree of dignity to their lives."[55] UNHCR has seen extraordinary growth in its resources since the beginning of the 1990s. It can afford to do the job well, especially where it can draw upon the expertise of well-placed and experienced NGOs to assist. But are there staff positions whose primary function is to do the cultural work of communication, translation, and interpretation across all aspects of humanitarian assistance? Administration, protection, social services, and field staff are all assumed to be gender sensitive and culturally competent in the areas for which they are responsible, but there is not yet sufficient political prerogative or resource allocation to work through the gender and cultural implications of programming on a situation-by-situation basis. This needs to be made a priority. Effective assistance requires as much engagement with the cultural politics, geopolitics, and history of the place where people are adversely affected as with the political and logistical challenges of finding and providing relief.

Women whose bodies, families, and communities bear the violent inscriptions of war and displacement are neither universal subjects nor essentialized subjects in distinct locations. The conditions, locations, and responses to displacement are political: Where openings exist, concrete links can be made across, within, and between categories and spatialized hierarchies of difference. The antagonism between culture as a universal and as cultural difference is longstanding. In the realm of refugee relief and humanitarian response, it can be resolved neither by simply introducing worldwide approaches nor by treating categories of difference, such as gender and culture, in a fixed and isolated manner. Engaging gender, cultural, and other axes of difference in humanitarian emergencies demands operational guidelines that are subject to transformation when they meet the reality and the subjects of displacement. It requires taking differences more seriously and implementing cultural workers who, alongside the water and sanitation experts, logistics personnel, protection officers, and health workers, negotiate, communicate, and collaborate with those affected.

4

In the Field: Camps, Compounds, and Other Spaces

Refugee camps are one temporary solution to the plight of displaced people throughout Africa. At the end of 1994, Kenya alone sheltered more than 250,000 refugees in camps located, for the most part, at the geographical and economic margins of the country. Refugees exchange the rights and entitlements of citizenship for safety in camps administered by UNHCR and supported by donations from countries in Europe and North America and from Japan. As prima facie refugees, they are spatially segregated in border camps and excluded from participating in Kenyan society.[1] This chapter focuses on the negotiation of space in three camps and its specific relation to gender and political status. I weave a partial picture of the field in which refugees move and live. The deliberate organization and calibration of spaces for refugees, Kenyan citizens, and international staff forge connections between the discursive and material sites of power in and around the refugee camps.

In 1994, "[a]s in past years, Kenyan authorities threatened to arrest any refugees living outside of designated camps and occasionally conducted sweeps in urban areas to find Somali refugees."[2] The Kenyan government insists that all prima facie refugees—whose status is designated by UNHCR, not by refugee law or by the Kenyan government—live in camps where they are prohibited from seeking employment or moving around the country. Instead, they are provided with food twice a month, basic medical services, primary schooling, and some housing materials, most of which are paid for by donor governments in Japan, Europe, and North America. The findings of one evaluation suggest that camps and border sites in Kenya attracted both Kenyan Somalis and Somalians in 1993 because of the relative wealth of these locations.[3] Given the very basic provisions of the camps, this observation highlights the relative poverty of the Northeast Province in comparison to other Kenyan provinces and alludes to the strategic use of the camps by refugees and others.

As political spaces of economic dependency and activity, refugee camps embody a tension between discourses of universality and particularity. They are material expressions of the international refugee regime, on the one hand, and segregated spaces of cultural and political otherness on the other. In these spaces, Somali cultural practices meet UN protocols on Kenyan soil. Encounters are not simply a matter of cultural contact but are constitutive of hierarchical political, economic, and social relations of power.[4] "Households are situated in a system of redistribution which is materially and discursively structured according to local and supra-local understandings of the rights and needs of particular sorts of persons."[5] The spaces of refugee camps are *in policy and in practice* (though these are not necessarily the same) structured according to supralocal understandings of local needs. That is to say, the UNHCR organizes camps, ostensibly with the shelter, provision, and protection needs of refugees in mind. But on the ground their organization looks quite different. Once inside the camps, it appears that they meet the security and logistical needs of the humanitarian organizations at least as much as those of refugees. Refugees living in the camps are both incorporated by and incorporate this supralocal geography through their own cultural practices, which include a gendered distribution of labor and specific expressions of social organization.

TO THE FIELD

Just as there is tension between discourses of universality and particularity—the shared language and entitlements of human rights versus distinguishing cultural practices—a discursive distance between "here" and "there," "us" and "them," confounds any singular understanding of culture. "The field" is a diffuse and problematic term for geographers, anthropologists, and other researchers who travel in a privileged way across cultures. For some, "the field" is a place impossibly outside of the power relations that organize "home." Without home, there can be no field. This separation is untenable when cultures come together to occupy the same spaces. As cultures dispersed across space and scattered over time, diasporas have for centuries defied the equation nation-culture = state-territory. Yet the continued existence of area studies in many disciplines—especially geography—reifies "the field" and extends the arguably masculine gaze of researchers.[6] Geographer Cindy Katz contends that "I am always, everywhere, in 'the field.'"[7] Katz challenges the marking off of the field as a separate time and space by asking what constitutes it. She employs a "politics of engagement" to illustrate her project: "The aim is not to bound a site of common culture and turn it into a museum/mausoleum, but to locate and pry apart some of the differences, not just between one site and elsewhere but within it as well."[8]

The notion of the field is thus rendered deeply problematic. Nonetheless, the term is used by virtually every UNHCR staff member; it is employed frequently by staff throughout the organization to refer to a range of discrete locations at varying scales. A Finn leaving headquarters in Geneva to work for UNHCR in Nairobi was presented with a farewell card wishing him well in the field. Although Nairobi is a large city with every amenity available to a large expatriate population, it is nonetheless a satellite of Geneva, and therefore, a field. In the Nairobi branch office, staff often visited from the field, meaning a smaller suboffice servicing refugee camps or a UNHCR outpost within the regional jurisdiction of the branch office. I worked, for example, as a "field officer" at a UNHCR outpost in Somalia. At yet a finer scale, in the UNHCR office in the town of Dadaab—a central administration point serving three camps—staff assigned to work with refugees would often spend the day in the field, that is, the camps. Within the organization and depending on one's post and location, "the field" has a multitude of meanings, most of which are predicated on geographical distance from a perceived center. In UNHCR's case, the center is the top of the spatial hierarchy of the organization. One can imagine a series of linked maps: at once discontinuous but connected as fields.

Before moving into the camps, this chapter begins by exploring some existing analyses of feminist subjectivities within the discipline of geography, analyses that provide relevant reference points for this research. I situate myself in relation to these fields of power and introduce different spatial, cultural, and political relations in the camps as a context for the subsequent discussion of refugee camp design.

INTERROGATING GEOGRAPHY: INSIDE AND OUTSIDE THE PROJECT

Feminist geographers have analyzed their often contradictory positions within their discipline as being simultaneously inside and outside the project.[9] They are at once purveyors of geographical knowledge and methods based on the traditions of the discipline in which they have been steeped and, as feminists, critical of the production and content of knowledge claims in geography. They are positioned simultaneously within what can be viewed as irreconcilable intellectual or political projects. Reconciliation is not, in my view, a goal or practice of feminist geography. Rather, feminist geography is a post-disciplinary orientation of critical engagement open to those who take seriously all the kinds of material and discursive constellations of power that produce and reproduce social and spatial hierarchies and inequalities at a multitude of scales.

As a feminist and a geographer, I conducted fieldwork in Kenya. The everyday survival strategies of refugee women living in camps and of professional women working for UNHCR constituted an important focus of my research. My main motivation to conduct research stemmed from observations of and reservations about refugee operations that I had encountered while employed in humanitarian work. I was and remain concerned that the means by which refugees are managed by humanitarian agencies reinscribe neocolonial and counterproductive relations of power predicated on a hierarchy of cultures in the camp and on major asymmetries of power linked to gender and political status. Though I was an insider to refugee operations, having worked for two agencies, I was also critical of these operations. I was both inside and outside the project of providing humanitarian assistance.

In the camps, I found that the everyday experiences and struggles of refugee women were often invisible, inaudible, and secondary to other issues and actors in the camps. They were less likely than men to speak English; they had less access to camp jobs and fewer opportunities to be involved in camp decision making and consultations with relief organizations. Many of these refugee women were, in a different sense, both inside and outside the humanitarian project of the refugee camp. Though there were (and are) a number of UNHCR and CARE policies aimed at supporting and promoting refugee women, I found that camp operations were generally inattentive to the conditions of work and home for these women. As a frontline relief worker myself, I received no formal training or policy documents relating to refugee women.

These paradoxical positionings problematize both epistemological and political issues, but from a feminist perspective, they do not go far enough in taking apart the construction of "refugee woman." A less dichotomous and state-centric way to talk about connections and differences without homogenizing or appropriating subjects is sorely needed.[10] An approach that forges links between locations and among subjects is integral to this project, despite very real differences in political status, cultural background, and resources. Though feminist geographers claim locations both inside and outside the project, the affinities and tensions between geographical and discursive locations are more transnational and deterritorialized than these binary locations of inside and outside imply.[11]

TROUBLED TRANSLATIONS

Translation and interpretation between researchers and refugees pose questions and raise issues of theory and politics that warrant an entire book. Aware that translation is heavily invested with unequal power relations and a site for questions of representation, power, and historicity,[12] my research nonetheless attempts to incorporate some two dozen interviews with refugee women, all of which were contingent upon the availability and skills of one translator. Sherene Razack tells of the "perils of storytelling for refugee women" in particular.[13] She calls for an interrogation of the construction of subjectivity on the part of those who collect and use stories, as well as a more careful examination of how we come to know what we know given the unequal relations among groups differentiated by nationality, ethnicity, class, gender, and so on. Interviews often serve to authenticate research findings by appropriating subjugated knowledges from essentialized "native informants."[14] At least as problematic as cultural appropriation is the uncomfortable realization that the interview process reinscribes the same power relations that I aimed to critique and contest from the outset.[15] Interviews exact the same kind of performances from refugees as do the relief agencies that organize access to food, medical services, and other needs. Consent becomes almost meaningless in the wholly unequal relationship between interviewer and interviewee.

Language translation poses other difficulties in the camps. Translation is a critical activity for UNHCR and all other international agencies' daily operations.[16] Almost all my face-to-face interactions with refugees required a translator. Often discussions and disagreements occurred solely around the issue of whose translator, "ours" or "theirs," would interpret. On one occasion an incensed UNHCR local staff discovered that a rape incident had been translated to the police as "spousal assault." As Norma Alarcón notes, "The act of translating, which often introduces different concepts and perceptions, displaces and may even do violence to local knowledge through language. In the process, these may be assessed as false or inauthentic."[17] Refugees' displacement is both a corporeal and cultural condition. In an effort to avoid the further cultural displacement vis-à-vis the research process, I tested my proposed questions before commencing the interviews by having the translator, a Somali woman from the area who moved between cultures daily, review and assess whether they were conceptually and culturally translatable.[18] "Language is not a neutral medium that passes freely and easily into the private property of the speaker's intentions; it is populated—over populated with the intentions of others. Expropriating, forcing it to submit to one's own intentions and accents, is a difficult and complicated process."[19] Neither translation nor the differences in cultural and professional positions of the people involved were neutral; nor were the languages employed.

Selected interviews follow a discussion of modes of organizing humanitarian space, including an imaginary geography of management based on UNHCR's policy of protection for refugee women, a supralocal geography that minds the security of UNHCR expatriates and efficient logistics, and finally a geography defined by mobility stories that trace refugee women's movements within and beyond the social and physical infrastructure provided by UNHCR and other NGOs. Refugee routines in the camp are shaped by clan affiliation and culturally informed divisions of labor that are highly gendered, but they are also defined by the superimposed layout of the camps, the supplies provided for subsistence, and the political status of refugees, which circumscribes their spatial separation. UNHCR's planning policy aimed at protecting women in refugee camps is, I maintain, stronger on paper than on the ground. How refugee work is organized, tasks distributed, and strategies of maintaining refugee households enacted within this context constitutes a substantive part of this chapter. I aim to multiply the dichotomous positions of "inside/outside" and to unsettle the anatomical categories of gender, class, and race by invoking connections among subjects. Yes, gender matters; citizenship and political status also matter, as does the built space of refugee camps. But how, if at all, can they be linked by a feminist geography?

WHOSE GEOGRAPHY?

Pastoral nomadism does not fit easily into either the traditional model of refugee resettlement or the traditional UNHCR definition of its responsibility.
— NETHERLANDS DEVELOPMENT CORPORATION,
"HUMANITARIAN AID TO SOMALIA"

The vast majority of refugees in Kenya have prima facie status. This has two main implications. First, refugees are spatially segregated from Kenyan society by being required to live in border camps designated by the government of Kenya. Second, this sublegal status restricts not only their mobility but also their access to employment and their ability to generate an independent livelihood. They exchange the rights of citizenship for safety in camps. As Caren Kaplan notes, "To put it bluntly, few of us can live without a passport or an identity card of some sort and fewer of us can manage without employment. Our access to these signs and practices is deeply uneven and hardly carnivalesque.[20] Nowhere are Kaplan's observations more fitting than in Kenyan refugee camps. Without a Somalian government to safeguard the entitlements of citizenship in their own country, Somali refugees flee to Kenya, where they are relegated to isolated camps financed by donor countries thousands of miles away. Mobility and access to employment are officially unavailable to prima facie refugees. Within the context of the camps, UNHCR attempts to make the best of the situation.

In some cases, when a large influx of refugees cross a border unexpectedly, camps are established without the luxury of planning (see figure 4.1). Liboi camp, very close to the Somalian border on the Kenyan side, grew exponentially and haphazardly as Ifo, Hagadera, and Dagahaley camps were under construction. Problems of crowding, poor sanitation, and related disease plagued the camp in 1992. Mortality rates soared while relief staff scrambled to improve conditions in the camp and, in turn, stabilize the health of the refugee population.

UNHCR has established general guidelines for organizing camps where planning is possible. Some of these guidelines emphasize the safety of refugee women:

> The physical circumstances in which refugees are housed affect their safety. Too often refugee women face dangers stemming from poor design of camps: for example, communal housing that provides no privacy for women; location of basic services and facilities such as latrines at an unsafe distance from where refugee women are housed . . . construction of barriers and even the mining of the perimeters of camps even when refugees must go beyond those borders to obtain firewood or other items.[21]

Figure 4.1. Refugees from Somalia/Liboi camp. Courtesy UNHCR/22043/ 05.1992/P. Moumtzis.

Awareness of the importance of built space is evident in UNHCR's *Guidelines on the Protection of Refugee Women,* which enumerate several questions that planners and administrators should consider in establishing camps. Possible program interventions the guidelines list include

- Conserve to the extent possible the original community from the country of origin within the new site.

- Consult with the refugees as to the preferred physical and social organization of the camp. Ensure that women are consulted during this process, and when possible, have female staff talk with community workers.

- Ensure that basic services/facilities at the site are located in such a manner that refugee women do not become vulnerable to attack when they need to avail themselves of these services/facilities.[22]

How to conserve local community in the context of pervasive supralocal planning exigencies is not expounded here. A checklist of questions to consider in assessing physical layout is included in the guidelines. Site planners are asked to consider: "How is the camp or other place of settlement physically organized? Is the camp organized in a manner similar to what the refugees are accustomed to in their villages and townships? Have refugees been consulted?"[23] Consultation with refugees about camp design is difficult if they are absent from the Nairobi offices and proposed camp sites where layout is conceived and debated. "Back in the putative 'center,' metropolitans have the luxury of manipulating the images of links and disjunctures, fantasizing *contact* with difference while maintaining a comfortable distance."[24] Despite good intentions, these considerations suggest that only lip service is paid to refugee input.

The guidelines are ironically overshadowed by an approach that addresses the security and logistical concerns of expatriate workers and relief agencies in the Dadaab camps. Maps of the Dagahaley, Hagadera, and Ifo camps (figures 4.2–4.4) illustrate the clustering of services at one edge of each of the camps, easily accessible by road but less accessible to refugees on foot.[25] Staff offices are located close to roads and near Kenyan police bases to ensure safety during the day.[26] In the evenings, staff members who work in the camps return to the main UNHCR compound located in the town of Dadaab. The rationale for such sociospatial organization is security for staff and

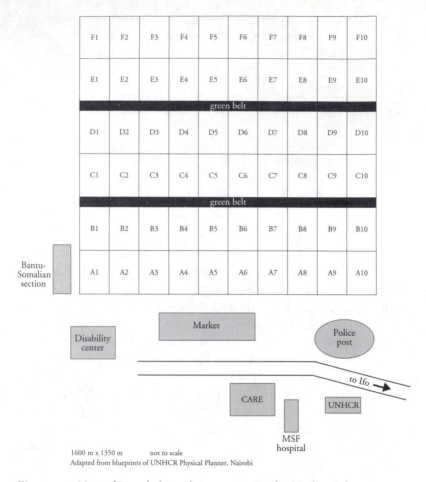

Figure 4.2. Map of Dagahaley refugee camp. Credit: Nadine Schuurman.

protection of supplies. This border area has a history of insecurity based on geopolitics and Shifta banditry. Refugees living in camps situated in this region have not been immune to theft and assaults. Equipment and cash stores maintained by UNHCR and other agencies represent an inviting target. In the event of an uprising or violent protest, staff can be more easily evacuated from a location on a road and near a Kenyan police post than from offices and services centrally situated in the camps.

Most of the residences and catering facilities for humanitarian

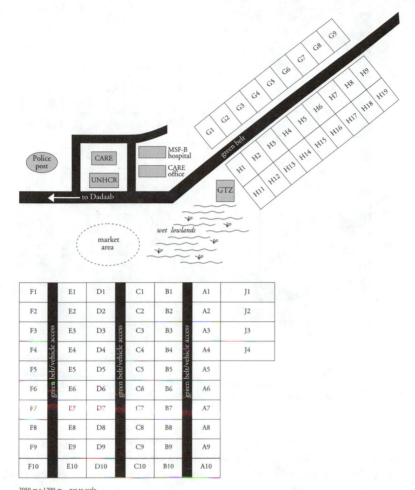

Figure 4.3. Map of Hagadera refugee camp. Credit: Nadine Schuurman.

workers are separate from the camps. Each organization has its own central compound in Dadaab. UNHCR's main compound used to be a collection of tented sleeping and eating quarters. The new compound, completed in 1994, features permanent buildings, including both a central office and a residential section (see figures 4.5 and 4.6).[27] It is fortified with two security fences made of dry acacia bushes, which have sharp spikes that easily puncture the skin and

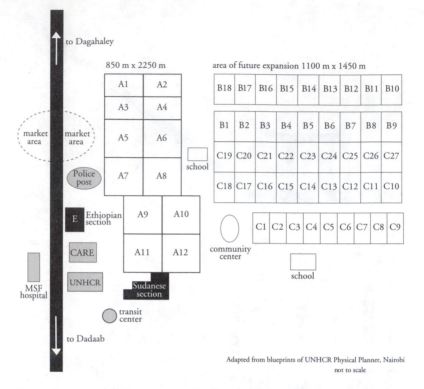

Figure 4.4. Map of Ifo refugee camp. Credit: Nadine Schuurman.

that stick tenaciously once caught on clothing. A large staff of guards is stationed at the entrance gates to various sections of the compound. At night, a number of armed guards provide extra security. Like the UNHCR day offices located in the camps, the compound can be evacuated quickly if necessary.[28] The main UNHCR office is located within yet another fence inside the compound. The office of the most senior UNHCR staff member has two doors, yet no direct access from the office foyer. In the event of an incident, these doors provide escape routes in addition to the building's main entrance. To the extent that violent confrontation is anticipated, the design represents a geography of fear.

Access into and out of the camps is also important for logistical reasons. Accommodating transportation and delivery to the camps

Figure 4.5. Shared housing for expatriates, UNHCR compound. Author's photograph.

Figure 4.6. Dining hall, UNHCR compound. Author's photograph.

is a major consideration. Food commodities, for examples, are trucked from the Kenyan port of Mombasa to the camps, off-loaded, and stored in large secure tents known as Rubb Halls. These food storage areas tend to be located close to roads on the perimeter of camps rather than centrally, close to the refugee population for whom the food is intended. Situating the storage areas near the police post seemingly minimizes the potential of theft. The question remains, however: security, convenience, and service for whom? More crudely put, whose geography is this? In 1994, CARE reported that 41 percent of households in the Dadaab camps were headed by women.[29] Yet planning on the basis of strategic evacuations and logistical considerations points to an arguably disembodied and masculinist mode of operation. The security of refugee women in the camps is not of the same order, nor optic, as that of relief workers, whose safety is organized on the basis of a confrontational, quasi-military model.[30]

Moving to a finer scale, I suggest that the spatial organization and *segregation* of the camps shape the social routines and income-earning strategies of refugees, women in particular. Access to health care, food rations, police protection, and other services is concentrated in a single area in each of the camps. This arrangement is secure for UN, NGO, and other refugee relief staff, but inconvenient and potentially dangerous for many refugees. Moreover, the organization of the camp can exacerbate the workload of refugee women.[31] Somali women are largely responsible for maintaining the household. This includes caring for children, searching for firewood, collecting water, cooking, and queuing for food rations twice a month. Children often assist their mothers with these tasks. Girls, in particular, carry out some of these jobs independently of their mothers as part of the household distribution of work. This arrangement helps explain the three-to-one ratio of school attendance rates between refugee boys and girls in camps.[32] Simultaneous demands on women refugees necessitate this kind of time-space coordination. Because firewood is required to cook the food staples donated and distributed by international bodies, women have to leave the camps, often for hours at a time, to collect wood. This, in turn, raises questions not only about the local suitability of foreign foodstuffs provided by international donors but also about the physical safety of refugee women as they forage for wood in remote areas beyond the perimeters of the camp. The layout of the camps, with a concentration of major services, shapes the daily routines of refugee women.

In Kenya, there is a glaring discrepancy between the planning guidelines outlined by UNHCR and practical measures to organize and secure the camp. To illustrate this third geography, that of refugee women negotiating these supralocal designs at a local level, I employ selected responses from twenty-five interviews I conducted with refugee women in the three Dadaab camps, Ifo, Hagadera, and Dagahaley. Through a translator, I asked women randomly selected from all three camps exactly what they had done the previous day and for how long. I also asked about the economy of the household, the adequacy of food rations distributed by CARE, and how the family covered any deficits. In what ways are patterns of mobility constituted *through* gender relations defined by social organization, access to resources, and political status? Though the brief geographical stories offered here are imperfect sketches of refugee women's work, my intent is to document time-space constraints and strategies that women employ under these conditions.[33]

The texts presented are based on the verbatim translations of the interpreter, and as such are presented in the third person. This strategy of representation—one which inserts both the interpreter and my own cultural distance from the interviewee—is a deliberate effort to render visible, transparent, and problematic the process of translation and the power relations that interviews involve.

> How do you inscribe difference without bursting into a series of euphoric narcissistic accounts of yourself and your own kind? Without indulging in a marketable romanticism or in a naive whining about your condition? In other words, how do you forget without annihilating? Between the twin chasms of navel-gazing and navel-erasing, the ground is narrow and slippery.[34]

In making connections across differences, the ground was and is indeed slippery. Such connections among people of unequal positionings offer the possibility of feminist affinity and politics but risk reinscribing authoritative relationships of imperial pasts and contemporary cultural politics in the region. Nonetheless, imperfect engagement is better than no engagement at all based on paralyzing angst.

The selection of responses presented here illustrates how space is negotiated during a given day and some of the activities and income-earning strategies women employed. The addresses of the women interviewed are based on section location, a notation used by the women themselves, and are noted so that approximate distances to markets, food distribution tents, and hospitals can be ascertained with reference to the camp maps (see again figures 4.2–4.4). I avoided asking questions that UNHCR and NGOs often posed, such as those pertaining to household size and composition, so that I might distinguish my research from the surveillance roles of administering agencies. Though one cost of this approach is the absence of biographical detail about refugee families, the purpose of my study was not to develop a description of their households but to understand the influence of the humanitarian agencies on their lives. My questions focused on the ways that UNHCR and NGO practices of camp design, organization, and provision of supplies affected the routines of refugee women. All of the refugee women interviewed were at home when approached by the interpreter and myself.

Interview 1

[Ifo camp, Section A6, young Somali woman with baby] She rises at five to prepare tea and breakfast, tea alone yesterday because there was no wheat flour in the last food distribution. After an hour washing clothes and children, she grinds and mills sorghum for lunch. While lunch is cooking, she goes to look for firewood, which takes about three hours. She eats lunch with the family and relaxes until 3:30, when she goes to look for water. She returns two hours later and starts supper, which is eaten between 7 and 7:30. Then they visit as a family and go to sleep between 8:30 and 9 [see figures 4.7 and 4.8].

Interview 2

[Hagadera camp, Section D3, young Somali woman with baby; the woman is grinding sorghum into flour upon our arrival.] She wakes up at six. Until nine she is preparing breakfast, washing utensils, and cleaning the compound—sweeping and such. Between nine and ten she goes for water. From ten to twelve, she grinds sorghum (as she is now). From twelve to two, she prepares, cooks, and eats lunch. Then she goes for firewood until four. At four she goes back home to prepare tea and sorghum again until six. By 7:30 supper is eaten and finished. She is sleeping by nine.

Figure 4.7. Refugee woman carrying firewood. Author's photograph.

Figure 4.8. Waiting for water. Courtesy UNHCR.

It is worth noting that sorghum, like whole grain wheat, is one of the most labor-intensive foods to prepare because it has to be ground and milled by hand. In the camps among Somalian refugees, this work is a female responsibility and, as these excerpts suggest, consumes a large part of daily routine. Rice is both the easiest to cook and the most popular staple among Somalis. It has also become a rare ration during food distributions in the Dadaab camps. Both staples do, of course, require cooking with water and wood, which are also collected by women.

Interview 3

[Dagahaley Camp, Section F10, young Somali woman with baby] She awakens at six and has her prayers first. She then prepares tea for the children, washes the utensils, cleans the house and bathes the children until about nine. She collects water, and at about 9:30 starts the process of preparing sorghum for the noon meal. At noon she begins cooking for about an hour; everyone eats at two and then rests. After three, the same grinding of sorghum for the evening meal begins. More water is fetched, and she cooks dinner. The children are fed by eight. She then visits with the neighbours for a while and goes to sleep by nine.

Sometimes her husband collects firewood to sell, but it is dangerous because bandits rob and sometimes attack people collecting firewood. This woman is part of a group of other women that formed in order to meet additional income needs. In a group of about five, each woman contributes an equal portion of her ration after a distribution. The total sum is sold at the market and the money is given to one of the women. The system rotates so that each woman eventually benefits by having access to credit.[35]

An informal economy of trade is evident from this interview. The credit afforded these women allows them to buy household items, such as tea, footwear, and clothing, that are not generally provided by relief agencies. And the supplies of some items distributed by CARE in the camps, such as cooking oil, often need to be supplemented. Women are largely responsible for maintaining the household and earning additional income to meet other needs.

Where are the men in this picture? Given that in the social organization of Somali families, one man may have more than one wife, many households are led by women. One cannot speak of gender divisions of work, however, without accounting for men's activities in the camps. My request to UNHCR staff in Nairobi and Dadaab for more information to fill this gap was met with this response:

> It's not the same for all groups of men. The Somali men are different from the Sudanese, and so on. As far as the Dadaab camps go, a lot of men are just wandering around meeting other men. They talk politics and what have you in the shade under the tree or they go to the local café to rest for a coffee and to play some games (chess, cards, and local games). Some men have jobs with CARE and other NGOs.[36]

The men's absence from the homes at which the interviews took place was evident. Their daily activities were, as this transcript suggests, more difficult to trace. The following interviews illustrate the geographies of refugee women who did not appear to have much active male support in their households:

Interview 4

[Ifo camp, Section A6, a young Somali woman] She is awake by five, lights the fire, and makes tea and food for the family. By seven she leaves to look for firewood—which takes about three hours—and then takes the wood to the market to sell. She returns home by noon, prepares lunch, and takes a bit of rest until three, when she goes to fetch water. This also takes three hours because there is a queue. Supper is prepared and the family eats by seven. Up until about nine she talks with her neighbours who lived within the same fenced compound. Then, she is ready for sleeping.

The official ration is not enough. She sells firewood to buy extra food.

Interview 5

[Ifo camp, Section A6, an old woman; the interview format varies somewhat from the others because the woman thought she was too old to be relevant to the questions posed.] This woman has two grandsons who are orphans. She has a ration card for a family of five. She doesn't go to the market [to earn extra money]. She does washing and cooking, though not to the same extent as younger women. Her neighbours collect firewood in bulk and give her some. She also receives help from the Al-Haramein [an NGO nearby] with her firewood supply. Sometimes she sells sorghum, but the price is very low.

Though anecdotal as evidence, interviews such as this one pointed to informal support systems for households at a disadvantage. Refugees living in the same area sometimes shared water and firewood when they were in scarce supply. NGOs like Al-Haramein and CARE make some effort to identify vulnerable refugees and assist them where possible.

Interview 6

[Dagahaley camp, Section D4, young woman with baby] She rises at six; she has a maid who cooks in the kitchen. Yesterday someone— the husband of a pregnant woman—came to her house and asked her to come to Section C5 where the pregnant woman lived. [She has a job with the French medical NGO as a traditional birth attendant, or TBA]. She stayed there until nine, after which she went for help. A vehicle was called to take the woman to the hospital where she gave birth. The traditional birth attendant stayed with her until eleven when she returned to the house. She rested, had lunch, and at three began to build a new *tukul* [hut], which took about an hour. She built another one today, the one in which we're sitting. They are for the coming hot season and for Ramadan. At four she returned to work, stayed until six, and then came home. She bathed herself and her kids while the maid cooked. The family ate supper and stayed around the house. At eight they slept.

Though refugee women with jobs are few, their earned income affords them extras, such as the services of a "maid" in this example. According to the interpreter with whom I conducted the interview, domestic help is common among more affluent families in Somali society. Usually, the help is a young unmarried woman who works and lives with a family in exchange for room and board and a small stipend.

Interview 7

[Dagahaley camp, Section D5, a Bantu-Somalian woman] She woke up at 6 A.M., made breakfast and cleaned house until 8:30. Then she went for water, which took two hours, until 10:30. Afterwards she went to the market to buy wheat flour in order to make a local bread which she sells. Returning at noon, she made lunch and finished eating. Then she went back for water, which took from 2 P.M. to 6 P.M., but she came back empty-handed. [I asked why the water problem; she said the population is dense there, and the water pressure was very low]. She made supper for the family, arranged the beds for the children, and afterwards slept.

The considerable time and effort required to collect water and firewood is exacerbated by population concentration in the desert-based camps. Decentralized water taps are located within the camp perimeter, usually within 500 meters from any given refugee *tukul* (hut). Nonetheless, lines can be long and pressure poor at some distribution points. Firewood is often sold in the local refugee camp markets but must otherwise be collected well beyond the boundaries of the camps. Refugee women cover up to fifteen kilometers on a single journey to gather firewood.[37]

Just as industrial geography and sociology once spoke of "cathedrals in the desert," referring to culturally, economically, and geographically inappropriate projects established in the name of "development," refugee camps are desert cities similarly unsuited to highly concentrated human populations. Though a sizable aquifer runs below the desert floor in the Dadaab area where the camps are situated, providing ample supplies of water and wood for some 100,000 visiting refugees is an obvious environmental challenge. What is less obvious is the shift in demand for these commodities based on the kinds of external food aid imported. Both the Somali Kenyans and many of the Somali refugees living in the Dadaab area have a largely nomadic background based on economies of livestock, camels and cattle in particular. The staple foods of the population are meat and milk from these sources, the latter of which requires neither wood nor water to prepare. Large amounts of wheat, rice, corn-soy blend, dried kidney beans, and other nonperishable food aid arrive from other oversupplied regions of the world, but in Kenyan camps their preparation poses serious environmental questions. Each of these commodities can only be prepared with considerable amounts of water and wood, whose paucity is thereby exacerbated. The daily collection of these resources becomes increasingly difficult for refugee women.[38]

Interview 8

[Hagadera camp, Section E2, a Bantu-Somalian woman with a new-born baby; the woman is standing pounding sorghum as we arrive.] She wakes up at seven. From seven to eight she prepares breakfast and the family eats it. Between eight and nine she goes for water; from nine to twelve she prepares sorghum; crushing it, making it into powder. Between twelve and two she cooks and eats lunch. From two to three she went [sic] back for water; from four o'clock is supper preparation and bathing of children until five. By six supper is ready and she makes sure the little ones are fed because they go to sleep earlier. Up until 7:30 the elder people have supper. From 7:30 until 8 she chats with the children and her people [I didn't clarify the possessive adjective here but assume it means other Bantu-Somalians with whom she shares a fenced compound]. She goes to sleep between eight and nine. To earn extra money, she begins some days by fetching and selling jerry cans of water to other households. She usually sells six cans [twenty liters each] at three shillings each in a morning. This gives her enough money [U.S.$0.33] to buy someone else's bulk firewood off a donkey cart, which she then sells in smaller bundles in the market.

This elaborate income-generating arrangement suggests spatial constraints and possibly security considerations. Rather than stray far from the camp to collect her own firewood, before sunrise and with children in tow, this woman hauls water closer to home to earn the seed money required to buy bulk firewood from someone else. The tiny amounts of money accrued in each exchange are part of an informal economy that is constituted through the spatially circumscribed and artificially endowed formal economy of the camp. The sale of refugee labor and of donated commodities provide the basis for trade in the camps. Based on the collection of water and wood and the selling of food aid, ad hoc markets carrying a range of provisions— cigarettes, spices, tea, candies, and camel's milk among them—have been established in all of the camps. Refugee women's work is not simply a struggle to meet multiple household and income demands. While work is convoluted by the spatial segregation and organization of the camps, refugee women employ elaborate strategies to make ends meet. Credit schemes and labor-intensive entrepreneurial activities of various kinds are evidence of a vital informal economy.

As in most cultural contexts, Somali cultural practices code household work as women's responsibility, but women's work cannot simply be reduced to the gendered division of labor. One can describe the temporary urban spaces of the desert camps as expressions of an imperial order characterized by foreign foodstuffs and a design that suits the administrators and suppliers at least as much as the refugees. It at once exacerbates the burden of work that women do and reinscribes their routines.

These representations of Somalian refugees try to avoid dissecting the daily routines of women refugees or incorporating them into imperial geographies in the same way that other researchers have drawn and quartered other cultures.[39] At one time, my intention was to represent the lives of these women in such a way that the repetition and duress of their work could be felt in the repetition of lean, prosaic prose. Such a strategy, however, risks textualizing a very corporeal and often dangerous set of routines shaped by social stature, subordinate legal status in relation to Kenyans, and corresponding spatial containment.

What becomes clear from these selected geographies of refugee work is that a significant amount of time is spent performing the tasks that allow basic subsistence and survival in the camps. The design of the temporary urban spaces of the desert camps contribute to this work. Characterized by foreign foodstuffs, a corresponding high demand for wood and water, and a concentrated population, the camps are anything but an attempt to "conserve to the extent possible the original community from the country of origin within the new site."[40] The nomadic practices of many Somalis, including their reliance on meat and milk, are not incorporated into the organization of the camps. Rather, the refugees who seek asylum are incorporated into a geography of humanitarian assistance (see figure 4.9). "The body repeats the landscape. They are the source of each other and create each other."[41] A supralocal order prevails.

There are at least two geographies to consider here: a grid of intelligibility and control defined by the supralocal humanitarian organizations operating in the area, UNHCR in particular, and the multiple movements of refugees informed by locations of gender and culture negotiated within this design. These geographies, I suggest, are complicated by the political status of refugees and the hierarchy of cultures that characterizes the camps.

SUPRACITIZEN AND SUBCITIZEN: BORDER SUBJECTS

Once an individual, a human being, becomes a refugee, it is as though he has become a member of another race, some other sub-human group. You talk of rights of refugees as though human rights did not exist which are broader and more important. . . . One individual's protection is as important as making a camp for ten thousand people.

— ZIA RIZVI, "THE PROTECTION OF REFUGEES"

Citizenship and legal status, or nonstatus, as it were, are critical factors shaping one's geographical placement in the wake of displace-

Figure 4.9. Daily routine in the camps. Courtesy UNHCR/21052/ 05.1991/B. Press.

ment. The movements and economic activities of refugee women, many of whom fall outside the project of camp planning and operations, illustrate how and for whom refugee camps are organized. Migrant status is significant: Refugees are forced migrants; expatriates are voluntary migrants. Refugee subcitizens, who have no legal status in the law of the country in which they reside, are administered through a suprastate institutional framework by the supracitizens who work ostensibly for them. These concepts introduce a simplified politics of citizenship that illustrates the unequal positioning and spacing of particular groups under the banner of UN humanism. Somali refugees, local Kenyans, and international staff are ranked hierarchically on the basis of citizenship and the access to employment this status enables. The cadre of international professional supracitizens who assist refugees in the camps is made up of employees from around the world, many of whom carry the coveted light blue *laisser passer* UN passport. In contrast, the mobility of forced migrants is highly circumscribed by legal, geographical, and administrative parameters. As prima facie refugees, they are required to abide by the stipulations of the Kenyan government and the isolation of camp life these invoke. "Supracitizens" and "subcitizens" are not simply descriptions of two distinct groups found in the camps; they represent linked but unequal identities.

In a very different way, the staff who work in these camps are also displaced. They are not forced, but voluntary migrants. Accordingly, their position is much more privileged. They are for the most part professionals being remunerated for difficult jobs. To compare these distinct groups of displaced people at all is to risk blurring the acute differences between them. Nonetheless, the expatriate stories warrant telling. They too are symptomatic of the spatial organization of camps in isolated border regions.

Over breakfast one morning at the UNHCR compound in Dadaab, a serious comparison of long-distance phone call charges and longings for home consumed the four women employees with whom I sat. Some had children; others had partners. They moved on to recite from memory a litany of airfares—imagined getaways—to desirable destinations: Addis, U.S.$542; Bombay, U.S.$480; the Seychelles, Dubai. . . . Unlike the phone calls, these imagined geographies for the most part excluded home. Isolation and hardship in the desert camps could be rewarded by compensating trips to nearby, available destinations. These women had endured much: They spoke of their experiences of malaria, reactions to medication, and other physical ailments they said were symptomatic of Dadaab. At a professional level, their initiative was sometimes obstructed, their innovations were resisted, and hierarchical discipline was maintained. Though these employees were extremely privileged compared to the refugees they assisted, they were also near the bottom of the professional organization chart at UNHCR. Dadaab is a nonfamily "E" duty station in UNHCR parlance: the least desirable of locations. UN staff and refugees may coexist in one general location, but they have different political status and cultural backgrounds, which separate them socially and geographically.

The range that these extreme migrant positions represent introduces a larger debate among critical scholars, between those who want to align themselves with the subaltern postcolonial subject, in this case with refugees, and those who insist that such an attempt becomes only a refined version of the very discourse it seeks to displace.[42] My project falls somewhere in between. Certain refugee subject positions—particularly those of women—are under erasure. Rather than align myself with refugees against the humanitarian corps that aims to assist them, however, my objective is to expose the different geographies that each of these "sides" produces and analyze the common space of refugee camps in relation to social and political status. The politically unequal and arguably neocolonial encounters between "un-stated" refugees, centrally and locally hired Kenyans, and "ex-patriate" employees introduce an intense case of cultural politics that provide the basis for some modest claims about the significance and signification of these subjects.

A cultural politics of negotiation, subversion, and indifference mark the spaces of text and territory in the camps: "[A]lthough there may be surveillance, fixity is not achieved."[43] How humanitarian discourses organize the space of these camps, and whom they include and exclude are my principal concerns in the section that follows. Who are the actors and interlocutors, and who is excluded from these subject positions?

Serving the camps are a number of medical, social, and legal humanitarian agencies assisting refugees. They all communicate by handheld radios. Each organization is named according to the alphabetical vocabulary of international radio code. Each international appellation corresponds to a physical space, usually a compound or base camp. Thus, staff working for the High Commissioner for Refugees are referred to on the walkie-talkie handsets as the "hotels," most of whom live at the UNHCR compound. CARE employees who distribute food and provide social services are the "charlies," staff of a medical NGO from France were "foxtrots," and so forth. Each employee authorized to carry a handset is assigned a call sign: a combination of the organization's radio name as well as numbers and sometimes letters designating a particular person. The more elaborate and lengthy one's call sign, the less important one's rank. All refugee agencies use one common channel for calling others. When contact is made, employees switch to another shared channel to discuss particular matters. These conversations are by no means private, as other workers can move to the same channel and listen in, although they are limited to the few staff members working in the camps who have handsets.[44] In addition, UNHCR has its own discursive space, an exclusive channel on the handsets, to convey information on private or internal matters. The radio network is the most vital communication link in the camps and is so pervasive among relief workers that many people are referred to by their call signs rather than their names.

The great irony of this international radio language, which literally and figuratively maps an intensely local field, is that there is no call sign or designated name for the refugees themselves, though their existence is the very raison d'être of this humanitarian exercise. Edward Said notes of outcast populations that "their existence always counts, though their names and identities do not, they are profitable without fully being there."[45] "[N]aming is part of the human rituals of incorporation, and the unnamed remains less human than the inhuman or sub-human."[46] This erasure points to the un-stated condition of refugees in more than a political sense. As technology and language, the radio is constitutive of subject positions.

Supracitizens, citizens, and subcitizens have differential access to mobility and to the power relations that shape the geography of refugee camps. Refugee subcitizens have forcibly migrated across borders to safety and sustenance. International supracitizens have flown across borders to well-remunerated jobs carried out in often harsh conditions. Kenyan citizens find work where refugees and relief agencies have moved in. The power to move is shaped on a broader scale by the mobility of money and information, the color of one's passport and skin. To those without identity documents and citizenship, entitlements are few and mobility restricted. They are likely to cross the Kenyan border on foot and to be escorted by UNHCR in the back of a truck to a nearby camp. The minimal status of prima facie refugees is differentiated by gendered routines of work, by nationality, and by ethnicity.

Despite the language of international human rights and universal entitlement, subject positions in the camps are discursively and geographically spaced out. These locations are material expressions of international law and transnational subjectivities, marked also by the segregation of cultural, political, and gender difference. The routines of refugee women are circumscribed by supralocal camp organization, positions of unequal political status, and gendered divisions of labor. They are at once relegated to the camps by Kenyan government rules and left with little choice but to leave the camps regularly in search of firewood in order to cook foods distributed by the relief agencies. Camp design is expressive of the logistical and security considerations of international staff, despite the lip service paid to policies aimed at promoting and safeguarding refugee women. These women perform gendered routines of household work exacerbated by camp layout and mediated by their own survival strategies.

The daily routines of refugee women presented in this chapter cannot simply be reduced to an economy of women's work and to culturally defined divisions of labor. The built space and layout of the camps organize refugee women's work in important ways. This chapter concludes by proposing a direction for feminist geographers, one that works through difference rather than on either side of it. In analyzing UNHCR operations, it invites engagement with "others" rather than simply accepting, accommodating, or managing otherness as diversity.

> A notion of links between locations and subjects deconstructs the long-standing marxist cultural hegemony model by demonstrating the impossibility of finding a pure position or site of subjectivity outside the economic and cultural dynamics that structure modernity. . . . it is through transnationality that feminists can resist the practices of modernity—i.e. nationalism, modernism, imperialism, etc.—that have been so repressive to women.[47]

There is no "pure position or site of subjectivity outside" the power relations that structure the field. Rather, I may be complicit, subversive, accepting, and critical, but I am always connected to the field that the camps represent. My complicity lies in my privileged position in relation to the refugee women who clean my room and wash my clothes during my stay in the camps. My criticism of camp operations is evinced in the pointed but evenhanded discussion papers I circulated to UNHCR staff during the period of my research and in the debates that revealed my feminist sensibilities as a researcher. In this context, I am a small part of the camps' construction and reconstruction through the arguments, actions, and affinities in which I engage.

UNHCR's policies concerned with refugee women's welfare represent the organization's best intentions toward achieving participatory structures, gender equity, and camp designs conducive to refugee needs. It is committed to these ideas on paper. In practice, camp design and organization emphasize supracitizen control and management, from a distance, of refugee difference. The space of the camps is divided between refugees and nonrefugees. Though this separation may be a practical response to security concerns on the part of international staff, it is cause for critical reflection. If the camps are not safe enough for expatriates, are they sufficiently secure for the refugees who live in them? Transnational feminist practices demand enacting connections of this kind, rather than the management of refugees' differences.

The design of refugee camps in northeast Kenya shapes gender relations in the camps. The gendered division of labor and locally derived relations of domination also influence the lives of women living in the camps. This chapter has touched upon the political and material gulf that separates refugees from the staff hired to assist them. One response to this segregated construction of the camps is to annihilate the space that separates sub- and supracitizens, both in the material sense by creating proximity and in the political sense by engaging refugees as subjects and interlocutors rather than as helpless, hapless "others." At one time, international staff at UNHCR and other NGOs did live within the perimeters of the camps. Since former military officers were hired as security advisers by UNHCR in Nairobi, the separation of the two groups has become a priority. The creation of rigid lines of social and spatial distinction between Africans and Europeans (as well as expatriates of other nationalities) echoes practices of white settlers in Kenya during the colonial period.[48]

The liberal humanist construction of united nations, human rights, and equality for all becomes rhetorical in the refugee camps where humanitarianism is practiced. Borders and distinctions continue to be made: "Boundaries are drawn by mapping practices; 'objects' do not pre-exist as such. Objects are boundary projects."[49] To examine a border or boundary between supra- and subcitizens is to expose its "mapping practices." The discursive distance between refugees and humanitarian staff inscribes corresponding physical boundaries. The mapping practices of the Kenyan camps are predicated on this distance and the gulf between Somali refugees, Kenyan locals, and international relief staff. "Objectivity is not about disengagement, but about mutual *and* usually unequal structuring."[50] Having identified an axis of political difference that separates refugees from humanitarian staff, in the next chapter I document mapping practices and examples of unequal structuring that preclude engagement between groups in the refugee camps.

5

Ordering Disorder: Sitreps, Headcounts, and Other Instruments

Colonial discourse, with its emphasis on Third World inferiority, has re-emerged in the language of the international development agencies.

—JANE PARPART, "POST-MODERNISM, GENDER, AND DEVELOPMENT"

[D]iscipline was never more important or more valorized than at the moment when it became important to manage a population. . . . we need to see things not in terms of the replacement of a society of sovereignty by a disciplinary society and the subsequent replacement of a disciplinary society by a society of government; in reality one has a triangle, sovereignty-discipline-government, which has as its primary target the population and as its essential mechanism the apparatuses of security.

—MICHEL FOUCAULT, "GOVERNMENTALITY"

There is no pure, apolitical, unadulterated way to deliver humanitarian assistance.[1] Relief agencies cannot operate outside the networks of power in the refugee camps and war zones in which they work. In areas of conflict and displacement, local power brokers often control certain territory or facilities, and require "compensation" for their "cooperation." In 1992, CARE hired planes to transport staff and supplies into Baidoa—famine capital of Somalia at the time. CARE was required, in turn, to pay a landing fee to a self-appointed local authority each and every time a plane used the airstrip. In order to move around the town safely, the organization

117

also had to hire self-appointed security who drove "technicals"—
jeeps with submachine guns mounted on the back. To these self-
proclaimed authorities, relief agencies were either allies or enemies.
To be an ally, one had to pay. "Because of the need to negotiate with
armed groups for access to displaced people and other conflict-
affected populations, aid agencies often implicitly accept that a proportion of their relief will go to the very groups which are waging
war."[2]

Similar kinds of negotiation occur at virtually every site of humanitarian relief. Indigenous social and political structures inevitably
clash with those introduced by international humanitarian agencies.
The mandates of UN and nongovernmental organizations operating
in conflict zones to do humanitarian, rather than political, work are
at serious risk of being compromised, if not undermined, by the politics of humanitarian engagement on the ground. Humanitarian assistance is political: It is part and parcel of the power relations among
governments, opposition forces, and other nonstate actors.

Refugee camps, too, require a politics of engagement, though on
quite different terms. Chapter 4 sought to illustrate the cultural hierarchies and spatialized politics evident in the camps among local
Kenyans, refugees, and the relatively privileged international staff
that assists refugees. Following from that analysis of camp layout
and cultural politics, this chapter addresses some of the ways in
which refugee operations in the field are organized and reported.
Citing on-the-ground practices and the findings of selected reports, I
begin by outlining links between practices of managing displaced
people and constellations of colonial power. This chapter addresses
power relations in Kenyan refugee camps from a postcolonial perspective, linking the liberal, humanitarian present with the colonial
civilizing missions of the past. By placing current humanitarian operations within this framework, I elucidate their links with colonial and
neocolonial relations.

The chapter focuses on practices *within* the camps, including
management and discipline and the implementation they entail. One
specific objective is to analyze the production of official refugee reports and to examine their content as ways of knowing about a subject population. The most powerful if not persuasive technologies of
recording and reporting the field are exercised by UNHCR and its

partner agencies. These modalities of representation are predicated on control, vision, and distance, but the techniques of surveillance and control employed in the camps do not constitute a closed system of discipline and management. Containment—whether political, economic, or social—is tenuous at best and does not create a community. In the final section, I challenge the assumption that refugee camps are communities.

LINKING POSTCOLONIALISM AND HUMAN DISPLACEMENT

Postcolonialism has been described as a movement that aims to decolonize the mind. It is an attempt to refute and reconstruct the ethnocentrism of traditional European thought and historiography in relation to former colonies. "Postcolonialism is distinguished, not by a clean leap into another discourse, but by its critical reaccentuation of colonial and anti-colonial languages."[3] It is not simply a condition that follows colonialism temporally, applying equally to all formerly colonized locations. Rather, it refuses the simple diffusion of a global culture and instead underscores the continued relevance of history and geography.

> [I]t can be argued that colonial power, far from being monolithic, seizes upon, enlists, and combines a range of discourses, knowledges, and signifying practices (scientific, religious, aesthetic) which are not formally or ideologically aligned with colonial administration, but from which the demarcation and regulation of difference can be appropriated and utilized by colonial power. . . . there can be no global theory of colonial culture, only localized theories and historically specific accounts that provide insight into varied articulations of colonialist and countercolonial representations and practices.[4]

Postcolonial approaches subvert the liberal framework of law, democracy, and human rights to the extent that these are absolute values or moral positions.[5] They attempt to unravel colonialism as a coherent, uninterrupted history, and they suggest ways in which colonial pasts are connected to the liberal present. Such approaches expose the inequalities of cultural, national, and gender hierarchies and the practices they sanction. For example, how is it that the voices of refugees themselves are so rarely heard in academic journals, despite efforts to include them and authors sympathetic to their conditions of displacement? Like Gayatri Chakravorty Spivak, I would argue that the subject positions of refugees are effaced through the production of expert commentary on humanitarian crises.[6] Scripts are written about them, speaking of them but not to them; women in postcolonial locations are particularly susceptible to subaltern status: "Between patriarchy and imperialism, subject-constitution and object-formation, the figure of the woman disappears, not into a pristine nothingness, but into a violent shuttling which is the displaced figuration of the 'third-world woman' caught between tradition and modernization."[7] Just as histories of formerly colonized countries have often been written by authors from their respective colonizing nations, or motherlands, so too is the field of refugee studies populated primarily by scholars located in Europe, North America, Japan, Australia, and New Zealand, with some obvious exceptions. This writing relationship and these relations of power are not easily rectified, nor are they necessarily ignored by scholars of refugee studies. The point is that refugee subjects do not simply have experience that can be transparently recorded; rather, they are produced by their experience and represented in very particular ways.

Anthropologist Liisa Malkki exposes the limits of liberal traditions of refugee assistance and of refugee studies through an analysis of material discourse within a loosely Foucauldian context. She takes apart the meanings of displacement, noting the term's decentered and pathological connotations in relation to the order of nation-states and their centered citizens. Malkki's analysis extends further to the refugee camp, which she contends became "a standardized, generalizable technology of power in the management of mass displacement."[8] Because refugees are constructed as aberrations of the nation-state, they are often construed as in need of therapeutic treatment for their condition. "The refugee camp is a technology of 'care and control.' . . . a technology of power entailing the management of space and movement—for 'peoples out of place.'"[9] Malkki's critical theorization of refugees is important to refugee studies because it provides cause for reexamination of the ways refugees are represented, written, and situated in academic and humanitarian circles.

Employing Michel Foucault's concept of governmentality, Nicholas Thomas notes that "[t]he observer, or observing colonizer, commands a knowledge of groups such as institutional inmates, welfare recipients, and the colonized, that is intimately linked with a classification and diagnosis of the inferiority or inadequacy of the latter, that establishes the need for management.[10] Though he does not mention refugees per se, his analysis reiterates the "care and control" management ethos Malkki outlines. In the spirit of both Malkki and Thomas, this chapter takes the governance of refugee camps in Kenya as its object of inquiry and seeks to link it with colonial practices of administration and order.

KNOWLEDGE AND POWER: TECHNOLOGIES OF KNOWING

The production of maps, statistics, and assessments by professionals at UNHCR is, I believe, performed with the welfare of refugees in mind. Nonetheless, their production often occurs without reference to the historical configurations of power that preceded them. In the context of refugee camps, cartography, counting, and recording are all acts of management, if not surveillance. They enact controversial power relations between refugees and humanitarian agencies. These strategic tools represent the field of refugee camps as orderly and comparable to other fields managed in various parts of the globe: "Facts are presented in standardized ways, so that they can be retold if necessary. In this sense, facts must be seen as an aspect of social organization, a practice of knowing that, through the use of ready-made categories, constructs an object as external to the knower and independent of him or her."[11] Indeed, accounts are often retold in humanitarian circles, as information is passed from field offices to regional locations and ultimately to head offices. Standardization is crucial to the integrity of the information-gathering process, but it occurs at the expense of accounting for local historical contexts.

In line with the observation that refugees are portrayed as needing care and maintenance, Barbara Harrell-Bond has observed that "[o]utsiders view African refugees as *helpless;* as needing outsiders to plan for them and to take care of them. This assumption is the cornerstone of nearly all appeals for funds."[12] Getting funding is certainly one rationale for presenting this image of helplessness, but other relations of power operating in the camps are also predicated on notions of paternalism.

ORDERING DISORDER

The onset of a humanitarian crisis, such as the civil war, famine, and human displacement in Somalia, can provide a political rationale for external intervention or assistance. In Kenya, the official job of ordering disorder, of organizing and assisting Somali refugees, belongs to UNHCR. It is a difficult job characterized by the basic task of matching refugee needs with appropriate resources, but it is mired in more diffuse political relations at different scales. UNHCR responds to crises and solicits resources to support its operations. Despite the involvement of various governments, NGOs, vendors, and UN partner agencies in most major crises of displacement, UNHCR has tended to be the main transfer point of assistance to refugees. The organization is, therefore, responsible to those contributors as well as to the refugees whom it has the mandate to assist. This is admittedly a tall order. UNHCR has to perform multiple tasks under often difficult conditions and is held increasingly accountable for its performance. Performance in this context involves not only the achievement of ends but also the use of suitable means.

In the case of widespread displacement, such as the displacement of Somalis to Kenya and of Rwandans to the former Zaire, the expansive network of government donors in the humanitarian sector effectively hires UNHCR as its agent in emergency situations. One outcome of this arrangement is an established and ongoing interest in the number of refugees or displaced persons for whom UNHCR is responsible. While UNHCR is by far the most visible agency in most refugee emergencies, the visibility of the displaced people it assists is also a primary concern. Refugee statistics are the basis for funding proposals, allocation, and planning. Refugee operations embody a language of arithmetical calculation and therapy that transposes particular events and activities in the field into standardized reports, statistics, and community development projects suitable for consumption at the UNHCR branch office in Nairobi and headquarters in Geneva. Information from a particular location and context is standardized and made comparable to reports from other places.

The tension between cultural particularity and universality introduced in chapter 3 is evident in the tension between distinctive politicocultural practices in the camps and standard UNHCR reporting procedures. Standard information—in the sense of being both usual and comparable—is collected. These procedures are part of the organization's institutional culture. Some examples include headcounts, situation reports ("sitreps"), and refugee "biodata"—(personal information pertaining to one's asylum claim, usually collected for purposes of determining legal status). Biodata is solicited by protection officers who interview asylum seekers individually and is used in the assessment of their claims. Both headcounts and sitreps apply to more aggregate populations of displaced persons, and each will be discussed within the context of field reporting.

Transposing the field into text or image is concerned with two tasks: micropolitical analysis and micropolitical intervention.[13] Indeed, governmentality inquires by means of management and codes of information: "written reports, drawings, pictures, numbers, charts, statistics. This information must be of a particular form—stable, mobile, combinable and comparable."[14] The excerpt from the Country Operations Plan for Kenya quoted in Chapter 1 is worth reiterating because it alludes to some of the technologies of surveillance, control, and management of refugees in postindependence Kenya:

> The Branch Office [in Kenya] has addressed the intractable problem of discrepancies between feeding figures, registered numbers, and total populations, by camp site as well as by overall caseload and nationality, through physical headcounts and registration of refugees in the camps. These discrepancies are due to acts of refugee sabotage; double registration within camps and between camps; and inflation of the number of dependants on ration cards in a bid to maximize their entitlements to food and other relief assistance distributed in the camps.[15]

UNHCR meticulously orders the field through exercises of counting, calculating, and coding refugees. Though this short excerpt is not necessarily representative of all UNHCR activities, refugees are represented in this operations plan as statistical and moral deviations. The report speaks directly to Foucault's tripartite concern with security, territory, and population in his analysis of "governmentality":

> By this word I mean three things:
>
> 1. The ensemble formed by the institutions, procedures, analyses and reflections, the calculations and tactics that allow the exercise of this very specific albeit complex form of power, which has as its target population, as its principal form of knowledge political economy, and as its essential technical means apparatuses of security.
>
> 2. The tendency which . . . has steadily led towards the preeminence over all other forms (sovereignty, discipline, etc.) of this type of power which may be termed government, resulting, on the one hand, in the formation of a whole series of specific governmental apparatuses, and on the other, in the development of a whole complex of *savoirs*.

3. The process, or rather the result of the process, through which the state of justice of the Middle Ages, transformed into the administrative state during the fifteenth and sixteenth centuries, gradually becomes "governmentalized."[16]

Though refugees and the camps in which they live are "un-stated," both are managed by an international governing apparatus, in which the Office of UNHCR is a major player.

Michel Foucault outlines the critical shift in modes of governance, from juridical models of sovereignty imposed from above to instrumental modes of spacing people to achieve certain ends.[17] Foucault posits the reorientation of government away from territorial concerns of statehood toward a different sphere of power, that of population. Furthering Foucault's argument, "[T]he family is re-configured as the basic unit of a *population,* and re-emerges not as a *model* of government but as an *instrument* of government. Knowledge of the family provides the basis for a statistical accounting of the population as a whole. Thus the population, its pursuits and products, its very life, become appropriate objects of state management."[18]

Given UNHCR's job as executor of humanitarian relief, it is at the center of refugee emergencies: "a centre of ordering is a place which *monitors* a periphery, *represents* that periphery, and makes calculations."[19] Benedict Anderson contends that the census, map, and museum constituted the "grammar" of the colonial state and were instruments for coding and controlling the colonized.[20] Like Timothy Mitchell, he underscores the importance of visibility.[21] Anderson cites the example of Indonesian novelist Pramoedya Ananta Toer's *Glass House,* comparing it to Jeremy Bentham's Panopticon: "For the colonial state did not merely aspire to create, under its control, a human landscape of perfect visibility; the condition of this 'visibility' was that everyone, everything, had as it were a serial number."[22] In recording the field, an emphasis on vision is not misplaced. Technologies of vision are used to calculate refugee populations and map the grid design of the camps onto the desert floor (see figures 5.1–5.2). A more grounded view (figure 5.3) shows the camp inhabitants at work in a much messier, less orderly context. Aerial photos provide a basis for counting refugee huts and subsequently estimating the population, one of several methods used to report the field.[23] Also, the construction of neat rows of refugee shelters is an attempt to create order.

Figure 5.1. UNHCR at Dadaab: aerial view of compound. Author's photograph.

Figure 5.2. Aerial view of Ifo camp before refugees arrive: geometric order. Courtesy UNHCR.

Figure 5.3. The "messiness" of refugee living in one camp. Courtesy UNHCR.

HEADCOUNTS

There is ample evidence that refugees are contained and counted according to codes they resent and resist. Headcounts, which serve as census-taking exercises, provide an excellent example. A field officer from UNHCR, who had just been part of a headcount process, described the exercise to me in Nairobi; the description is paraphrased here:

> In June 1993 at Mandera refugee camp in northern Kenya, a headcount of Somali refugees was discretely organized by UNHCR. The purpose of the exercise was to determine the actual size of the population and thus to reduce the inflated number of false ration cards circulating in the camp. The plan was devised secretly, so that refugees would not subvert the counting process.
>
> At five in the morning approximately 200 Kenyan police and army personnel surrounded the camp. Six counting centers had been set up. All refugees were awakened and instructed to move to the nearest center, each of which was fenced and guarded. UNHCR staff, many of whom had been flown in from other locations to assist, communicated by walkie-talkie between the centers. Their first objective was to get all refugees inside any one of the six fenced sites. Refugees then filed through narrow corridors through which only one person at a time could pass. Here, they were counted—their hands marked with ink to signify this—and moved to the next area cordoned off within the fenced center. Registration numbers were allocated, ration cards issued, and refugees released back into the camp. The exercise was complete by early morning.

This scenario has been enacted repeatedly in Kenyan refugee camps up to as recently as December 1994. According to senior UNHCR staff in Nairobi, headcounts are standard practice.[24] UNHCR has also recently published a registration guide outlining the planning and practice of a refugee census.[25] It illustrates ways of structuring the processing centers in order to execute the task efficiently (see figures 5.4 and 5.5).

Historically, headcounts have been problematic for UNHCR and other administering agencies.[26] Accurate refugee numbers are important for procuring funds and food rations and for planning purposes, but refugees have not willingly subjected themselves to the methods these counts employ. In Kakuma camp—sanctuary for predominantly Christian Sudanese refugees fleeing General Omar El-Bashir's regime—refugees subverted the census process on two occasions, in April and June 1994. On one occasion they tore apart the enclosures built for the exercise, and on the other they kidnapped the staff participating in the headcount. Refugees argued that the rounding up of people into fenced lots did not respect basic human dignity and reminded them of the slavery of their people under Arab rule.[27] The Sudanese refugees vehemently resisted UNHCR's efforts to subjugate them to what they considered demoralizing headcounts. At Kakuma, UNHCR officials finally had to consort with leaders of the Sudanese

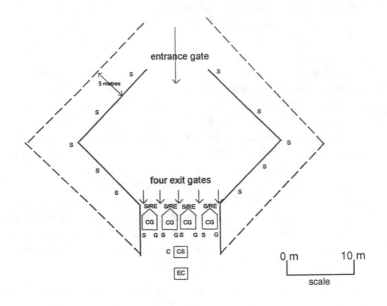

----- Bush fence/rope
___ Pole and wire fence
S   Security Guard
CG   Coupon Giver
RE   Refugee Elder
G   Gate Guard
CS   Coupon Supplier
C   Coupon Guard
EC   Enclosure Supervisor

Figure 5.4. Sample plan of a registration enclosure. Courtesy UNHCR. From UNHCR, Registration: A Practical Guide for Field Staff *(Geneva, May 1994).*

People's Liberation Army (SPLA) after the two failed attempts at a camp census. Meeting with political groups contravenes UNHCR official policy, but given the SPLA's significant influence in the camp, UNHCR staff felt they had little choice.[28] The SPLA representatives refused to agree to the use of enclosures. Instead, they suggested that churches in the camp be fenced and used for the registration process. The churches are, of course, powerful political symbols in the war between the Islamic fundamentalist El-Bashir government forces in the north and the Sudanese of Christian and indigenous beliefs in the

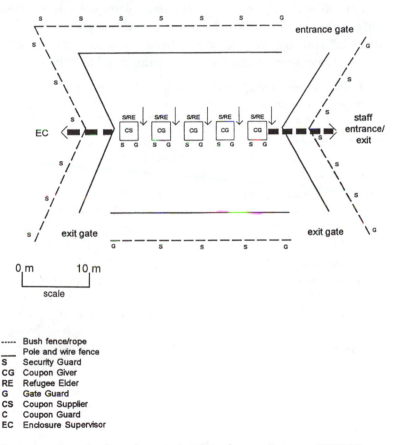

Figure 5.5. Sample plan of a registration enclosure. Courtesy UNHCR. From UNHCR, Registration: A Practical Guide for Field Staff (Geneva, May 1994).

south. In the end, separate arrangements had to be made for registration of Muslim refugees in the camp, but the churches were used as counting centers, and the exercise was completed quickly and uneventfully on December 15, 1994. The Sudanese refugees' analysis in action is perhaps the strongest critique of UNHCR operations in the field to date, and yet their responses did nothing to change the basic procedures used for conducting headcounts.

UNHCR's registration guide outlines how to manage "difficult populations" during camp census exercises through the use of enclosures into which refugees are herded in order to be counted.[29] Both Somali and Sudanese refugees have been classified as difficult populations by UNHCR. The registration guide explains the role of "shepherds," who act as ushers to move refugees in the proper direction. "Banders" are those who attach wristbands to refugees inside the enclosures. Other terms defined in the registration guide include

- *Fixing.* A rapid, and approximate, means of defining and limiting a target population so that persons of concern can be more readily identified for further registration.

- *Fixing token.* A preprinted card issued to individual refugees in order to define their entitlement to registration. No information is collected during a distribution of fixing tokens.

- *Registration.* The process of identifying and documenting individuals and families of concern to UNHCR by which systematic information is obtained to facilitate protection, program planning and verification.

- *Registration Card.* Card issued to a refugee head of household giving individual identification number, indicating the number of persons in the family and also used as a beneficiary card for rations and other distributions. The identification number is linked to a registration form, which contains fuller information on the household.

- *Shepherd/Usher.* A refugee, respected within the community, who is responsible for ensuring that refugees know what to do during a registration exercise.

The language of "fixing" seems odd, given that people displaced from their homes are being literally attached to the space of the temporary camps through this process. On a more practical level, it becomes clear that headcounts are a coercive exercise conducted by humanitarian staff on the bodies of refugees. The "us"/"them" distinction is clearly drawn.

Headcounts are common to UNHCR refugee operations in the region, though practices do vary. The excerpt that follows is taken from my field notes and is based on an interview with a UNHCR staff member in Nairobi. It illustrates some of the politics of counting among Rwandan refugees in Tanzania:

> In Benaco, Tanzania, UNHCR conducted a headcount among Rwandan refugees. Wristbands were used to count 300,000 people, mostly Hutu refugees. An information campaign was launched [by UNHCR], but the Hutu translators of UNHCR's information interpreted wristband as "dogtag." The negative connotation thus created resistance among the refugee population. This was exacerbated by the [enemy] Rwanda Patriotic Front (RPF), whose Tutsi-led rebel group's radio broadcast announced that the wrist tags would leave permanent marks on refugees' wrists. When and if they returned to Rwanda, they would be hunted down on this basis. The whole exercise collapsed with 300 expats in place for the exercise. The coordination team met with the "commune leaders" (big shot politicos from the former Rwandan government, the ones who were responsible for the dogtag translations) and had a long meeting in a Rubb hall full of people.
>
> Both the former government and the RPF [enemies of each other] were undermining UNHCR's efforts. UNHCR maintained that "if there is no registration, there will be no food distribution. Donors will not give food." Still, little progress was made until finally two of the "troublemakers"/leaders were allowed to speak (as a last resort, co-opt the enemy). UNHCR was given the go-ahead. . . . The next day the [counting] exercise went well.[30]

The war between opposing forces in Rwanda was literally played out in the refugee camps. Though UNHCR usually conducts an information campaign to announce and explain the rationale for headcounts, the groups to be counted, in this case, insisted on the negotiation of this process on political terms.

STANDARDIZING THE SITUATED: SITREPS

Another technology of representing refugee operations in the field is the situation report, or sitrep. These weekly information reports are filed by UNHCR staff in various field offices to the Nairobi branch office, where they are compiled into a single summary and forwarded to headquarters in Geneva.[31] They provide a picture of the refugee population through statistics and descriptions of camp conditions and activities that document the work being done by UNHCR staff at each location. Reporting formats are standardized across fields and consistent in content. Measurement is usually quantitative and aggregate. Statistics are a standard part of any sitrep, and a major characteristic of sitreps is their apparent precision: project details, plentiful statistics, and specific dates. As such, they at once simulate and assimilate *particular* experiences at very different refugee camps in a variety of locations into a more *universal* narrative, both in terms of consumption and coherence. Yet in Kenya, nationality, class, and material conditions vary enormously between the coastal and border camps for specific refugee groups.

An excerpt follows from a typical regional sitrep, this one filed in 1994 by the UNHCR office in Nairobi to Geneva:[32]

TERTIO. STATISTICS: REFUGEE/RETURNEE/DISPLACED PERSONS:

AAA. MOVEMENT OF REFUGEES INTO KENYA DURING PERIOD
- 613 NEW ARRIVALS IN KAKUMA FROM SUDAN
- 4 NEW ARRIVALS IN KAKUMA FROM ETHIOPIA
- 17 NEW ARRIVALS IN KAKUMA FROM UGANDA
- 3 NEW ARRIVALS IN KAKUMA FROM ZAIRE

637 NEW ARRIVALS INTO KENYA DURING THE PERIOD 18 FEB–3 MARCH

BBB. REPATRIATION.
A TOTAL OF 11,491 REFUGEES VOLUNTARILY LEFT MANDERA FOR VARIOUS DESTINATIONS. A TOTAL OF 9,398 REPATRIATED SPONTANEOUSLY WITH UNHCR ASSISTANCE WHILE 489 REPATRIATED VOLUNTARILY IN ORGANISED CONVOYS TO LUUQ, 92 TO BURHACHIE, 637 TO BARDERA, 207 TO GARBA HARE, 575 TO BURDHOBO AND 93 TO MOYALE.

CCC. INTERCAMP TRANSFER.
ON 18 FEB A CONVOY OF 25 TRUCKS LEFT FOR DADAAB WITH 1049 REFUGEES ABOARD. ON 24 FEB ANOTHER CONVOY OF 1133 LEFT MANDERA AND ARRIVED DADAAB ON 27 FEB.

DDD. TOTAL NUMBER OF REFUGEES IN KENYA:
A) ASSISTED IN CAMPS:
NORTH, NORTHEAST AND NORTHWEST:
LIBOI   44,840 (MAINLY SOMALIS)

IFO	29,900 (MAINLY SOMALIS) (NEW FIGURE FOLLOWING HEADCOUNT)
DAGAHALEY	24,000 (MAINLY SOMALIS) (NEW FIGURE FOLLOWING HEADCOUNT)
HAGADERA	31,200 (MAINLY SOMALIS) (NEW FIGURE FOLLOWING HEADCOUNT)
KAKUMA	37,542 (MAINLY SUDANESE)
RUIRU	1,723 (MIXED)
COAST:—	
UTANGE	44,112 (SOMALIS AND ETHIOPIANS)
MARAFA	29,348 (SOMALIS AND NON-SOMALIS)
MOMBASA	6,149 (BARAWAS AND OTHER SOMALIS)
HATIMY	3,058 (SOMALIS—BARAWAS)
JOMVU	4,773 (BAJUNIS)
SWALEH NGURU	4,542 (BENADIR)
MAJENGO	1,547 (SOMALIS)

B) ASSISTED IN BORDER SITES

| MANDERA | 8,500 (MAINLY SOMALIS) |

C) NON-ASSISTED: NAIROBI AND MOMBASA (KNOWN TO UNHCR)— 20,000

(THE GOK ESTIMATES THIS FIGURE TO BE BETWEEN 100,000– 150,000 "FREELIVERS" IN NAIROBI AND MOMBASA)

GRAND TOTAL: 291,999 REFUGEES IN KENYA

Though sitreps contain more than just statistics (political developments, program progress reports, and staff updates are also included), sitrep statistics such as these do suggest a preoccupation with numbers and the meticulous classificatory schemata of humanitarian operations. They are formulated on the basis of headcounts and come to have both political meaning and importance in refugee planning. Consider the sitrep just illustrated: A grand total of 291,999 refugees have been committed to paper; this number can later be used as a measure of UNHCR's progress toward reducing the refugee population in Kenya when subsequent counts report other totals. As with the targets of affirmative action at UNHCR, numbering can have highly political objectives that relate more to organizational aspirations than to staff or client welfare. These statistics constitute, in one sense, "grids of intelligibility" that control and standardize information.[33]

OTHER ORDERS: THE SEARCH FOR COMMUNITY AMONG REFUGEES

Having analyzed UNHCR's rationale for and processes of coding the camps, I now turn to other community-based approaches to assisting refugees. "Community" is a term with multiple meanings and strategic uses. Marlee Kline has analyzed ways in which New Right governments tactically employ notions of community.[34] Strategies to privatize and off-load social service delivery at lower cost are predicated on the idea that the community can do it better and should have a say in such matters. Such tactics often rely on the volunteer or unpaid labor of community members, particularly women. Community development is often distinguished by participatory approaches and grassroots projects organized by members of a given community. In contrast to hierarchical top-down approaches, community-based development claims to include and represent the people affected—in this case, refugees. In Kenyan refugee camps, UNHCR is the lead agency that organizes and subcontracts service delivery to NGOs. Its reputation among NGOs varies, but as the organization with the mandate and money to spend, it tends to be viewed as the hegemon and bureaucrat of refugee assistance.

CARE is a major NGO player in most of the Kenyan refugee camps. Its Kenya-based office became involved in refugee assistance only in 1991. Lucrative transportation and refugee camp management contracts from UNHCR since that time have resulted in a more-than-twofold increase in its operating budget. At the beginning of 1995, more money circulated in the refugee assistance program (RAP) than in all of CARE's other development programs in Kenya combined. As an implementing partner for UNHCR, CARE managers are obliged, to a large extent, to do what UNHCR asks. Because of this, CARE tends to employ some of the same reporting procedures and ways of representing the field. For example, CARE's publicity on RAP reported: "From mid-1991 to late 1992, the refugee population increased from 21,000 in two border camps to over 425,000 in fourteen camps spread across Kenya. . . . By early 1994, CARE was serving a population of around 200,000."[35] CARE is responsible for the transport and distribution of refugee food, the provision of essential social services, and for adequate water and sanitation in all camps except those formerly located on the Kenyan coast. Its stated objective in the social services sector is "(t)o assure that all refugees are administered humanely and efficiently and equipped with vital skills and knowledge for repatriation."[36] This echoes UNHCR's pledge to provide "a full-fledged care and maintenance programme" to refugees in established camps.[37] Anthropologist Liisa Malkki has argued that refugees are designated as liminal in the categorical order of nation-states. As an aberration of this order, they become the object of therapeutic interventions. Refugee subjects are constituted as dysfunctional, not because of the trauma or violence they may have experienced but because of their membership in the category "refugee."

Given its well-established mandate for community development work, CARE does incorporate some community-based approaches to refugee assistance. In particular, the agency contracted a pair of consultants in 1994 to conduct a community consultation with refugees in the Dadaab camps to examine "the appropriateness and effectiveness of SSEP [CARE's Social Services and Education Programme] in meeting the needs of the refugee community."[38] The questions the consultants ask overlapped with many of those I had initially posed in my own research proposal. The consultants, however, had the advantage of speaking fluent Somali, enabling them to communicate directly with the majority of refugees. Their positioning was further enhanced by the politics of their locations: One was an American married to a Somali with whom she had several children and the other was an ethnic Somali himself. As independent and in some respects "inside" commentators, in their final report they present pictures of the field quite different from those of official UNHCR reports and other NGO assessments. Their community focus emphasizes quality over quantity and is critical of the statistical focus of both UNHCR and CARE. They indicate a preference for community-based research methods: "[I]t is recommended that future investigations should utilize the techniques of action research and of participatory research, and should emphasize the collection of qualitative rather than quantitative data."[39]

The consultants challenge others' quantitative approaches to data collection, but they note that refugees also demonstrated a lack of support for their own survey techniques: "[Q]uestionnaires appeared to alienate participants. Participants expressed exasperation at the eternal round of interviewers filling out forms, while tangible results benefiting the respondents themselves were negligible, or non-existent. Some expressed a feeling of exploitation." However, the major areas of concern raised by refugees during the consultation revolved around fuel, sexual violence, and safety:

> The issues of energy, sexual assault and security are so interrelated that they were normally presented together. As land surrounding the camps becomes more and more denuded, women must go further and further to collect firewood. This increases their chances of encountering "shiftas" who threaten them, beat them, sexually assault and sometimes abduct them. Men who collect firewood in place of their female family members are beaten, threatened and sometimes killed.
>
> The refugees find themselves in an almost impossible situation in attempting to meet their requirement for energy. Neither HCR [UNHCR] nor CARE provide any kind of cookstove or any kind of fuel. The refugees understand that they have been told that they are no longer allowed to collect firewood from the areas surrounding the camps. When refugees are attacked, the "shiftas" tell them it is because they are collecting firewood which is prohibited. When sexual assaults are reported to the [Kenyan] security forces, the response is often, *"You are raping our trees, so you got what you deserved."*[40]

The assault and rape of refugees who are living on Kenyan soil are seemingly warranted by refugee "violence" toward the Kenyan environment. This tension, however, goes beyond a simple "us"/"them" division. The isolated and segregated location of camps exacerbates these relationships by defining refugees as "others" and restricting them to the lands officially designated for refugee use. Beyond the perimeters of the camps, refugees are seen to be trespassing. The provision of foreign foodstuffs that require firewood for cooking in a semiarid area with few trees to speak of is not figured into the equation. The refugees are not considered a legitimate part of the human landscape outside the camps.

The consultants' report reiterates some of the problems presented in the individual refugee testimonies discussed in chapter 4. It extends the question, "Whose geography?" in terms of camp organization to the politics of land and resource utilization, a question of entitlement. Refugees in the Kenyan camps clearly present competition and breed resentment among some locals with whom they share scarce resources. In the excerpt just quoted, the consultants place the blame on CARE and UNHCR for not providing fuel or a method by which to cook food in a self-sufficient manner. The implication is not that the food supply is necessarily inappropriate but that those who provide it are obliged to provide the means to prepare it. The report goes on to make some interesting connections between refugee safety, the household requirement for firewood, and fencing as a means of ensuring some security:

> "Shiftas" also attack inside the camps, especially at night. These attacks generally include robbing and looting, as well as sexual assaults, beatings and killings. Blocks/sections well inside the camp and with adequate fencing appear to have less of a security problem inside the camp than blocks/sections on the edges of the camp and with inadequate fencing. Some of the newer areas reported having not yet received fencing. Others said that having repeatedly been thwarted in their attempts to collect firewood, they had been forced to use their fencing for firewood.[41]

The report clearly speaks on behalf of Somali refugees. On the one hand, it criticizes the quantitative methods and control over programs that the relief agencies employ and argues that they do not provide sufficient resources (that is, fuel) to support refugee households.[42] On the other, the consultants perceive the perils of too much dependency given the long history of foreign aid to Somalia:

> The collective self-esteem of the Somali community has been undermined by decades of aid dependency, and the national humiliation experienced on account of the civil war and the ensuing international intervention. The humiliations of refugee life have further contributed to undermining self-confidence. In addition, the traditional aid approach has generally encouraged its recipients to represent themselves as helpless victims of circumstance. Some Somalis have been representing themselves in this way for so long that, along with convincing the donors of its reality, they've also convinced themselves. This has eventually led to a diminution of their individual and collective capacities and human potential, as their energy and intelligence are increasingly directed towards manipulating donors for "freebies."[43]

This is a damning critique of both donors and recipients, in this case the refugee relief agencies and the Somalis they serve. The way out of this apparent conundrum is, according to the authors, through "community-managed programmes."[44] What this proposed solution fails to account for is that a refugee camp is not a self-identified community. It is an institution generated by the international refugee regime. Its subjects are recognized in international law but have no political status in the country that hosts them. Iris Marion Young contends that the ideal of community privileges unity over difference. She defines community in her own terms as "the unoppressive city" defined by "openness to unassimilated otherness."[45] Recognizing that ideal notions of community can be exclusionary, a refugee camp can be thought of as a noncommunity of the excluded. Refugees are legally subordinated and spatially segregated in ways that preclude their participation in the local economy, polity, and society.

SIMULATING COMMUNITY: REFUGEE SELF-MANAGEMENT

One initiative to redress top-down management and to create a more accountable relationship between donors, relief agencies, and refugees in the camps is a project proposed by CARE called Refugee (or Community) Self-Management. It represents a bold, if imperfect, initiative that aims to forge a direct link between donors who fund refugee camps and the refugees who live in them. Refugee Self-Management aims to redistribute decision-making power by increasing refugee participation and decreasing the role of agencies in determining priorities and projects in the camps. It assumes that a refugee camp can, or does, operate as a village or civil society, and it employs such community-development principles as self-governance and democratic decision making.

The gist of the proposal is the promotion of refugee self-determination through democratic process. Decision-making power related to refugee camp affairs would be transferred to a democratically elected group of representatives from among the refugee "community." The proposal outlines a sharing of responsibilities whereby refugee representatives could decide how to spend available funds for social, economic, and infrastructural development of the camps. The aid agencies, which are responsible to both donors and refugees, would then provide these goods and services as decided upon by the refugees. Under the plan, refugees would participate in decision making, but material resources and funds to enact or follow through on decisions would remain under the control of the international agencies.[46] In this case, CARE would ultimately have a veto power which could block any decisions that it deemed unacceptable.

The proposal of Refugee Self-Management has been met with

some resistance. Much debate and disagreement took place among UNHCR staff at the administering suboffice in Dadaab based on its proposed redistribution of power. UNHCR responses to CARE's proposal were mixed and measured. One UNHCR officer in Dadaab argued that "we have a triangle of responsibility; there is UNHCR which looks after the political decisions and operations; it is responsible for peacekeeping and controlling the political games in the camps. NGOs provide resources and services, and the Government of Kenya simply provides security. We have succeeded in breaking up the traditional structures of power [in the camps]."[47] In his mind, UNHCR is effectively the governing body of the three camps. Refugee Self-Management is viewed by this staff member as dangerous because it poses the possibility of redirecting this power and re-instituting elders' enclaves of supposedly autocratic power.

A field officer working for UNHCR in Dadaab echoed this sentiment. In his view, CARE's idea of Refugee Self-Management "may be possible in five to six years. Now deals are made to 'get' what they [refugees] want. People are only a 'community' for one meeting, purely for exigency. [The CARE staff person responsible for the initiative] is in a grey zone where there is room for hijacking." He views refugees with suspicion and considers the camps, in his words, "a war zone."[48]

Another UNHCR officer in Dadaab was more positive about the idea: "Refugees are part of a culture that has learned to be dependent, and we taught them that." She hints at the idea that refugee camps *produce* refugee behaviors. Her argument echoes that of other critics of dependency among refugees, namely that there is nothing intrinsically dependent or impoverished about refugees' culture at the prerefugee stage.[49]

During my fieldwork in the camps and based on my earlier exposure to camp culture working for CARE, I developed an analysis of the power relations and gendered outcomes of this initiative that raises three main criticisms: First, a refugee camp is not a community; second, the transfer of camp governance from organizations to refugee leaders cannot exclude control of economic resources; and third, the proposed structures of Refugee Self-Management would not represent the interests of some segments of the camp population, notably women. In the first instance, refugee camps in Kenya are not self-identified communities. In the camps, I noted evidence of communal interests and refugee cooperation—organized, for example, among refugees of common nationality, subclan affiliation, or proximate physical location. But a refugee camp is an institution organized as a temporary solution to displacement. In a recent publication, UNHCR admits this fact: "Refugee camps and settlements are not, of course, 'normal' places, particularly in situations where the population has little or no access to land or wage labour, and must therefore rely on external assistance."[50] Camps are, arguably, part of a strategy to contain refugee "foreigners" enforced by the Kenyan government and administered by UNHCR and its implementing partners. UNHCR has a mandate to provide material assistance and legal protection in conjunction with the government of Kenya. The government insists that refugees reside in the camps. They are the subjects of a tacit and unsatisfactory policy of containment by which camps are enforced "colonies," not communities defined by voluntary association. Communities do not usually have, by definition, greater or lesser legal status and entitlement than other groups. In Kenya, many citizens live in communities; refugees live in camps. Citizens move without restriction; they have political and economic relationships to the historically contingent places in which they live, and access to land, jobs, and resources whereby they often generate self-sufficient, if interdependent, livelihoods.

In the case of Somali refugees in Kenyan camps, none of these criteria applies. In exchange for temporary asylum and the provision of basic needs, refugees forfeit a number of entitlements. Cultural politics among the refugee, local, and humanitarian groups that share and negotiate the space of the camps only complicate any power-sharing agreement or notion of a unified community. Young warns that "the desire for unity or wholeness in discourse generates borders, dichotomies, and exclusions."[51] Though UNHCR and CARE desire such unity on occasion, the various cultural groups present in the camps are hierarchically positioned and partitioned based largely on political status. At times, staff members at CARE and UNHCR maintained that a refugee camp could be treated as a trustworthy community. On other occasions, they treated refugees as institutional subjects who could not be trusted. The inconsistency of refugee treatment by the international humanitarian groups does nothing to engender trust on the part of the refugees. One moment they are asked to become leaders and decision makers in the camp; the next they are herded behind barricades by armed police and army personnel in order to be counted for a UNHCR census.

Headcounts in the camps provide a clear example of how one administrative practice contradicts another, namely, any sense of camp as community. In civic societies, community leaders generally do not conduct a census of their population by coercing, containing, and then counting their members. As Trinh Minh-ha puts it, "participate or perish."[52] Refugees may oblige those who organize them, but the relationship is hardly one based on accepted leadership or participant-oriented decision making. Though a refugee camp is not formally a war zone, it is a venue of intense cultural and organizational politics where refugees operate in their own self-interest and participate in the exercises tied to goods offered to them by relief agencies accordingly. Headcounts are the basis for issuing ration cards, which entitle refugees to food and nonfood items. It thus makes sense that they would maximize this entitlement by resisting counting procedures that might reduce the number of extra ration cards circulating in the camps. Equally, NGOs depend on donor support and supplies, which must be judiciously distributed. Their objective of obtaining an accurate refugee census is also reasonable, though other means of achieving this could be negotiated.[53] The strategies of both parties, however, allude to the politics of institutions, not communities.

My second criticism of the Refugee Self-Management initiative relates to the separation of political power from economic resources. Anthony Giddens distinguishes between authoritative and allocative resources as dual structures of domination in his theory of structuration.[54] Dominion over the social world and dominion over the material world are two sets of resources that combine differently across societies, but they occur together during different historical periods and modes of production. Responsibility for meaningful decision making cannot be separated from the resources necessary to carry out the decisions taken. In the 1960s, many African states gained nominal national independence, but they inherited the colonial economic structures of former European administrations.[55] Similarly, if CARE and UNHCR are unwilling to relinquish any of the economic means that would enable refugee self-management to occur, they will defeat the proposed objectives of refugee self-governance and democratic process, and potentially reproduce a neocolonial power structure.[56] This is not to say that constructive change is not useful and important in a milieu characterized by refugee dependency and disciplinary techniques on the part of humanitarian agencies. To succeed, however, a thorough self-examination and reformation of the institutions that manage refugees needs to occur before external-ized power-sharing agreements, such as Refugee Self-Management, are introduced.

My final criticism of Refugee Self-Management concerns struc-tures of refugee representation. Broadly based participation in camp decision making and projects—particularly by and for women—cannot be limited to the democratic structure of elected committees. The refugee self-management project proposes various committees of democratically elected members from the refugee population. During my research in the three camps, I found that much discussion revolved around "Who will represent whom?" and "What will the relationship among committees be?" The majority of refugees, espe-cially women, do not generally attend these consultations. Refugee men are more likely to have the time, the language skills necessary to converse with NGOs and participate in political processes, and the social authority to attend. The community development structures of opportunity, participation, and access are distorted by the institu-tional setting of the camps and the gender division of labor within the camps.

As outlined in the interviews with refugee women presented in chapter 4, informal, collaborative self-management initiatives were al-ready evident in the camps. These included collective rotating credit schemes, small solo shops set up in the camp markets, individual col-lection and sale of firewood, and assistance to neighbors or family members who are pregnant, infirm, or elderly. Refugee women have created their own community-based arrangements, outside the offi-cial discourse of Refugee Self-Management and its allotted circuits of refugee participation. They nonetheless remain largely excluded from so-called democratic process by their gendered cultural posi-tioning. The vast majority of Somali refugee women in these border camps are unlikely to ever be part of the official self-management scheme proposed by CARE. One might argue that the refugees fur-thest from the these centers of institutionalized power, namely, women, are quite capable of self-management. Certainly no one is helping them at the moment. This is not to say, however, that they receive equitable treatment and material assistance relative to other refugees in the camp.

The democratic election of leaders is likely to reproduce and rein-scribe the power of those refugees already in positions of authority and relative privilege in the camps. The refugee elite in the camps do not see a need for elections. I attended one meeting between refugee agencies and camp elders where the latter group submitted a list of those refugees they had unilaterally decided should be representa-tives to CARE. Most of those on the list were the same male elders in attendance. They also noted the remuneration expected. Agency staff members were naively perturbed with the elders' self-appointment and expectation of pay. CARE had assumed that the work would be done for the welfare of the community, and thus on a volunteer basis. Agency staff were paid for their work in the camps, but the proposal did not include refugee remuneration. Where the communi-ty took over governance responsibilities, the terms were ultimately determined by the agency.

While partial to the *idea* of refugee self-governance based on my own background in community organization and planning, I harbor skepticism about the willingness of the aid agencies to give away any meaningful decision-making power to refugees, particularly with re-spect to the allocation of resources. No formal link of accountability to the refugees on the part of agencies would exist to ensure that power is shared on an ongoing basis. Unlike donors, who provide the resources to run the camps and attach certain conditions to those resources, refugees remain recipients who get what they are per-ceived to need. I am also concerned that such changes might rein-scribe women's subordination in the camps. To assume that prin-ciples of community development and organization are directly transferable to refugee camps is problematic. Though camps as com-munities may be desirable, this notion of community is not viable. CARE's initiative recognizes that the relations of power that charac-terize the status quo are problematic, but it does not address the dif-ferences in political status and affiliation that produce these rela-tions of power.

CONTRADICTIONS AND TENSIONS IN THE FIELD

Practices of institutional control of camps by donors and agencies sometimes contradict the principles of community self-management and refugee participation. How can UNHCR credibly conduct head-counts one week and discuss the sharing of decision making with refugee leaders the next? One rather obscure paragraph in the Country Operation's Manual for Kenya illustrates this contradiction perfectly:

Sanitation

Maintenance of sanitary facilities and camp cleanliness will continue to play an important role in the overall welfare and health of the refugees during 1995. Sanitation activities will focus on greater community participation in maintaining the camps in as sanitary a condition as can be expected. Refugees have already started to keep latrines on a family/compound basis, significantly reducing the incidence of looting [theft] of superstructures. This trend will be encouraged during 1995.

Surveys will be conducted on a regular basis to assess the need for rehabilitation/construction of latrines in the camps to maintain a ratio of 16 persons per latrine.[57]

The logic of the first paragraph contradicts the second. Responsibility for maintaining facilities on the basis of social organization proves more effective than allocation based on ratios per abstract segment of population. Yet there is a constant revisiting of this language and logic in UNHCR operations. Encouraged by UNHCR staff members with whom I became friends, I wrote the following commentary, both to submit as a memo to the UNHCR Representative and for my field notes. The excerpt below speaks to some of these contradictions and the tensions they raise in the context of the camps.

Contradictions and Tensions in the Field
January 1995

To focus on headcounts and refugee statistics one moment and refugee participation and community approaches the next poses a contradiction for UNHCR. Headcounts and statistics infer a monitoring role mainly concerned with technical information, control, and surveillance. On the other hand, participatory planning methods suggest a collaborative approach to camp operations with space for negotiation and discussion among UNHCR, NGOs, and refugees. This contradiction must be acknowledged and addressed if UNHCR wants to meet its existing mandate *and* incorporate the changes introduced by new UNHCR policies and training programs. The two approaches are not mutually exclusive. . . . each does, however, operate according to a different type of logic and subsequently each distributes power through different structures. . . .

The contradiction should not be viewed as a contest of "counting" (for reasons of control) versus "cultivating" (in order to elicit refugee input), or quantity (statistics) versus quality (effectiveness); both systems are part of UNHCR culture. Nonetheless, this contradiction has proven extremely divisive among staff working in the field, and is a drain to already scarce staff resources available. Change which incorporates *both* approaches needs to be developed; defending one approach against the other is counterproductive to field operations. [Emphasis in original]

The conciliatory tone of this text speaks to two very distinct camps among UNHCR staff in the Dadaab camps. There are those who guard the importance of control and security concerns at UNHCR and those concerned principally with refugee welfare who employ community-based approaches in the camps: government for the refugees versus government by the refugees. The commentary from my field notes continues:

One myth that needs to be clarified is that a refugee camp is not a community. A refugee camp is an *institution* created specifically for the purpose of providing protection and assistance to a group of people who are not citizens of the country in which they are living. . . .

The second myth that requires critical examination is the claim of refugee dependency and idleness. Household interviews conducted so far in the three Dadaab camps suggest that women working at home grinding sorghum, collecting water, searching for firewood, cooking and cleaning are anything but idle. This is, of course, a gendered routine, and it may be true that refugee men are often not gainfully occupied.

The dependency, where it exists, should not be blamed on the refugees. Rather, the institution of the refugee camp *produces* refugee subjects and behaviors. Mobility for *prima facie* refugees is severely curtailed; they are legally required to stay in the camps. They live on marginally productive land in a semi-arid region of Kenya which is also geographically marginal—far from the educational, medical, and consular services of Nairobi and the coast. Unlike refugee camps in, for example, Northern Uganda where Sudanese refugees have been allocated farmland by the government, refugees in Kenya cannot produce food for their own needs. Access to productive land is critical to long-term self-sufficiency, but camps in Kenya are only temporary measures to provide safety and assistance to refugees. These conditions of containment and marginalization highlight some of the artificially imposed constraints which shape camp planning and refugee participation.

. . . Refugees are not citizens who have the right to work and freedom to move within the country. They do not have access to land to provide for their own needs. Nor are they criminals or prisoners who need to be controlled through coercion. A refugee camp is not a war zone. Field staff must be careful to balance the organizational needs for information with respect for refugees and their participation in programme development.

This argument against coercion in the camps exposes my own point of view with respect to refugee operations. Senior UNHCR officials are concerned about refugee dependency in the camps.[58] What they sometimes refuse to take responsibility for are the structural and legal reasons for this reliance. The government of Kenya effectively exiles refugees to remote border regions and prohibits them from living outside of the camps. As displaced people without permanent legal status in the country, refugees are given few options. They must either accept the terms UNHCR offers—which includes dependence on foreign foodstuffs and spatial segregation in the camps—or go underground to create an unofficial livelihood elsewhere. Though I did discuss my motivations for writing this memo with a senior UNHCR official in Nairobi, no reaction or formal response was forthcoming.

FINAL REMARKS

This chapter has explored some of the ways in which the space of refugee camps is coded and represented. On the one hand, technologies of vision serve surveillance functions, particularly in calculating refugee populations. Comparable and frequent statistical reports are also part of an attempt to order disorder. These strategies characterize the salient mode of reporting the field. On the other hand, community-based consultations and Refugee Self-Management are promoted by CARE. The report prepared by the consultants is critical of quantitative assessments of refugee operations and wary of refugee research in general. A review of the Refugee Self-Management initiative exposes competing assumptions of "community." This and other CARE initiatives contrast vividly with the more coercive control and quantitative measure of refugees. My own field notes analyze the relationship between UNHCR and the CARE consultants by juxtaposing the former's emphasis on monitoring from above with the latter's emphasis on grassroots community work. Movement between the universal practices of UNHCR and the particularities of Somali culture and society are posited as either/or approaches. My own analysis calls for some linkages between the two. Constructive negotiation is a necessary, but not sufficient, measure. The intensely uneven relations of power within the camps and the cultural politics they generate render such negotiations rhetorical. The subversion of unity myths—such as a refugee community—is a strategic departure point toward forging links across differences.

UNHCR's registration guide outlines a counting process (fixing) followed by a subsequent collection of refugee information. The counting process is important and political, precisely because it determines food and other entitlements. But UNHCR positions itself precariously by treating the refugees as partners in community decision making, on the one hand, and as prisoners of the camps in which they live, on the other. This fundamental contradiction in the ways in which power is deployed poses a major dilemma for humanitarian organizations. At what point do charitable acts of humanitarian assistance become neocolonial technologies of control? The line is fine.

The demands on UNHCR are greater than on most UN agencies. Staff must respond quickly and effectively to emergency situations, solicit support and funding to pay for these operations, and conduct itself in an efficient, accountable manner. Remarkably, it achieves many of its objectives. But response, management, and fund-raising responsibilities fail to ensure that the modes and means of delivering assistance—*how* operations are carried out—are in keeping with the spirit of the ultimate objectives.

In chapter 6, the efficacy and relevance of camps is challenged by leaving the field behind. The movement and activities of Somali refugees outside the legal and institutional structures of the formal camp setting accentuate their efforts to establish normal, as opposed to normalized, lives outside their country and beyond the camps to which they are assigned.

6

Crossing Borders in Theory and Practice

This chapter is an attempt to think outside the logic of camps, counting, and control. I examine some of the ways in which refugees deal with their displacement and outline a theoretical approach that defies borders, much as refugees defy the categories and locations to which they are assigned. Many of the findings presented here are based on serendipitous encounters that occurred during the course of the research. As such, they represent the edges of my research, which move away from a central focus in more diffuse directions. Accordingly, a theoretical approach that decenters the state and pays attention to these "unauthorized" movements is sketched toward the end of the chapter. Though I make no major claims based on the anecdotal evidence amassed, the encounters surveyed are nonetheless suggestive of the unofficial movements of refugees and of theoretical approaches that cross accepted boundaries. The geography of refugees' lived experience stands in stark contrast to the order of the camps and to the neat categories of assistance, destitute populations, and research concerned with refugee mobility. Somali refugee movements in Kenya challenge the notion that the boundaries of the camps are impermeable. The containment and order attempted by UNHCR and the Kenyan government are anything but complete. Having established that a refugee camp is not a community, I present findings that suggest that Somali refugees make communal connections beyond the perimeter of the camps and in some cases, overseas.

Refugees remake the places in which they find themselves. The research illustrates that the livelihoods they establish outside the camps also have the effect of disordering some of the Kenyan communities and urban spaces to which they move. The findings presented, in turn, point to transnational approaches and unconventional detours that open up avenues for a transformative politics of displacement.

Kenya shares borders with Somalia, Ethiopia, Sudan, Uganda, and Tanzania. As such, it serves as a gathering place and potential country of asylum for displaced persons from all of these countries. Nairobi is the consulate capital of the region, where high commissions and embassies station their immigration officers to screen refugee applicants for resettlement. This geography of asylum makes Kenya in general and Nairobi in particular attractive places for refugees. The Kenyan government has attempted to maintain strict control of refugees by containing them in camps, but the reality is that not all refugees live in the camps. Despite efforts to order disorder within the camps, their borders remain porous to refugee movements. Though some live in the camps, many refugees opt for other arrangements. In order to recognize some of the paths and patterns of Somali refugee activity outside the camps, I recount here stories of transplanted Somalis within and beyond Kenya's borders.

In Kenya, Somalians fleeing the perils of civil war have crossed a political border; crossing the border makes them refugees, but not all of them live in the camp spaces to which they are technically confined. By working and living outside the camps in Kenyan society, many refugees cross less clearly defined cultural and material borders in intensely local ways. Concentrations of Somalian refugees in Kenyan cities attest to the establishment of homes beyond the confines of the camps. Though UNHCR maintains that camps are intended only as "temporary solutions," camps in Kenya have become an entrenched stopgap measure in the absence of viable permanent solutions for most refugees. The ambitious, often risky, journeys of refugees beyond established borders illustrates that the conceptual-political-material space of the camp is untenable as anything more than an immediate response to crises of human displacement.[1]

In the absence of Cold War funding and superpower support for refugee populations, increased humanitarian intervention across sovereign international borders has attempted to contain potential refugees by protecting them at home. The dismal record of UNHCR's Cross-Border Operation, which created a preventive zone to discourage further refugee flows into Kenya and to encourage refugee repatriation from Kenya, provides convincing evidence that such measures have limited purchase. Both sets of safe spaces—camps and UN safe areas—may serve a geopolitical purpose by isolating the problem, but neither approximates a solution. "Refugees and displaced people are the human barometer of political stability, of justice and order in much of the world,"[2] but they are not simply passive indicators of geopolitical conflict. The new settlement of diasporic populations affected by displacement remakes places. This is particularly evident in urban areas of Kenya, where some Somali refugees have relocated. In crossing the borders between camp and city, they unsettle the order, containment, and administration of displaced persons by the Kenyan government and UN authorities. Not only have government authorities demonstrated their intolerance of Somali refugees, but Kenyans living in proximate areas have also expressed their resentment, particularly with respect to issues of housing, business practices, and land.

THE STATE OF SOMALIA

Almost a decade of civil war in Somalia, coupled with the loss of the country's strategic importance to and resources from its former superpower patrons, has contributed to the demise of its social and physical infrastructure: "Following the end of the Cold War, Somalia has become an international commodity—an object of compassion—but has no means of exercising diplomatic leverage."[3] In the late 1980s, almost half of Somalia's gross domestic product (GDP) consisted of official development assistance. It also received emergency food, refugee, and military assistance.[4] In 1990, the per capita GDP was U.S.$120, making it one of the poorest countries in the world.[5] External assistance from donor countries has decreased since UN peacekeeping forces withdrew in March 1995. Though selected NGOs continue to work in the country, budgets and humanitarian projects have been comparatively small-scale.

Somalia remains without a government or basic public services, as fighting continues and clan-based militias vie for control of key areas in the capital and along the coast.[6] Even though such conflict precludes the possibility of repatriation for many Somali refugees currently in Kenya, the political economy of the country is not particularly attractive to prospective returnees, nor indeed, to many people living there. In August 1996 self-declared president General Mohammed Farah Aideed was shot dead in Mogadishu. His death only exacerbated instability in the Somalian capital, as control of the city was renegotiated among warring factions. Fighting intensified in December 1996, killing 300 people and wounding 1,000 others. This violence was the worst in Mogadishu since 1992.[7] Renewed fighting in 1998 did not bode well for Somali refugees still living in Kenya.

Futhermore, humanitarian efforts within Somalia have been seriously undermined by a lack of security. In 1997, an international staff member of MSF was killed in June; two international aid workers were kidnapped in July; two Somali relief workers were killed in August; and seven expatriate NGO workers were abducted during the months of November and December. A UNICEF plane was also shot at in August.[8]

Continued fighting in Mogadishu and Kismayu has made repatri-

Figure 6.1. Somali refugees at Utange camp: going home. Author's photograph.

ation unsafe for many refugees.[9] In more stable areas, UNHCR has assisted refugees with repatriation, although this flow slowed to a trickle in 1997, with only 200 Somalis repatriated (see figure 6.1).[10] With the closing of Utange and Marafa camps on the Kenyan coast, refugees have had to either repatriate or move to one of the Dadaab camps. Many have chosen to live unofficially in urban areas. According to the Kenyan government, refugees on the coast adversely affect tourism and the environment.[11] Most Somali refugees living in coastal camps have refused UNHCR invitations to repatriate to Somalia or to relocate in the remote border camps. In fact, significant numbers of refugees—between 30,000 and 40,000 Somalis—moved *from* the Dadaab camps to the coastal camps in 1993. A UNHCR staff member in Mombasa explained that this movement was partly the result of refugees' perception that opportunities to resettle in the United States were better in the coastal camps. He also noted that many refugees living in and near Mombasa are funded by relatives and contacts abroad and are not dependent on humanitarian assistance.[12] Given the collapse of public telecommunications, postal services, and banking operations in Somalia, Mombasa offers a reasonably secure and well-connected location for the transfer of money and information from these global contacts to refugees.

Reports suggest that some Somalis are traveling to South Africa, Yemen, Malawi, and Ethiopia.[13] In 1995, the Australian High Commission in Pretoria expected a 250 percent increase in refugee claims at its office for that year, 70 percent of this from the Horn of Africa.[14] These numbers did not raise alarm on the part of South African authorities nor the High Commission's staff, as the actual numbers selected in Pretoria for refugee resettlement in Australia were small. Nonetheless, they mark movement. Unauthorized migrations across camp and other borders signal refugee strategies to locate themselves favorably for a chance at citizenship or to gain convention refugee status. Given the options of repatriation to Somalia or camp living, many Somali refugees are choosing neither and moving unofficially in other directions.

The forced migration of a segment of the Somalian population, and the piggyback flow of unknown size of other Somalians searching for a viable livelihood, has shifted the boundaries of the Somali nation—that is, as a cultural group—southward into Kenya and somewhat westward into Ethiopia. In addition to the camps, evidence also suggests the informal settlement of many Somalians in Kenya and others in Ethiopia.[15] The relatively new government in Ethiopia, led by President Meles Zenawi, apparently does not have the administrative machinery in place to be discerning in such instances. The movement of Somalians southward is more significant in size and has important implications for Kenyan housing markets, local business, and cultural politics in urban areas.

BORDER CROSSINGS AND CLASHES

Although segregation can be temporarily imposed as a sociopolitical arrangement, it can never be absolute, especially on the level of culture. All utterances inescapably take place against the background of the possible responses of other social and ethnic points of view.
— ELLA SHOHAT AND ROBERT STAM, *UNTHINKING EUROCENTRISM: MULTICULTURALISM AND THE MEDIA*

The line between refugee camps and local, Kenyan-held property is fine. In a country of more than forty distinct ethnic groups, cultural difference is the rule, not the exception, but when refugees proceed too far across camp boundaries, there can be trouble. Tensions between Somalian refugees and local Kenyans along the coast mounted in 1995, as more refugees arrived at Utange camp just north of Mombasa. Many were not registered with UNHCR at this location and did not have ration cards. The arrival of additional refugees into the already overcrowded Utange camp generated an overflow population, some of whom had constructed houses at the perimeter of the camp, just outside the official camp boundary, at the time of my visit. On two occasions local citizens burned these borders back into stark view by setting fire to refugee houses situated on Kenyan land.[16] The state land adjacent to the camp belongs to a Kenyan prison. Close by, in a tiny camp called Swaleh Nguru, which was built to accommodate Benadir refugees of Somalian nationality, two fires were set within one week during my visit in January 1995. Another act of arson in the area killed two people in 1997.[17] The materiality of borders between cultures and subjects becomes evident. They are reinscribed through violent acts of "clarification."

Barbara Harlow notes that prisons, factories, and buses are often the primary sites of cultural confrontation that "delineate a liminal geopolitical space, created by historical circumstances and contested by multiple parties with divergent political agendas."[18] Her points of cultural interface and tension suggest corresponding interstitial spaces between the cultures of refugees and locals along the Kenyan coast. Bus stops, or "*matatu* stages" as they are called in Kenya, are the places where contact between refugees and locals occurs most regularly. Refugees commute back and forth into Mombasa, often to trade and earn an income by selling in the market.

In Kenya, the marketplace replaces the factory as a central site of cultural and economic confrontation. Somalian refugees often undercut the prices of Kenyan vendors. One Red Cross delegate noted that goods sold by Somalians are one-third to one-half as expensive as those sold in the shops.[19] In part, this can be explained by lower overhead, as Somalian refugees usually sell their goods in the outdoor public market, offering everything from bed sheets and blenders to radio cassette decks. Their low prices are also an expression of the fact that many of the goods Somalians sell have come clandestinely to Kenya through Somalia, avoiding the import duties that Kenyan vendors must pay at the port. In the Northeast Province, where the Liboi border crossing was officially closed during one of my visits, police reported that several commodities were being illegally smuggled across the border by women with camels and men leading donkey carts. The UNHCR office in Mombasa receives daily complaints from Kenyan shopkeepers about Somalian sellers intensifying competition and capturing their trade.[20] Whereas formal businesses in Mombasa are undercut by informal trade, other informal self-employment initiatives in and near the camps flourish. Local Kenyans find work selling services to Somali refugees. Prison land, *matatus* (buses), and the Mombasa marketplace are all sites of confrontation and cooperation between refugees and local Kenyans. Where refugees impinge on Kenyan land, boundaries are "clarified" by setting fire to refugee housing. Cultures clash, official boundaries are transgressed, borders are contested by Somalian refugees and reaffirmed by Kenyan residents.

Within the camps, cultural difference and confrontation emerge at even more nuanced levels. In Utange camp near Mombasa, the Kenyan Red Cross's camp manager hired ten Masai guards to provide security for the camp, admittedly more to protect the Kenyan staff working in the camp than to safeguard the refugees.[21] The

Masai constitute one of the many Kenyan ethnic groups, and they are historically renowned for their skills as fierce fighters. Their nomadic background and fierce independence during British rule proved to be effective resistance to the colonization of Masai land. Several non-Masai Kenyans I spoke to feared the Masai, who still hunt with spears, shields, and other traditional weaponry. In this particular case, the hiring of Masai guards in full warrior costume pitted one set of fears against another. Though many urban Kenyans feared Masai Kenyans, they saw the Somali refugees as an even greater threat. The camp management was not interested in cooperation despite differences, or affiliation, as Edward Said advocates, but in safety from difference at a secure distance.[22]

Refugees who remain in the camps do not uncritically accept the authority of the aid relationship. In order to receive their basic entitlements of food and nonfood items, refugees have to meet certain terms of the humanitarian organizations whose mandate it is to assist them. As one Red Cross worker put it bluntly: "[T]he Somalis are hated by every delegate [international staff member]."[23] The feeling may well be mutual. Nonetheless, expatriate relief workers and administrators generally view work with Somali refugees as difficult. Such jobs are seen as hardship posts that may earn them "credit" toward future opportunities or serve as a punitive posting for past mistakes. Somalis have a reputation of talking back to relief workers, rejecting the charity script of the needy *and* grateful. Trinh Minh-ha contends that "[t]he 'needy' cannot always afford to refuse, so they persist in accepting ungratefully."[24] The actions of Somalian refugees toward humanitarian staff unsettle the charitable, hierarchical relationship of power between the Western donors and Somali refugees.

Across the border, evidence of political resistance to the U.S. and UN intervention in Somalia has been expressed in the public demonstrations held in Mogadishu. Somali women in particular displayed their support for General Aideed and disdain for the UN presence in the Somalian capital in 1993. This geography of protest, however, was uneven as Somali women in Bardera demonstrated in *support* of UN activities in the country (see figure 6.2). Their region of southern Somalia was subject to attack and pillage by Aideed and his troops in September 1992. Unlike in the capital, UN operations in the Gedo and Bai areas of southern Somalia were popular with civilian beneficiaries.

Figure 6.2. Somali women in Bardera rally in support of the United States and the United Nations. Author's photograph.

REFUGEES ON THE MOVE: SOMALIS IN THE CITY

Displacing is a way of surviving. It is an impossible, truthful story of living in-between regimens of truth.
            —TRINH T. MINH-HA, "COTTON AND IRON"

Early in 1995, UNHCR estimated that 110,000 Somali refugees live in the three Dadaab camps located in the Northeast Province. Some 75,000 refugees lived in the coastal camps, while others had homes in Mombasa and Nairobi. Despite Kenyan government regulations that refugees live in border camps, estimates of the number of these illegal urban refugees ranged from 20,000 to 100,000. Many Kenyans and Somalians buy and sell identity papers, which are used as evidence of nationality. For Kenyans, a refugee ration card represents an opportunity to collect basic foodstuffs and to access services otherwise unavailable to them. They can purchase ration cards discreetly at the markets set up in the camps. One UNHCR field officer estimated that roughly 40 percent of the Somalis in camps along the Kenyan-Somalian border are actually Kenyan nationals from surrounding areas.[25] According to refugee sources in the Dadaab camps, a ration card to feed a family of five cost KSh 2,000 (approximately U.S.$45) in November 1994. Closer to urban markets, prices were higher. Prior to the government announcement in August 1994 that Utange camp near Mombasa would close, a ration card to feed a family of seven in that camp sold for KSh 7,500 (U.S.$170). After the announcement, which signaled the finite life of the ration cards, the price of the same card plummeted to KSh 1,500 (U.S.$35).[26]

Identity cards are sold or traded to refugees for other reasons. Somalian refugees buy Kenyan identity cards for their political value. A Kenyan identity card can facilitate greater mobility, and in some cases, make it possible to work, given that Somalian (prima facie) refugees may not legally do so. When traveling outside the camps, refugees are less likely to be harassed by authorities if they hold some kind of Kenyan identity documents. A number of Somalis from both sides of the border have dual status, holding both Kenyan and Somalian identities at once. The material and political entitlements of these various identity cards have given rise to a thriving economy of falsified documents. In Nairobi, false UNHCR protection letters, which give individual refugees the right to stay in Kenya, are bought and sold.[27]

Evidence of the commuting habits of refugees points to regular movements between camp and city on the Kenyan coast. At Utange camp, two refugee leaders described the difference between Marafa camp, some forty kilometers from the coastal town of Malindi, and Utange camp, located just outside of Mombasa, in this way: "Marafa is a real camp, not a suburb like Utange." At Utange, I met with one refugee woman who described her typical day to me.[28] After cleaning and preparing breakfast, she leaves home at 8 A.M. and travels to Mombasa. There she buys vegetables wholesale and then sells them retail in the city market. She spends three to four hours in Mombasa selling her produce. When everything is sold, she then returns to the camp and prepares lunch for herself and her children. She spends the remainder of the day looking after the children and preparing dinner.

In January 1995 after visiting Marafa camp, I stopped in the tourist town of Malindi. Just outside the fenced property of a garage, where I waited for my lift with a Red Cross employee, was a small shop where I purchased a ginger soda and struck up a conversation with a young Somali man. I told him of my trip to Marafa that day. He explained that he commuted daily from Marafa camp to work in the shop owned by his brother. His brother, meanwhile, operated another small business in Malindi. Though not officially allowed to hold employment in Kenya, these young men were part of a burgeoning informal economy that involved regular commuting. Like the woman from Utange, the economy of home in the camps was tied to jobs in adjacent urban areas.

Not all Somali refugees commute between city and camp. Rather, they find homes in neighborhoods of Mombasa and Nairobi. Socioeconomic status, gender, and class are factors determining who remains in the camps and who sets up independent households in urban centers. As one Red Cross official commented on those he saw as the privileged refugees living near Mombasa, "these are the distressed gentlefolk" of the refugee population.[29] Access to basic services, such as education or job training, can be used to justify refugees' presence in the city *as long as they are able to pay for themselves and their families to stay there.* This special allowance is based on an agreement between the Kenyan government and UNHCR, a result of some cajoling on the part of the latter in conjunction with a local refugee service organization. Although the government initially refused any exceptions to refugee camp residence, the agreement reached authorizes temporary stays in the city under certain conditions. These conditions include the need for access to medical treatment, education, or training; reasons related to resettlement; court appearances; family reunification; security; intercamp transfer; or employment as an interpreter with a refugee organization. While creating a better life for a few individuals and their families, the agreement also creates privileged spaces for refugees with money. Families who have sufficient funds to maintain a household and pay school fees for their children or enroll in employment-related training themselves have a good chance of being authorized by UNHCR to stay in the city.

In Kenya, refugee access to the city vis-à-vis this agreement is also gendered. Just as refugee women are less likely to access resettlement programs because of their lower skill level or because small children and no husband accompany them,[30] the resources and mobility required to take advantage of this agreement limit its application. As James Hathaway points out: "All but a very small minority of refugees—predominantly young, male, and mobile—either find protection in states adjoining their own, or are [unable] to escape at all."[31] With a significant proportion (reportedly 40 percent) of the households in the Dadaab camps female-headed, this is an even more important consideration. Given the social and political organization of daily routine in the camps, men's mobility tends to be greater than that of women.

An unexpected outcome of this policy has been that many refugees who want to live in the city but who are without the funds to finance the conditions of the agreement have convinced health practitioners in the camps that they require urban-based medical services for mental illness. Medical personnel in the camps are usually trained in emergency response and primary health care and are not always well-positioned to assess these cases. A psychiatrist in Nairobi to whom many refugee patients are referred by UNHCR noted that at least 50 percent of the refugee patients he saw were *not* legitimate cases.[32] Opportunities to live in the city on a temporary basis with international humanitarian support are clearly desirable to many refugees. Access to them, however, remains very uneven and is based almost exclusively on socioeconomic status.

During the course of my research, a number of people commented on the effect the arrival of Somalians has had in terms of housing in Kenyan urban areas.³³ The *Standard on Sunday,* a local Kenyan newspaper, perhaps best summarized the perceived impact of their settlement:

> Soaring housing rents have condemned about 40% of Nairobi residents to a life in the slums. . . . An influx of foreigners, especially Somali refugees, into Nairobi has worsened the situation. A one-bedroom flat in Eastleigh, for example, which had been renting at Shs [Kenyan shillings] 1,000 a month, now goes for 7,500 because of the high demand for houses by Somalis. . . . As a result, most *residents displaced by the Somali refugees* are progressively joining shanty life in the neighboring Mathare Valley or Kitui Village.³⁴

The great irony of this account is that Somalian refugees, themselves displaced from their country of origin, are believed to have, in turn, displaced Kenyans of a lower socioeconomic status. Somali refugees have begun to gentrify the lower-class Nairobi suburb of Eastleigh. In Mombasa, UNHCR recorded a rise in housing prices, and as noted, intense competition from Somali entrepreneurs in the local market. Utange camp near Mombasa has become a diasporic suburb of the Somali nation in which relatives from abroad provide support, as information and foreign exchange are sent to Somalis settled in Kenya via fax machines, telephones, and cables to Kenyan banks. Both Nairobi and Mombasa serve as satellite financial centers for the transfer of moneys from abroad. In a related example, Somali refugees living in Uganda refused to be transferred to a camp outside Kampala because it "had no telephones or basic communications which were important to the Somalis since most lived off handouts sent to them by their relatives in Europe, Canada and the United States."³⁵ Their decisions to integrate locally, at least in the short term, are shaped and financed by access to resources at a more global level.

This first section of the chapter has drawn out what were the unexpected findings at the edges of my research. It illustrates that the containment of the refugee camps is by no means complete. There is a significant gap between official programs and places for refugees and the locations of everyday living. Somali refugees have links outside the Kenyan camps and, in certain cases, outside the country. Some actively seek to live in cities, establishing homes and finding jobs. UNHCR has done its best to implement ad hoc measures that make education and job training in the cities possible, but only for a select few. Others commute from camp to city on a regular basis, highlighting the porosity of the officially sanctioned safe spaces of the camps. These attempts to create livelihoods independent from the camps have been met with some hostility by Kenyans, who perceive Somali refugees as a threat to their businesses, housing markets, and land.

Evidence that they are circumventing Kenya altogether, opting out of the camps and for other destinations, points in part to the camps' gross ineffectiveness in meeting people's needs. UNHCR camps are not intended to be long-term settlements, but in the absence of other alternatives, they have become well-established Band-Aid solutions that leak. For many Somali refugees, Ethiopian citizenship, asylum in South Africa, and potential resettlement abroad look better than temporary status in Kenya. In the face of a crumbled state structure, a precarious economy at home, and continued fighting in certain areas, Somali refugees are on the move, abandoning the camps and seeking alternate arrangements elsewhere. In the next section, the experience of refugees beyond the borders of their home states and away from the state-sanctioned refugee camps are explored in the theoretical context of transnationalism.

BEYOND BORDERS: TRANSNATIONALISM
AND THE DETERRITORIALIZATION OF NATION

[A]nxiety abounds today about this most unnatural miscegenation of core and periphery, First and Third Worlds, development and underdevelopment, miscegenation whose hybrid progeny now occupy the same space and time.
— KRISTIN KOPTIUCH, "'CULTURAL DEFENSE'
AND CRIMINOLOGICAL DISPLACEMENTS"

Territorial place-based identity, particularly when conflated with race, gender, religious and class differentiation, is one of the most pervasive bases for both progressive political mobilization and reactionary exclusionary politics.
— DAVID HARVEY, "FROM SPACE TO PLACE AND BACK AGAIN"

Nationness may still be the most universally legitimate value in the political life of our time.[36] Imagined communities and their displacement, however, often undermine the normative territory and temporality of the nation-state. The nation-state is challenged by the increasingly transnational relations of production, trade, and international migration, both voluntary and involuntary. "Regions and region-states increasingly override national borders and older territorial forms and create special economic zones of uneven development and transcultural hybridity."[37] State-centric notions of community, economy, and polity no longer suffice. Yet as state borders are broken down, in this case, by forced migration, and as the primacy of the nation-state as the basis for social, economic, and political organization appears untenable, as in Somalia, how can the displacement and dispersion of refugees be theorized in a relevant and political context?

Migrant identities are constituted by more than one geographical location and more than one appellation.[38] Concepts of "immigrant" and "refugee" are defined by juridical and political apparatuses of national governments, premised upon the territoriality of nations, and predicated on the political borders of individual states. They are pure categories of migrant status that do not capture the contradictions of historical and geographical experience nor the politics of the borders that define them. A refugee is defined as one who is outside the borders of her nation-state due to violence or persecution and displaced from what has become the centered norm of citizenship, or "placement," within her country. An immigrant is seen as replacing one nationalist identification with another.[39] He is a newcomer, a former outsider now authorized to participate in, if not belong, to the host society. The refugee is expelled from her state; the immigrant is incorporated into his. Both are territorially rooted, sometimes overlapping, conceptions of migrant status defined by narratives of nation. Forced migrants may cross national borders, but they also move between conventional identity markers of nationality, ethnicity, culture, gender, and class. What often gets lost in discussions of immigration, refugee law, and international migration more generally are the transnational processes, politics, and multiple positionings that transcend or subvert the primacy of the nation-state as the de facto unit of migrant identity. Cognizant of its inadequacy, geographers have begun to challenge the primacy of the nation-state as the venue for political change and action.[40]

In stunning contrast to efforts in the 1960s to forge a pan-Somali state that would annex the Ogaden area of Ethiopia and much of Kenya's Northeast Province inhabited by ethnic Somalis, the Somali nation has dispersed on a scale unimaginable in the neorealist framework of conventional geopolitics. As Homi K. Bhabha provocatively contends, certain groups of people are *themselves* the shifting boundary that contests the boundaries of the modern nation:

> At this point I must give way to the *vox populi:* to a relatively unspo-
> ken tradition of the people of the pagus—colonials, postcolonials, mi-
> grants, minorities—wandering peoples who will not be contained
> within the *Heim* of the national culture and its unisonant discourse,
> *but are themselves the marks of a shifting boundary* that alienates the
> frontiers of the modern nation.[41]

The idea of refugees delineating a new border, contesting the existing Kenyan-Somalian frontier, is ironic. The possibility of forced
migration as conquest seems contradictory, although Somali occupation of this area may have historical and political meanings beyond
the notion of displacement. At the same time, that people must cross
a border in order to claim refugee status has the effect of reinforcing
the border's legitimacy.

TRANSNATIONALISM AND TRANSMIGRANTS: AN OVERVIEW

As discussed in chapter 2, the theoretical literature emerging from
discussions of displacement and traveling cultures is comprehensive
and somewhat controversial. The meanings of exile, diaspora, and
transnational identity have been debated and discussed at length,
with critics charging that such concepts engender theoretical tourism
and cultural relativism. In an effort to avoid the perils and pitfalls of
celebrating displacement or assimilating diasporic histories into immigrant ideologies, any "theories of exile must delineate the material
conditions of displacement that generate subject positions."[42] Transnational displacement has corporeal, social, political, and economic
identities and geographically specific historical markers.

In the 1980s, transnationalism emerged from a synthesis of two
dominant modes of thought: postmodernism, which emphasized
new, more fragmented relations between knowledge and power enabled by new technology; and Marxist critiques, which paid attention to the material transformations associated with increasingly
global capitalism.[43] One might argue that the critiques from which it
stems and transnationalism itself represent yet another white, Western neocolonial attempt to strip non-Western peoples of their national identities in order to subjugate them further.[44] This is a potential
danger. If, however, transnationalism and its hybrid cultural forms

are contextualized as a form of local response and remaking of global and international forces, as Néstor García Canclini contends, they hold out the possibility of a transformative politics.[45]

Though some notable anthropologists have focused upon refugees within a context that problematizes the identities and boundaries of nations,[46] most authors in the field of transnationalism are concerned with migrant circuits of movement related to their economic activity, with its obvious connections to social relations, and in cultural studies, to the construction and politics of diasporic subjectivities. Both sets of analysis are important to demonstrate the imbrication of migrant identities and the power relations that position these identities unequally in economies of "nations unbound."[47]

Nina Glick Schiller and her colleagues have argued that a distinctive kind of migrating population is emerging: *transmigrants,* who maintain a number of different ethnic, national, and racial identities. Host and home societies are connected through networks not circumscribed by conventional political boundaries. The authors' conceptualization of transnationalism foregrounds the emergence of an increasingly globalized capitalist system and with it increased flows of social, cultural, and political life. These processes of globalization exact a critical rethinking of migration studies. Michael Kearney adds a distinction between globalization and transnationalism: "[W]hereas global processes are largely decentered from specific national territories and take place in a global space, transnational processes are anchored in and transcend one or more nation-states."[48] Globalization can easily lead to the erasure of the local.[49] Whereas globalization discourse renders transnational migrants largely irrelevant (except perhaps as a labor source), transnationalism views them as constitutive of distinct social, cultural, political, and economic spaces that do not adhere to the more straightforward categories of nation, class, ethnicity, and gender.

Transnational migration is underscored by a number of politicized processes. It can be (1) a survival strategy in the face of economic or political insecurity; (2) a response to social (and, I would add, political) exclusion in countries of origin; and (3) an expression of racialized exclusion in North America.[50] Sociologist Luin Goldring defines "transnational communities" as dense social fields consisting of people, money, goods, and information that are constructed and maintained by migrants over time, across space, and through circuits that repeatedly cross borders. Focusing on the patterns of return migration for Mexican workers employed in Las Animas, California, Goldring chronicles the creation and maintenance of a transnational social space across the U.S.-Mexican border.[51]

Feminist authors theorize and politicize transnationalism from within cultural studies by employing a more explicitly postmodern approach to migration and its politics. "Transnational feminist practices," for example, focus on "the effects of mobile capital as well as the multiple subjectivities that replace the European unitary subject."[52] Processes that constitute and fragment migrant subjectivity are analyzed within the purview of the geopolitics of postmodernity. Modalities that construct centers and margins, like First and Third World, are challenged by transnational subjectivities that examine ways that women are constructed in subordination or positioned unequally in discourses of nationalism or the patriarchal state. Though these authors acknowledge the risks of abandoning identity politics, they contend that existing categories of identification elude the representation of certain histories and obfuscate the links among diasporic subjects in transnational culture. Such approaches to transnationalism examine the processes that contribute to identity formation and the unequal links that constitute these maps of power.

The materiality and corporeality of transnationalism, together with these critical interventions, create a vibrant theoretical and political surface for both subjects who defy national boundaries and those tracing the meanings of their movements. The emerging literature on transnationalism, however, tends to focus on economic and cultural analyses at the expense of political considerations. The conditions precipitating forced migration and the politics it produces are one example. Relatively little is said about refugees, whose politically induced migration involves elements of cultural dislocation and economic costs. Basch et al. note that political and economic crises often act as catalysts of migration and motivate people to maintain ties and return home, but their analysis of them does not address the problematic construction of "refugee" as an expression of national borders.[53] Transmigrants may support an opposition party or movement from afar, or they may return to participate in a new government, but questions of asymmetrical power relations that shape access to mobility, resources, and institutions across space, cultures, and nationalities remain largely unaddressed.[54]

Transnational migrants maintain multiple identities, moving across borders and often between cultures to create a single, imagined social field, politically displaced and geographically distributed. By maintaining identities that link them to more than one nation, they challenge academic orderings, territorially fixed notions of nation, and assimilationist narratives of immigration.

MERGING TRANSNATIONALISM WITH GEOPOLITICS AND PRACTICE

This chapter has moved from the corporeal movements of refugees in Kenya beyond the authorized limits of the camps and the borders of the country, to a transnational theoretical orientation. Transnationalism pays attention to historical and geographical change that generates migration across the political boundaries of states and beyond the conventional categories they designate. It is an orientation that embraces a critical geopolitics of mobility. Following my earlier discussion of postcolonial theory and its links to refugee management in camps, transnationalism draws upon such theory and improves it by focusing on those dimensions of difference and dynamics of change across space that are specifically embodied in migration.

A transnational politics of mobility analyzes the unequal relations of power among locations and subjects involved in humanitarian provisions. These relations represent links among funders, service providers, and those in need but are also sites of political negotiation and contest that produce distinct spaces. Preventive zones, safe havens, safe corridors, and UN protected areas are some examples. They shape mobility, especially for displaced persons who are internationally recognized, designating where they will go and how and when they will be helped. Those displaced move on their own volition within parameters marked by political status, nationality, gender, class, and ethnicity.

Earlier in the chapter, I posed a rhetorical question: As state borders break down and the primacy of the nation-state as the basis for social, economic, and political organization is challenged, how can the displacement and dispersion of refugees be theorized in a relevant and political context? What are the perils of abandoning the existing modes of ordering disorder, and what alternatives can be conceived? The practical and political implications of this question are explored in the final chapter.

7

Beyond the Status Quo

[T]he United Nations is in the process of exemplifying the transmutation of national resources into transnational interests of a new and puzzling sort.
— ARJUN APPADURAI,
"SOVEREIGNTY WITHOUT TERRITORIALITY"

There is no such thing as love of the human race, only the love of this person or that, in this time and not in any other. . . . The problem is not to defend universality, but to give these abstract individuals the chance to become real, historical individuals again, with the social relations and the power to protect themselves. . . . The people who have no homeland must be given one; they cannot depend on the uncertain and fitful protection of a world conscience defending them as examples of the universal abstraction Man.
— MICHAEL IGNATIEFF, THE NEEDS OF STRANGERS

The current international humanitarian regime is clearly in crisis. Complex humanitarian emergencies have emerged without coordinated, consistent responses. Refugee protection and humanitarian assistance are not separate from ethnic tension, regional conflict, or state posturing. As official development assistance declines and multilateral humanitarian assistance increases, many countries appear to be distancing themselves from state-based obligations toward refugees. Rethinking state-centric assumptions of asylum is critical during this period of reflection and reform. On the one hand, material assistance should not become a substitute for international protection.

Every effort to meet the extant mandates for protection, however minimal or partial they are, must be made. On the other, it is clear that a humanitarian regime limited to state-based international law and human rights instruments is insufficient.

UNHCR's recognition that people displaced on different sides of a border may belong to the same group and face similar problems is a step in the right direction to the extent that it does not discriminate on the basis of political borders but, rather, provides aid on the basis of need. UNHCR risks militarizing humanitarian approaches and endangering lives, however, when it is complicit with the UN Security Council and UN member states in the formation of ad hoc protected areas and safe havens in conflict zones, areas that do not, or perhaps cannot, guarantee protection. Likewise, complacence in the face of militarized refugee camps defeats their purpose. In refugee camps, ad hoc arrangements to provide basic material assistance and limited protection to noncombatants can be effective as an immediate response to unexpected emergency situations that need to be stabilized. But by letting refugees sit in camps and by constructing permanent buildings to house UNHCR staff and offices, the organization is reneging on its mandate: to find permanent solutions for displaced persons. This final chapter synthesizes lessons learned from recent humanitarian efforts and theoretical insights with practical directions for change.

Despite the current shortcomings of humanitarian and refugee efforts, doing nothing at all is not an option. Official UN reform is politically important to ensure the very survival of the United Nations, but to date it does not focus either on the slippage between UNHCR's mandate and the geopolitical field in which it operates or on that between the organization's donors and its recipients. Trimming budgets and reducing administrative costs within UN organizations may be desirable, but such measures do not constitute significant change. Genuine, if unofficial, reform within humanitarian circles is underway. Independent evaluations commissioned by select UN organizations have become a preferred route to assessing operations, chronicling mistakes, and recommending changes.[1] Though these reports offer considerable insight and refreshing perspectives, most have been carried out by agencies other than UNHCR.[2] Given criticism and efforts by advocates of displaced persons, UNHCR has come to disdain some human rights groups and NGOs. Nonetheless, change cannot be conceived of without the meaningful participation of these and other groups, for their years of experience in particular places *before* an emergency occurs are invaluable. Many NGOs have become increasingly politicized in their bid to assist refugees and are unwilling to keep quiet in return for lucrative health care and other contracts. Some sources say that the NGOs considered noisiest by UNHCR have been penalized for their statements by having their contracts suspended. Issues raised by groups like Human Rights Watch, Amnesty International, Médecins sans Frontières, and independent assessors are unlikely to fall silent until a consistently collaborative, coordinated process is established with shared accountability.[3] The quagmire of politics among humanitarian players consumes, in my estimation, as much time and resources as do efforts to coordinate and assist displaced people on the ground. Similar struggles do exist in crisis situations, however, with competition for beneficiaries among NGOs and UN agencies and some duplication of effort where humanitarian responses are not coordinated.[4] These are wars we can do without. Though it is naive and probably undesirable to think there is a *single* vision of humanitarian principles and practices to which all groups will agree at all times and in all places, recognizing the need for consensus among a much wider group of actors is an essential first step toward more-effective humanitarian response.

The involvement of nonstate actors is vital in creating what has been called a "framework of consent for humanitarian action."[5] Independent commentators have questioned the very assumption that the UN system is primarily responsible for the coordination of complex humanitarian emergencies. They maintain that the participation of "political and military actors that are legally, morally and materially responsible for the welfare of affected populations, i.e. national governments, local governments, armies, and in some instances, rebel authorities" in conjunction with the wider UN system is required for effective coordination of emergency response.[6] A broader range of local involvement has also been proposed, tapping the knowledge and plans of indigenous NGOs, women's groups, media, local governing bodies, and faith-based organizations.[7]

Scholars of refugee law and humanitarian emergencies are working hard to identify and test protection arrangements that go beyond conventional "durable solutions" to include temporary protection.[8]

Many have documented the inadequacy of existing measures to manage forced migration. The "right to remain" and "preventive protection" may constitute two of the most politically popular and thus viable approaches in the short term, but neither is viable in legal or humanitarian contexts in the longer term. Atrocities such as the mass slaughter of internally displaced Hutus in Rwanda at Kibeho camp in April 1995 and the widespread killing of Bosnian Muslims in the so-called safe area in Srebrenica that same summer will only mount as live experiments in humanitarian response continue. These extraordinary failures should not lead to a paralysis of the United Nations, however; in the absence of agreed-upon humanitarian principles and with degraded protection measures for displaced persons, yet more tragic outcomes can be expected.

> [C]ontinued international failure to tackle the political and security dimensions of the crisis, combined with sustained use of humanitarian assistance in the resultant policy vacuum, undermines the credibility, reputation, and long-term viability of humanitarian action, to deleterious consequence for the lives and livelihoods of those who humanitarian action is supposed to protect and assist.[9]

Complacence in the face of genocide in Rwanda followed by indiscriminate humanitarian assistance for both refugees and perpetrators of the genocide did not make sense in terms of protection, nor did it appear to be conceived within any kind of consensual political framework. As they did in Somalia, UN humanitarian agencies have learned a lesson of humility during the recent series of crises in central Africa: Their efforts alone cannot solve the problems of displacement. Where UN organizations intervene in conditions of ongoing conflict, they invariably participate in it.

THE IMPETUS FOR CHANGE

Humanitarianism is the site at which older projects of development and relief are being contested and recast in the face of new geopolitical and neoliberal realities. In this book I have outlined a number of current issues, dilemmas, and responses in the realm of refugee protection and humanitarian action. Existing international law pertaining to refugees emerged from the political context and conditions of displacement in Europe after World War II. Since then, the locations and kinds of conflict that generate displacement have changed, as has the geopolitical landscape. In keeping with these changes, particularly the nature and scale of forced migration in the Third World, various ad hoc measures have been introduced to accommodate displaced persons who do not fit the conditions and criteria outlined in the 1951 Convention Relating to the Status of Refugees and its 1967 Protocol. The convention definition of refugee remains the international standard used by states in determining who is a refugee, but it is becoming increasingly irrelevant to late-twentieth-century crises and to the characteristics of refugees they produce.[10]

The end of the Cold War marked a shift in responses to forced migration and in the geopolitics that generate human displacement in new ways. Put another way, the limits and leakage of state-based conceptions of international law and conventional geopolitics have been exposed. UNHCR has, in a sense, provided critical responses to human crises where no state apparatus exists. The organization transforms national funds into a multinational rapid-reaction force to meet the unexpected migration of people within and across the borders of nation-states. At the same time as it crosses borders flying the light blue flag of "united nations," the UN remains a powerful venue for the territorial nation-states that make up its membership and pay its bills. "What is puzzling . . . is that national resources given over to an organization intended to be a vehicle of international wishes are subsidizing activities that might actually reduce national control over a growing number of 'trouble spots.'"[11] The devolution of responsibility for refugees and displaced persons from states to such multilateral organizations as UNHCR represents a reinvention of states in different guises.

States have inserted a discursive and geographical distance between themselves and those displaced by political conflict or widespread violence. As neoliberal policies shape the social and economic climate at home, governments are keen to minimize their obligations and to prevent beneficiaries from materializing where possible.[12] This approach is in no way a conspiracy of states against the stateless and vulnerable; rather, it is a tactic of state transformation and political survival. Donor governments to the United Nations provide assistance to refugees and other displaced persons in camps "over there." This assistance is managed and disseminated through a nominally apolitical medium, namely, UNHCR, an agency that relies heavily on donations from these same countries for its basic operations. This incarnation of the state as, on the one hand, part of a multilateral organization, and, on the other, a sovereign fortress against involuntary migrants is an interesting, if insufficient, response to current conditions of displacement.

The Office of UNHCR has been called upon to extend its formal mandate and expand its operations to assist displaced people who are not technically refugees. International humanitarian interventions inside the borders of sovereign countries at war are examples of preventive protection and are part of a strategy to reduce the numbers of refugees and states' obligations toward them. At the same time, prevailing political problems—including civil war, related famine, and widespread fear of violence—increase the magnitude and complexity of need for humanitarian assistance across borders.

The existing international refugee regime has been likened to a 1950s car still running, but not very well, in the 1990s.[13] Ad hoc discretionary measures to assist refugees are too fickle and politically driven to ensure any consistency in humanitarian provisions and human rights enforcement. Under the status quo, fairness and consistency are predicated on benchmarks of entitlement determined by consenting parties, namely, states. Human rights conventions and international law pertaining to displaced persons change at a gradual pace in response to new social, economic, and political conditions. Nonetheless, they represent the basis for one "ethic of encounter" in situations of mass displacement. The importance and relevance of both international refugee law and human rights instruments must be revived to avoid impromptu, piecemeal provision of assistance to displaced persons in the post–Cold War period. They remain useful, if insufficient, tools because they are historically contingent and geographically inclusive. What is crucial, however, is that these tools not be hailed as universal values for all of humankind but, rather, serve as enforceable standards and guidelines for action. They are a means of connection and cooperation across difference, but they are also objects of debate, contest, and change.

This objective requires a continued contribution by UNHCR, which is well positioned to engage in a politics of location to protect human life. UNHCR has already begun this work, for example, in conjunction with the special representative of the UN secretary-general on internally displaced persons, by addressing ways to assist internally displaced people.[14] The claims of universal values and universal subjects, in contrast, are the salient symptoms of UN humanism. These claims embody a European geography that does not apply to most humanitarian emergencies in the 1990s. Crises of human displacement at the end of the twentieth century are more likely to occur outside Europe, creating refugees and other involuntary migrants who fall outside the convention definition of refugee. The evidence presented in this book shows that the European case after World War II was not the template crisis from which all subsequent emergencies and responses could be derived.

Rather than imposing closure on issues that are far from being resolved, I pose questions raised by the research as a means of provoking the reimagination of humanitarian operations in the current context. These questions and ideas speak from an ongoing commitment to the theoretical, political, and practical issues of humanitarian assistance for displaced people.

SHIFTING GROUND: THE POLICY VACUUM

In the late 1990s, the incongruent relationship between the conditions that generate involuntary migrants and the existing international laws to assist them is acutely apparent. In the absence of any agreed-upon principles and operational practices, UNHCR is well positioned to seek more than the input of NGOs and human rights groups. In collaboration with the recently renamed Office for the Coordination of Humanitarian Affairs (OCHA, formerly DHA), headed by a former senior UNHCR staff member, UNHCR has the opportunity to break out of the outmoded and state-centric categories of strict multilateralism and bilateralism and to establish a process that engages with other UN and non-UN organizations rather than merely including them in consultation. UNHCR itself acknowledges that "[w]hile the old rules of the game have evidently changed, the international community has found it extremely difficult to articulate a coherent set of principles and practices which are geared to contemporary circumstances."[15] Though UNHCR's "response-ability" and performance can be both applauded and criticized, it continues to operate without a set of agreed-upon criteria or framework of consensus among UN agencies, relevant governments, and nonstate actors. "UNHCR's founding statute makes it clear that the organization's work is humanitarian and entirely non-political."[16] In order to regain this status, it cannot continue to operate in isolation from other humanitarian actors or on a discretionary basis. To continue to operate without a specified, referenced mandate risks politicizing need and reducing humanitarian principles to popularity contests, especially if donor governments continue to earmark funds for specific crises of displacement. This has and will contribute to an uneven geography of humanitarian response. UNHCR has also recognized that "so long as reform continues in an ad hoc manner, it will remain prey to the limitations and contradictions of piecemeal change."[17] This conundrum is perhaps the greatest challenge to effective humanitarian operations.

In the African context, refugee eligibility involves a geographically circumscribed process of status determination. Individual case determination, based on the 1951 convention and its 1967 protocol, has largely been superseded by group status designations based on the regionally specific refugee definition outlined in the 1969 Organization for African Unity Convention. Prima facie refugee status was established by the Organization for African Unity Convention of 1969 as a protection measure to *complement* the refugee determination procedures of individual states. The status was never intended, however, to be used alone because it stipulates neither conclusive action nor solutions for refugees designated as such.

In the Horn of Africa, recognized groups of displaced persons outside their home countries are generally accorded prima facie refugee status and are administered and assisted by UNHCR and partner NGOs. However, prima facie status offers few, if any, permanent solutions to refugees. Somali refugees in Kenya with prima facie status are spatially segregated and isolated in remote border camps. In the absence of the quality and entitlements of legal status accorded to convention refugees, or some other regional alternative, their mobility is restricted. Though all refugees are subject to the laws and responsibilities of the state in which they reside, they are not criminals or prisoners of the state simply because they have been forced to move. They are invariably, however, subcitizens: "[S]econd-classness and third-classness are conditions of citizenship that are inevitable entailments of migration, however plural the ethnic ideology of the host state and however flexible its accommodation of refugees and other weakly documented visitors."[18]

Women refugees tend to be less mobile than their male counterparts and more responsible for household work. Accordingly, they are more adversely affected by camp organization. In order to cook, refugee women in the Dadaab camps must forage for wood beyond the perimeters of the desert-based camps; outside the camps, assault and rape are an ever-present risk. In the face of such violence, Kenyan authorities have, at times, been dismissive, blaming the refugees for taking wood that belongs to Kenyans. Refugees are not officially allowed to leave the camps or to seek employment nearby. The camps preclude any possibility of "capacity building," to use a buzzword in humanitarian circles. Very little social and economic infrastructure is developed in the camp context to enhance the lives of people living there on an ostensibly temporary basis or to improve conditions and build potentially autonomous organizations or institutions in the host country. Spatial segregation of and material assistance to refugees in camps provides no medium- or long-term solution to their situation. With the financial support of international donors and the reluctant cooperation of the Kenyan government, Somali refugees have become objects of discursive and material distancing strategies.

I have been somewhat critical of camp operations under the aegis of UNHCR. In the Kenyan camps, modes of ordering disorder—such as headcounts—resurrect colonial methods of managing "others." Incidents of coercion are consistent with neither UNHCR's mandate nor the community-based policies espoused at the organization's headquarters. The contradictory techniques of governing refugees through coercion, on the one hand, and through such cooperative schemes as refugee self-management, on the other, further complicate the situation. Though I appreciate the important role that UNHCR performs, that of providing immediate protection and short-term assistance to displaced persons, the lack of sufficient legal status and the concomitant restrictions of camp life prove problematic over time. Assistance cannot take the place of protection, nor can it be a sustainable stopgap measure that stalls the search for solutions, temporary or otherwise. Refugee camps are not solutions. Taking this analysis a step further, the problem is less with methods of counting in the camps than with the establishment of these strange temporary "cities" in the desert in the first place.

The most important criticism of the camps, then, is neither their design nor their management but their very conception as potentially long-term segregated safe spaces for refugees. This is not to say that safe havens within conflict zones are a better option. They are, in fact, more precarious in the safety and protection they afford. But as anything more than an immediate, emergency response to an unexpected influx of displaced people, camps are not satisfactory solutions. They can provide short-term safety, but they also institutionalize long-term exclusion, marginalization, and waste of both human and financial resources. Many refugees have been living in Kenyan camps for several years. Only a tiny proportion of refugees—fewer than 1 percent—are permanently resettled in countries like the United States, Canada, and Australia. And these numbers are declining.

UN HUMANISM OR POSTMODERN ETHICS?

The humankind-wide moral unity is thinkable, if at all, not as the end-product of globalizing the domain of political powers with ethical pretensions, but as the utopian horizon of deconstructing the "without us the deluge" claims of nation-states, nations-in-search-of-the-state, traditional communities and communities-in-search-of-a-tradition, tribes and neo-tribes, as well as their appointed and self-appointed spokesmen and prophets.
—ZYGMUNT BAUMAN, *POSTMODERN ETHICS*

What might the prognosis for UN humanism and humanitarian practice be? Lila Abu-Lughod argues that humanism in the West continues to be the language of human equality with the most moral force: "[W]e cannot abandon it yet, if only as a convention of writing."[19] I maintain that the political purchase of human rights instruments and international refugee law, as expressions of humanist thinking, are more than conventions of writing. UN interventions and assistance still command support and political legitimacy among Western governments, as can be measured in part by the financial resources UN agencies are able to solicit from them. International human rights and legal provisions for refugee asylum remain compelling, if imperfect, political instruments to which states consent. Although their initial formation is rooted in modern European notions of the universal subject and global progress based on human development, they can be viewed and used as historically contingent, changeable standards of human conduct. Political action takes culturally, historically, and geographically specific forms, but it is predicated upon some kind of shared dialogue.[20] Just as conditions and standards change, so too will the language of and players in this dialogue. The renewal and use of international laws and human rights instruments applicable to forced migrants is a necessary, if not sufficient, part of emerging responses to human displacement. In the absence of other geographically inclusive measures, these tools in the hands of UN, human rights, and nongovernmental organizations have the potential to minimize ad hoc status determinations and to provide common terms of reference for all concerned. Multilateral discretion, arguably the complement to these tools, places responsibility for involuntary migrants in the hands of UN agencies dependent on donor governments for funding and at a comfortable distance from these governments and the borders within which they govern. "Even if binding international instruments are lacking, there is a widely shared palpable gut feeling that no space is sovereign where egregious human rights violations occur."[21]

The affirmation of human rights instruments and international law relevant to displaced persons may actually reinscribe state boundaries and power to some extent. States are signatories to these conventions and declarations, yet the slippage between state and nation has been demonstrated. States do not necessarily act with the welfare of minority groups and political opponents in mind, and they are often part of the problem in civil conflicts that displace people. But in order to protect stateless refugees or internally displaced persons from uncertain, discretionary fates, some kind of consensual and changeable bottom line is required.

Refugee law and human rights provisions can arguably be reconstituted as expressions of postmodern ethics insofar as they enact changes over time and engage rather than deepen differences across locations. My understanding of postmodern ethics, however, departs somewhat from Zygmunt Bauman's project and includes a key role for UNHCR. It poses a transformative politics and set of practices that employ cultural workers alongside logisticians, medical personnel, and protection officers in conjunction with changeable, consensual, and contractual standards of conduct for the treatment of displaced people.

In order to engage difference, the application of international laws and human rights instruments cannot be subject to the popularity of a cause nor to a predisposition toward a particular place or people. These laws and instruments have the potential to be relevant tools of change if they apply to all contemporary refugees and internally displaced persons and not only to those who meet the criteria of the outdated convention definition of refugee or those whose conditions win the sympathy of donor countries.

Engaging difference requires not only human rights and legal instruments but also a range of organizations and staff to coordinate and activate appropriate responses. Stretched in every direction, UNHCR is a precariously balanced but vital agency in meeting humanitarian needs at the present time. Without established priorities and criteria for humanitarian intervention, UNHCR becomes a contractor of sorts to projects defined by donors or by other UN bodies. Where the agency works best, I argue, is in bridging the differences between the abstract, aspatial, and often outdated codes of legal and human rights and the particular exigencies of a given humanitarian crisis.

This in-between location is also a basis for further enhancing UNHCR's role. As noted, reinvigorating international instruments of law and human rights as political directives for action is a partial measure, but UNHCR's potential role as the link between these instruments and the varied political situations to which they might apply is the most significant. UNHCR has already proven its ability to adapt, customizing projects to the place and conditions in which they are implemented.[22] UNHCR can move between established criteria of humanitarian assistance and intervention, on the one hand, and specific places, people, and geopolitics on the other. In a more nuanced fashion, the UNHCR's Division of International Protection has recently supported a politics of location while retaining certain categories and mandates:

> Legal categories and institutional mandates retain all their relevance. . . . A comprehensive approach to coerced human displacement does not mean, however, that we should employ broad generalizations and undifferentiated treatment. No two humanitarian crises are ever the same, and a global approach to such complex situations requires, if anything, finer tools of analysis and a larger arsenal of flexible responses.[23]

Though I object to the militaristic notion of "arsenal" and the idea that flexible responses can be known a priori, this citation begins to acknowledge the importance of context and differentiation at UNHCR. To a significant extent, the Division of International Protection has renegotiated its own categories, admitted its limitations, and taken a closer look at the politics in and of place in relation to existing humanitarian codes. A politics of location is most useful when it is used to deconstruct any dominant hierarchy or hegemonic use of specific terms, in this case the idea that all refugees and their conditions of displacement basically require the same response.[24] As noted by a UNHCR senior staff member, it is "not whether you are a refugee but where you are. . . . it's all a question of space and distance."[25]

At the end of the twentieth century, the formal mandate of UNHCR appears sorely outdated, and its role in relation to OCHA, UNICEF, and other operational UN agencies remains ill defined. Yet the agency is well equipped to deal with an array of humanitarian emergencies on an ad hoc basis. The international refugee regime in some ways mirrors trends occurring at a national level today in a number of Western countries. As welfare states are restructured, so too are foreign aid programs, immigrant ceilings, and refugee sponsorships. State support for minimum standards and common provisions at home is increasingly being replaced by "user-pay" models of service delivery as well as by an emphasis on individual choice and responsibility. This shift from standard treatment to special needs has "institutionalized the *diversity* of fate."[26] Likewise, increasingly piecemeal approaches and responses to human displacement deepen the divide between those who donate and those who require assistance. Such approaches accentuate both the politicization of need and the politics of need, that is, questions of who is deserving and who has the power to decide.[27]

In the realm of humanitarian assistance, the distancing script that locates "us" and "them" involves a geographical and discursive divide. To assist displaced people at home by employing the language of preventive protection and the safe spaces it designates is to maintain a safe and less costly distance between "us" and "them." The ad hoc measures of humanitarian response, including prima facie status and UN-protected safe areas, are examples of the institutionalization of this "diversity of fate." UN interventions occur in selected locations, usually in politically defeated or less developed states. Legal status is accorded differentially to groups of displaced people over time and across space. The project of UN humanism and the distributions it espouses may be theoretically problematic and politically Eurocentric, but governments that relinquish responsibility for providing all but the most basic human needs—espousing a philoso-phy that one might call *neohumanism*—are in an even less defensible position. Neohumanism is characteristic of many neoliberal and post-welfare states. It describes the current trend whereby human well-being and development are qualified by the visibility and political popularity of people's need, as well as by the economic viability of measures employed to assist them. Neohumanism breeds ambiva-lence to and distance from the politics and privations of "others" in spite of connections among geographical and discursive locations in a shrinking world.

In an unprecedented and ironic move, Ted Turner, founder of CNN, recently announced that he would donate U.S.$1 billion to UN agencies.[28] The gift will be used to establish a foundation to fund UN programs aiding refugees and children, to clear land mines, and to fight disease. Turner called on the U.S. government to pay its out-standing debt of U.S.$1.5 billion to the United Nations. The fickle-ness of funding becomes apparent as CNN unexpectedly contributes to the organizations whose crises and pain it broadcasts while the U.S. government remains reluctant to pay its outstanding contribu-tion until what it considers to be appropriate reforms are made. Turner's donation to "charity" risks privatizing humanitarian fund-ing; at the same time, the U.S. government lobbies the United Na-tions to become more efficient and less costly. There is something un-settling about an unexpected billion-dollar donation from the most global television news station, on which displacement, famine, and other human tragedy are broadcast regularly. The CNN optic direct-ly affects the popularity and funding of humanitarian operations. The visual dissemination of extreme need from a distance evokes re-sponse, both on individual and governmental levels. As those in need approach "our" borders, however, they become more suspect. They threaten to take "our" jobs and are perceived to depend heavily on the social and educational services for which they do not pay. Human need is obfuscated as its proximity increases.

BEYOND RELIEF AND DEVELOPMENT

As the bipolar grid of intelligibility from the Cold War fades, humani-tarianism in the 1990s marked a renegotiation among states of their obligation to and contact with displaced populations. Is development, a Cold War discourse and tool of economic growth, over? Have the charity and compassion of relief been supplanted by coordinated responses to complex humanitarian emergencies? A decline in funding for official development assistance and a significant increase in money for humanitarian emergencies since the end of the Cold War suggest that this may be the case. Beginning in the 1970s, structural adjustment programs (SAPs) applied stringent conditions, such as public sector reduction, on loans to poorer countries. The lending institutions administering SAPs, the IMF and the World Bank, offer another example of the trend away from development assistance. Development programs and social spending were put on hold if they were not in line with fiscal realities.[29] Neoliberalism, which embraces unencumbered markets and the maintenance of a minimal state apparatus, embodies a narrower concept of the public good—limited to state, law, and money matters—than the one that underlies the conventional welfare state.[30] For the moment, funding humanitarian crises is in; funding development is out. Development belongs to the discourse of the welfare state, whereas humanitarian assistance suits the crisis-management strategies of postwelfare governments.

Neohumanism is symptomatic of the international refugee regime. Responses to human displacement and assistance to forced migrants speak the language of humanism: the protection of rights for all people. But the Kenyan study of UNHCR camps illustrates that on the ground practices stray far from this idea of protection. The infringement of rights implicit in counting methods and neocolonial controls over the refugee population in the camps is exacerbated by conditions of geographical isolation and social segregation based on subordinate legal status. Ironically, these camps, which are intended to provide asylum and uphold certain human rights, suspend other basic entitlements such as the right to work, to move freely, and to establish an independent livelihood. The discrepancy between a language of rights and the conditions of the camps is clear. Nor does this language fully address the current conditions of displacement generated by civil conflict, often occurring within state borders. The camps represent contradictory segregated spaces of ongoing displacement and assistance at once, what might also be thought of as *displaced assistance*.

SETTING A RESEARCH AGENDA

Beginning in 1991 with UN assistance to the Kurds in northern Iraq, there have been significant changes in the delivery of humanitarian assistance. UNHCR increasingly crosses international borders to assist displaced people at home, often in conflict zones. Responsibility for refugees has also shifted away from state governments toward multilateral organizations, such as UNHCR, as is indicated by huge increases in UN refugee relief and peacekeeping budgets and a decline in both the numbers of refugees being resettled in host countries and in official development assistance.[31] UNHCR has become the main multilateral organization responsible for forced migrants, both refugees who cross the boundaries of nation-states and, in many cases, internally displaced groups within countries at war. These conditions raise the following questions:

- *How temporary is temporary?* Given that refugee camps are only temporary solutions, as UNHCR maintains, what reasonable limits may be placed on the residence of prima facie refugees in camps and on the designation of such status itself? At what point should UNHCR and its member states be required to find a medium-term alternative, in keeping with basic human rights instruments, that would not preclude access to employment, mobility, and independent livelihood?

- *What are the alternatives?* Recognizing the broader definition of refugee in Africa, how might the existing option of temporary protection (TP) abroad or the possibility of temporary citizenship in another African country be arranged so that a refugee could enjoy basic rights of citizenship or nationality until residence in her or his own state becomes viable? Under such a plan, no one country could be expected to absorb all the refugees created by a given conflict. The proposal that burdens be shared, raised by refugee scholars,[32] could apply so that all signatory states to the 1951 Convention Relating to the Status of Refugees are made responsible for either hosting a certain proportion of refugees or paying to establish and support them on a temporary basis in a host country. A mechanism whereby both refugees and states have some say in who goes where would enhance the availability of support from other members of the same exiled group.

- *Is a transnational status for displaced persons possible?* Though the nation-state remains an important venue and body for granting legal status to refugees and displaced persons, its practical and theoretical limitations have been exposed. UNHCR has been the most active agency in the 1990s addressing the needs of refugees and other displaced persons who fall outside the existing state-based refugee regime. Could a transnational temporary status, determined by operational humanitarian agencies such as UNHCR and UNICEF and including human rights organizations, NGOs, and indigenous nonstate actors perhaps grant "persons of concern" status to certain groups of people who are in need of protection but who fall between the cracks of conventional borders? Such an option might be coordinated by OCHA, not replacing but complementing existing law and protection provisions. UN agencies have learned to cross borders and challenge sovereignty where humanitarian need and protection issues arise, but they alone cannot be the ones to identify legitimate need given the exigencies of funding noted earlier. While UNHCR and UNICEF remain inventions of states, their multilateral nature and voluntary funding bases render them more receptive to change.

UNHCR already uses the designation "persons of concern," as a kind of transnational status that applies to people assisted by the organization who fall outside the categories of "refugee" or "IDP."[33] The government of Thailand, for example, recognizes forced migrants from Burma as legitimate subjects of the international refugee regime only when they have been registered by UNHCR in Bangkok, granted legitimate persons of concern status, and transferred to the designated safe camp in Ratchaburi province. Without such status, displaced Burmese are treated as illegal migrants and subject to harassment by Thai police, especially when they make their way from the Thai-Burmese border to Bangkok.[34] The Thai government is not a signatory to the 1951 convention nor its 1967 protocol and does not recognize Burmese refugees for economic and political reasons. Could the UNHCR persons of concern designation be formalized and inculcated into a broader transnational system of temporary protection?

The questions above are predicated on the idea of a transnational politics of mobility conceived between the categories of nation-state and of international legal and human rights instruments. Global geographies of finance, geopolitics, and human displacement also challenge the categories of refugee and international borders as they were originally conceived. These questions admittedly sketch possibilities and fuel further debate rather than provide answers. They are, however, an attempt to think outside the box. Refugee scholars agree that the present political climate is not conducive to expanding the convention definition. Yet a temporary legal status that allows access to employment and mobility could engender more independent livelihoods. If anything, signatory states would be likely to restrict further eligibility for refugees in the current political climate. The principle of refugee burden sharing on a temporary basis is not new, but it should be carefully reviewed as a transnational response to displacement, a response orchestrated by UNHCR, NGOs, human rights organizations, legal scholars, and donor governments rather than states alone.

UNHCR: DEALING WITH DIFFERENCE

UNHCR is an organization undergoing immense change. As it moves from a welfare suprastate to a more fiscally transparent organization, it increasingly emphasizes the efficient management demanded by the donor governments which pay the bills. The difference between the demands of donors and the needs of refugees produces a distinct tension. Donors are predominantly governments, with geopolitical and economic agendas. Refugees are, by contrast, disenfranchised subjects of the international humanitarian regime. As an agency responsible to both sides, UNHCR is caught in the middle. This is, in my view, the primary basis for the antagonistic relations between UNHCR and organizations like MSF, Human Rights Watch, and Amnesty International. With few, if any, direct lines of accountability between those who pay for humanitarian assistance and those who receive it, "watchdog organizations" tend to step in when the protection or welfare of those in need appears to be compromised.

Given the claim that both government donors and refugee recipients are UNHCR's "clients," balancing and meeting both sets of needs is crucial to the agency's political survival and its effectiveness. If the demands of donors are met at the expense of protection and assistance to refugees or other displaced people, UNHCR risks operating within a framework whereby the economic viability and political popularity of a particular humanitarian emergency qualify efforts to improve the well-being of people at risk. On the other hand, if UNHCR engages in full-scale development work in cooperation with refugees, donor support is likely to wane because the organization will be viewed as exceeding its emergency and humanitarian mandates. With the popularity of the welfare state and its international corollary, development assistance, at its lowest since World War II, UNHCR has to navigate a precarious path between the excesses of social spending and the immediate needs of refugees and other displaced persons in need of protection.

UNHCR has traditionally focused its efforts on refugee welfare. Though assistance to refugees and displaced people remains the basis of its mandate, this perspective is changing dramatically. The demands of donors that the organization become more efficient are increasing, and they are being heard by UNHCR. The transition to more financial accountability at UNHCR mirrors current neoliberal economic trends within many industrialized countries. Taxpayer expectations that governments account for spending are high. Governments need proof that money has been wisely spent. Yet on a broader scale, refugees and displaced persons are not the taxpayers who are funding UN agencies. There is little, if any, constituency overlap between donors and refugees. UNHCR solicits funds and provides humanitarian assistance and protection with full accountability to its donors but with fewer such links to refugees and other recipients. This slippage allows for discretionary decision making regarding refugee status and camp operations. This same slippage between states and the stateless, the subject and abject, also opens up spaces among displaced people and for links that exceed the imaginary of territorial sovereignty. Despite UNHCR's sustained efforts to enact relevant policies, hire experienced staff, and take concrete steps to make the organization more responsive to donors and refugees alike, there is no formal mechanism that links refugee recipient needs or demands to UNHCR operations. Government donors are UNHCR's main clients; refugees and displaced people are its recipients.

FIELDING CHANGE

UNHCR is well positioned to recalibrate its policies and approaches to managing displacement in the field. The organization's tendency to domesticate gender and cultural differences under the twin policies of integration and multiculturalism is evident. The UN Family of Man is premised upon the idea that cultural and national difference is simply diversity and can be tolerated and managed because "We are all human beings"—a single human race. This notion of UN humanism is untenable. In the Kenyan camps, differences between refugees, locals, and international humanitarian staff are institutionalized and accentuated through administrative practices that mark and distinguish its subjects. Camp organization breaks down any notion of a common humanity, as political, material, and cultural differences between citizens and noncitizens are magnified rather than minimized. Things fall apart where a language of equality is undermined by spatially and socially distinct notions of "us" and "them," generated by administrative practices in camps and other protected areas. How ironic it is that the refugees should serve meals to the staff, visitors, and researchers from outside at the UNHCR compound, that the former tented camp occupied by UNHCR was catered by a Nairobi-based safari company, and that the planes used to transport supplies were the same ones hired by tour companies for weekend safaris to Kenya's Masai Mara Reserve.

One British-born pilot I met had been the district officer in colonial Kenya's Northern Frontier District thirty years earlier. He later turned to flying tourists on safari around Kenya, but given the decrease in tourism and the increase in UNHCR and NGO contracts he was now transporting humanitarian staff among various camps and outposts back in his old stomping ground. The connections between humanitarian management strategies and colonial practices in Kenya was stunning, yet their purposes were quite different. The fictional unity of a common humanity becomes clear as one group of people flies in and out of Kenyan refugee camps occupied by another group of people who are restricted to the camps. Acknowledging these unequal power relations and the axes of difference on which they are based is critical. Only then can the administrators and field staff working in the camps comprehend the full import of their actions as part of an ambiguously transnational project.

With respect to contemporary humanitarian operations, the unity in diversity approach of UNHCR is naively Eurocentric. Furthermore, refugee camps that feed, house, and provide some protection to involuntary migrants as dependents provide no solution to the problem of forced migration. Neocolonial and institutional practices of refugee management in the camps seemingly contradict UNHCR's humanitarian role. Practical, ongoing connections among nationalities are lacking, despite efforts to manage ethnic diversity. Simple geographical proximity and the social relations these tend to generate represent a move toward breaking down the category and meanings of nationality in the space of refugee camps.

MOVING AHEAD

To analyze the conditions and subjects of displacement in a more comprehensive framework, I have introduced the concept of a transnational politics of mobility. Uneven access to mobility is shaped not only by refugee status but also by relations of gender, socioeconomic status, and location. The geopolitics of mobility outlined earlier attempts to move beyond the binary geopolitical division of North and South and the outdated categories of First, Second, and Third Worlds to theorize unequal power relations in a transnational context. The politics of mobility apply not only to individual refugees but also to the positioning of hegemonic countries and regional blocks in relation to poorer, and arguably less-stable, areas.

Borders are being renegotiated at several levels. On the one hand, new states emerge in the absence of a Cold War climate. On the other, international bodies like the United Nations challenge and transform meanings of sovereignty in new ways by crossing existing state boundaries in order to assist people in peril. Multilateral interventions, often backed by the force of peacekeeping missions, represent a deepening divide in the relations of power between the hegemonic countries of the North, which decide to finance these endeavors, and the poorer countries that "host" them. Rather, participation and coordination of efforts among a wider group of humanitarian actors—a microcosm of civil society both within and across borders—constitute a more convincing option. Humanitarian activities and operations need to be in keeping with some agreed-upon principles of appropriate assistance to displaced persons. Otherwise, as Bauman warns, superior morality will continue to be the morality of the superior. Refugees in locations such as the Horn of Africa will simply stay in camps.

Despite my concerns about humanitarian responses to displacement, I retain a political and professional commitment to the project of safeguarding human life. My efforts have been directed at identifying emerging geopolitical change and organizational issues that inhibit UNHCR's effectiveness and the fair treatment of refugees, in particular women and people whose cultural backgrounds are not Euro-American. The intensity of humanitarian work derives, in part, from the contradictions and politics that shape responses to crises of displacement. As people, organizations, and countries become increasingly integrated into transnational networks of power, it becomes even more important that those rousted out of these circuits not simply be left in exclusion and isolation. Refugee camps do just that: They remove evidence of human displacement from view and contain "the problem" without resolution, as noncommunities of the excluded.

My objective has not been to criticize the efforts of those who work in the current humanitarian culture but to underscore contradictions and problems within this culture. At the same time, I have been wary of the state, of its primacy in international relations generally and humanitarian operations specifically. States are paradoxically positioned when they delegate responsibility for humanitarian activities to multilateral organizations and endorse their crossing of "other" countries' sovereign borders to assist people in need. But in relinquishing control of these functions and allowing sovereignty elsewhere to be transgressed, they implicitly challenge their own borders. The crisis of Rwanda and its aftermath highlight another dimension: Humanitarian operations demand a framework of consent and political solutions as well as resources to ensure protection and assistance to people at risk.

A transnational politics of mobility is grounded in material subjectivities and locations. It involves making connections across asymmetries in status and challenging the reproduction of unequal relations of power. A transnational politics of mobility involves the ongoing crossing of borders—political, cultural, economic, and social. What does this mean for operations in complex humanitarian emergencies? Though there is little question that professional efforts to save lives in a crisis situation are warranted in the short term, their deployment as a stopgap measure once a vulnerable population is stabilized is less tenable. I have attempted to illustrate the shortcomings and contradictions of such strategies where culture and gender are simply variations on a theme subsumed and managed under a humanist narrative of diversity. Categories of difference, such as gender and culture, cannot simply be filled in when humanitarian staff arrive on site.

Difference is distinct from diversity. It is about historically and geographically contingent meanings, timings, and approaches to a problem. It cannot be captured as a substantive category of "other" information. UNHCR can access cultural workers as well as medical staff, logistics specialists, and administrators. A cadre of employees

with both sets of skills—cultural and professional—needs to be cultivated further. Cultural politics, including gender politics, are inevitable in crisis situations, but they can be handled well by those
with the training, experience, or appropriate cultural capital to interpret the crisis conditions that humanitarian staffs face. This is not to
essentialize differences or to claim that possessing certain cultural
traits qualifies one to deal best with those possessing the same qualities. Rather, the experience and ability to work across differences
and through the exigencies of humanitarian crises by engaging them
through a variety of means should be recognized. Professionalization
of humanitarian personnel may be one step toward galvanizing the
critical mass of skill, knowledge, and experience required to respond
effectively to crises of displacement. More comprehensive training
and longer postings may be another step toward improving consistency and efficacy of humanitarian operations. Often the work of
nonemergency local and nongovernmental organizations precedes
that of humanitarian agencies. The knowledge humanitarian staff
members glean from these contacts is invaluable. Seeking more deliberate links with such organizations is vital.

There is no single project of human development or of emancipation from the oppressions brought on by poverty, displacement, colonialism, or conflict. Rather, the affinities and contests these unequal
power relations generate are historically and geographically contingent. They cross borders—both geographical and discursive—to
demonstrate affinity or to unsettle hegemonic sociospatial arrangements. "The global and the universal are not pre-existing empirical
qualities; they are deeply fraught, dangerous, and inescapable inventions."[35] Though arguably inescapable, the global and the universal
are negotiable, just as the dichotomies of North/South, modern/
traditional can be contested by forging affinities across these borderlines. Transnational feminist practices that attend to the mobility of
bodies, of money, and of power as well as to the colors, flags, and
performances that mark them provide tools for challenging existing
"inventions." Such a transnational politics generates strategic constellations of power that challenge the existing operations of humanitarian assistance in the Horn of Africa and elsewhere.

Notes

INTRODUCTION

1. Gayatri Chakravorty Spivak, "Can the Subaltern Speak?" in *Marxism and the Interpretation of Culture*, ed. C. Nelson and L. Grossberg (Urbana: University of Illinois Press, 1988), 271–313.

2. Felix Driver, "Discipline without Frontiers? Representations of the Mettray Reformatory Colony in Britain, 1840–1880," *Journal of Historical Sociology* 3, no. 3 (September 1990): 272–293.

3. Jonathan Stevenson, "Hope Restored in Somalia?" *Foreign Policy*, no. 91 (Summer 1993): 138–154.

4. Michael Shapiro, *Violent Cartographies: Mapping Cultures of War* (Minneapolis: University of Minnesota Press, 1997).

5. Gearóid Ó Tuathail, *Critical Geopolitics: The Politics of Writing Global Space* (Minneapolis: University of Minnesota Press, 1996); Shapiro, *Violent Cartographies*; Julie Murphy Erfani, "Globalizing Tenochtitlán? Feminist Geopolitics: Mexico City as Borderland," in *The U.S.-Mexico Border: Transcending Divisions, Contesting Identities*, ed. David Spener and Kathy Standt (Boulder, Colo: Lynne Rienner, 1998), 143–168; Roxanne Lynn Doty, *Imperial Encounters: The Politics of Representation in North-South Relations* (Minneapolis: University of Minnesota Press, 1996).

6. An extensive and important literature pertaining to the delivery of humanitarian relief and the organizations that respond to refugee needs has developed over the last dozen years. The findings of my research appear a decade after Barbara Harrell-Bond's landmark tome, *Imposing Aid: Emergency Assistance to Refugees*. Her study of Ugandan refugees in south Sudan

was a "first attempt to make an independent study of an emergency assistance programme"; Barbara Harrell-Bond, *Imposing Aid: Emergency Assistance to Refugees* (Oxford and New York and Nairobi: Oxford University Press, 1986), xii. Another remarkable work examining the genesis of the international refugee regime, its development, and limitations is Gil Loescher's *Beyond Charity: International Cooperation and the Global Refugee Crisis* (New York: Oxford University Press, 1993). The author addresses, in particular, two salient issues in humanitarian circles: the question of engaging political, or root, causes rather than offering palliative assistance and the question of where, if at all, development assistance fits with asylum. His careful, contemporary study of UNHCR is superseded in depth only by Louise Holborn's extensive two-volume history of UNHCR's work in *Refugees: A Problem of Our Time. The Work of UNHCR 1951–72* (Metuchen, N.J.: Scarecrow Press, 1975). Within the discipline of geography, a number of scholars have published research pertaining to refugee displacement. Not surprisingly, much of this body of work relates to refugees in the Horn of Africa, where forced migration has been widespread and large scale. In particular, see Johnathan Bascom, *Losing Place: Refugee Populations and Rural Transformations in East Africa* (Oxford and Providence, R.I.: Berghan Books, 1998); Richard Black and Vaughan Robinson, eds., *Geography and Refugees: Patterns and Processes of Change* (London and New York: Belhaven Press, 1993); T. Kuhlman, *Asylum or Aid? The Economic Integration of Ethiopian and Eritrean Refugees in the Sudan* (Aldershot, England: Avebury Publications, 1994), and *Burden or Boom? Eritrean Refugees in the Sudan* (London: Zed Books, 1990); John Rogge, ed., *Refugees: A Third World Dilemma* (Totowa, N.J.: Rowman and Allanheld, 1987), and *Too Many, Too Long: Sudan's Twenty-Year Refugee Dilemma* (Totowa, N.J.: Rowman and Allanheld, 1985).

7. Lila Abu-Lughod, "Writing against Culture," in *Recapturing Anthropology*, ed. R. G. Fox (Sante Fe, N.M.: School for American Research, 1991), 137–162; Allan Pred and Michael Watts, *Reworking Modernity* (New Brunswick, N.J.: Rutgers University Press, 1992).

8. UNHCR, *Registration: A Practical Guide for Field Staff* (Geneva, May 1994).

9. I am indebted to Julie Murphy Erfani's observation of the reinvention of statism under a multilateralist rubric. She points out that what might appear to be an initial contradiction turns out to be quite complementary; "statist multilateralism" seems most dedicated to preserving the sovereign authority of states by preventing cross-border movements of people. States in fact give up some sovereign authority to the United Nations in order to preserve this control over migration flows, which is an obvious aspect of

sovereignty. See also Saskia Sassen, *Losing Control? Sovereignty in an Age of Globalization* (New York: Columbia University Press, 1996).

10. The idea of distancing scripts is borrowed from Gearóid Ó Tuathail's work on representations of Bosnia-Herzegovina. Ó Tuathail provides a compelling argument that distancing scripts are used by media and humanitarian authorities to "other" refugees and displaced persons. He provides a detailed account of how one female journalist, Maggie O'Kane, attempts to counter this discursive strategy through her extremely vivid, human, and humane depictions and engagements with people affected by displacement in Bosnia. See his "An Anti-Geo-Political Eye: Maggie O'Kane in Bosnia, 1992–93," *Gender, Place, and Culture* 3, no. 2 (1996): 171–185.

11. Guy Goodwin-Gill, "United Nations Reform and the Future of Refugee Protection," online posting to forced migration listserve, June 4, 1997.

12. Ed Schenkenberg van Mierop, "Protection of Civilians in Conflict," in *World in Crisis: The Politics of Survival at the End of the Twentieth Century,* ed. Médecins sans Frontières/Doctors without Borders (New York and London: Routledge, 1997), 1–15, at 1.

13. Shapiro, *Violent Cartographies.*

14. Néstor García Canclini, *Hybrid Cultures: Strategies for Entering and Leaving Modernity* (Minneapolis: University of Minnesota Press, 1995), 54. Following Canclini, I want to suggest that transnational hybridities are a form of local response to and partial transformation of global (and international) forces and constraints in a world where cultural authenticity is neither possible nor emancipatory.

15. Murphy Erfani, "Globalizing Tenochtitlán?" 5. Murphy Erfani argues that classical geopolitics posits a neutral mind detached from a body that observes space "objectively." Her own feminist geopolitics focus on the interstices of mind and body as an inseparable borderland location of the corporeal subject (5–6).

16. Inderpal Grewal and Caren Kaplan, "Introduction: Transnational Feminist Practices and Questions of Postmodernity," in *Scattered Hegemonies: Postmodernity and Transnational Feminist Practices,* ed. I. Grewal and C. Kaplan (Minneapolis: University of Minnesota Press, 1994), 1–33.

17. Luin Goldring, "Blurring Borders: Constructing Transnational Community in the Process of Mexico-U.S. Migration," *Research in Community Psychology* 6 (1996): 69–104; Michael Kearney, "The Local and the Global: The Anthropology of Globalization and Transnationalism," *Annual Review of Anthropology* 24 (1995): 547–565; S. Shami, "Transnationalism and Refugee Studies: Rethinking Forced Migration and Identity in the Middle East," *Journal of Refugee Studies* 9, no. 1 (1996): 3–26.

18. Donna Haraway, "Situated Knowledges," in her *Simians, Cyborgs,*

and Women: The Reinvention of Nature (New York and London: Routledge, 1991), 183–201, at 201.

19. Cynthia Enloe, *The Morning After: Sexual Politics at the End of the Cold War* (Berkeley and Los Angeles: University of California Press, 1994), and *Bananas, Beaches, and Bases: Making Feminist Sense of International Politics* (Berkeley and Los Angeles: University of California Press, 1989); V. Spike Petersen, ed., *Gendered States: Feminist (Re)Visions of International Relations Theory* (Boulder, Colo.: Lynne Rienner, 1992); Jan Jindy Pettman, *Worlding Women: A Feminist International Politics* (London and New York: Routledge, 1996); Sandra Whitworth, *Feminism and International Relations: Towards a Political Economy of Gender in Multilateral Institutions* (Houndsmills, Basingstoke, Hampshire, and London: Macmillan, 1994).

20. Judith Butler, *Bodies That Matter: On the Discursive Limits of "Sex"* (New York: Routledge, 1993); Spivak, "Can the Subaltern Speak?"

21. UNHCR printed a public relations poster with a picture of a stylized refugee sheltered in a tent. The caption underneath reads: "UNHCR, a voice for the voiceless."

22. Donna Haraway, "The Promises of Monsters: A Regenerative Politics for Inappropriate/d Others" in *Cultural Studies,* ed. L. Grossberg, C. Nelson, and P. Treichler (New York: Routledge, 1992), 295–337.

23. See Michael Shapiro's discussion of the Gulf War and its representational strategies in "That Obscure Object of Violence," in *Violent Cartographies,* 73–105. For an incisive gender analysis of representational strategies employed during the Gulf War, see Matthew Sparke, "Writing Patriarchal Missiles: The Chauvinism of the 'Gulf War' and the Limits of Critique," *Environment and Planning A* 26, no. 7 (1994): 1061–1089.

24. Haraway, "Situated Knowledges."

25. Ó Tuathail, *Critical Geopolitics.*

26. U.S. responses to the first round of UN reform, announced in mid-1997, were not favorable; "UN Reform Plan Disappoints US," *Vancouver Sun* and *Washington Post,* July 17, 1997. See also UN General Assembly, *Renewing the United Nations: A Programme for Reform,* A/51/950, July 14, 1997, for the secretary-general's report on reform.

27. UNHCR, *The State of the World's Refugees: In Search of Solutions* (Oxford and New York: Oxford University Press, 1995), 48.

28. Ibid., 115.

29. Nira Yuval-Davis, "National Spaces and Collective Identities: Borders, Boundaries, Citizenship, and Gender Relations" (inaugural lecture at the University of Greenwich, presented May 22, 1997), 3.

30. Michael Ignatieff, *Blood and Belonging: Journeys into the New Nationalism* (New York: Farrar, Straus, and Giroux, 1993); Michael Watts,

"Mapping Identities: Place, Space, and Community in an African City," in *Geography of Identity*, ed. P. Yaeger (Ann Arbor: University of Michigan Press, 1996), 59–97.

31. Benedict Anderson, *Imagined Communities: Reflections on the Origin and Spread of Nationalism*, 2d ed. (London and New York: Verso, 1991).

32. Chantal Mouffe, "Post-Marxism: Democracy and Identity," *Environment and Planning D: Society and Space* 13 (1995): 259–265.

33. UNHCR, *The State of the World's Refugees: In Search of Solutions*.

34. A now-famous fax, dated January 11, 1994, from Major General Roméo Dallaire to UN Headquarters reported that the genocide was being organized in Rwanda well before the extermination began. Kofi Annan, then under-secretary-general for peacekeeping operations, has been questioned about the fax (to which he responded) and about the lack of UN action during the 1994 massacre. Several commentators on UN inertia in Rwanda noted that the crisis emerged in "the shadow of Somalia"; Philip Gourevitch, "The Genocide Fax," *The New Yorker*, May 11, 1998, 42–46, at 46. After peacekeeping operations in Somalia went awry in 1993, the White House produced Presidential Decision Directive 25, which effectively precluded any U.S. involvement in UN peacekeeping missions that were not directly linked to U.S. interests.

35. Roger Winter, "A Year in Review," in *World Refugee Survey, 1998* (Washington, D.C.: Immigration and Refugee Service of America, 1998), 14–19, at 16.

36. John Eriksson, *The International Response to Conflict and Genocide: Lessons from the Rwanda Experience* (Published by the Steering Committee of the Joint Evaluation of Emergency Assistance to Rwanda, March 1996); Sue Lautze and John Hammond, "Coping with Crisis, Coping with Aid: Capacity Building, Coping Mechanisms, and Dependency, Linking Relief and Development," report prepared for the UN Department of Humanitarian Affairs (DHA), December 1996; Mark Frohardt, *Reintegration and Human Rights in Post-Genocide Rwanda*, report issued by the U.S. Committee for Refugees, November 1997; Joanna Macrae and Mark Bradbury, "Aid in the Twilight Zone: A Critical Analysis of Humanitarian-Development Aid Linkages in Situations of Chronic Instability," report for UNICEF, February 10, 1998; and Sue Lautze, Bruce Jones, and Mark Duffield, *Strategic Humanitarian Coordination in the Great Lakes Region, 1996–97: An Independent Study for the Inter-Agency Standing Committee* (New York: Office for the Coordination of Humanitarian Affairs, 1998).

37. Timothy Mitchell, *Colonising Egypt*, paperback ed. (Berkeley and Los Angeles: University of California Press, 1991); Michel Foucault, *Discipline and Punish: The Birth of the Prison* (New York: Vintage Books, 1977), 81–82; Haraway, "Situated Knowledges." I agree with Foucault that "rather

than worry about the central spirit, I believe we must attempt to study the myriad of bodies which are constituted as peripheral subjects as a result of the effects of power" (98); exploring the domain and discourse of the "central spirit," in this case the management of people out of place, informs the production and distribution of bodies, whether they be refugees or internally displaced persons. The language of human rights and international law, according to Foucault's logic, is precisely the wrong place to study the disciplinary and regulatory relations of power. Foucault maintains that the very idea of power-as-right conceals the fact of domination and all the effects of domination. Accordingly, chapter 5 focuses on the camps as a site of techniques and instruments that distribute displaced bodies in particular ways.

1. SCRIPTING HUMANITARIANISM

1. Chantal Mouffe, "Post-Marxism: Democracy and Identity," *Environment and Planning D: Society and Space* 13 (1995): 259–265.

2. UNHCR, *The State of the World's Refugees: In Search of Solutions* (New York and Oxford: Oxford University Press, 1995), 70.

3. Ed Schenkenberg van Mierop, "Protection of Civilians in Conflict," in *World in Crisis: The Politics of Survival at the End of the Twentieth Century*, ed. Médecins sans Frontières/Doctors without Borders (New York and London: Routledge, 1997), 1–15, at 2.

4. Humanitarian law consists of the four Geneva Conventions of 1949 and the two Additional Protocols of 1977 and is applicable to civilians within their own country during conflict. Though humanitarian law codifies standards of conduct during war, standards that include protection for internally displaced people, it applies only to persons displaced because of armed conflict. It does not cover intercommunal violence or other cases of internal disturbances that create internal displacement. See Francis M. Deng, "The International Protection of the Internally Displaced," *International Journal of Refugee Law*, special issue (Summer 1995): 74–86, at 82.

5. Articles 13.2 and 14 of the UN Declaration for Human Rights outline these rights. Article 15 states that "(1) Everyone has the right to a nationality; (2) No one shall be arbitrarily deprived of his nationality nor denied the right to change his nationality." See Annex II.3 in UNHCR, *The State of the World's Refugees: The Challenge of Protection* (Toronto: Penguin, 1993).

6. Interview, senior manager, UNHCR, Geneva, October 18, 1994.

7. UNHCR, *The State of the World's Refugees: In Search of Solutions*, 48 and 115.

8. UNHCR does have a highly placed NGO coordinator within the or-

ganization, but this does not guarantee that NGOs have meaningful input at strategic planning sessions in early stages of a situation that requires response. The important role of the Office for the Coordination of Humanitarian Affairs (OCHA) is recognized and discussed later in the book.

9. Aristide Zolberg, "Migrants and Refugees: A Historical Perspective," *Refugees* 91 (December 1992): 36–39.

10. James Hathaway, *The Status of Refugee Law* (Markham and Vancouver: Butterworths, 1991).

11. Louise Holborn, *Refugees: A Problem of Our Time. The Work of UNHCR 1951–72* (Metuchen, N.J.: Scarecrow Press, 1975), 153.

12. Guy Goodwin-Gill, cited in James Hathaway, "Reconceiving Refugee Law as Human Rights Protection," *Journal of Refugee Studies* 4, no. 2 (1991): 113–131, at 116.

13. Hannah Arendt, *The Origins of Totalitarianism* (Cleveland and New York: Meridian, 1958), 288.

14. Ibid., 286 and 296.

15. Deng, "The International Protection of the Internally Displaced."

16. Hathaway, *The Status of Refugee Law.*

17. Ibid., 8.

18. The convention entered into force April 22, 1954; this excerpt is taken from note 27, Article 1(A)(1), cited in Hathaway, *The Status of Refugee Law,* 6.

19. Fifteen years later, in 1966, two legally binding human rights instruments were created to protect, on the one hand, civil and political rights, and on the other, economic, social, and cultural rights. The International Covenant on Civil and Political Rights most closely expresses the emphasis of the 1951 convention. It ensures respect for citizens regardless of such characteristics as language, religion, sex, or political opinion, as well as "the right to liberty of movement and freedom"; see UNHCR, *The State of the World's Refugees: The Challenge of Protection,* 164. The Covenant on Economic, Social, and Cultural Rights includes provisions that are more applicable to the so-called developing world than to Western countries, such as the right to food, shelter, and basic medical and educational services. The first covenant applies to individuals; the second refers to particular groups of people.

20. Hathaway, *The Status of Refugee Law,* 6.

21. Ibid., 9.

22. Article 2 of the Statute of the Office of UNHCR (1950) in UNHCR, *The State of the World's Refugees: The Challenge of Protection,* 162.

23. Holborn, *Refugees: A Problem of Our Time.*

24. Guy S. Goodwin-Gill, "The Language of Protection," *International Journal of Refugee Law* 1, no. 1 (1989): 6–19, at 10 and 12.

25. Holborn, *Refugees: A Problem of Our Time*, 838.

26. Ibid., 440.

27. Ibid., 294.

28. Ibid., 837.

29. Statement of R. Rochefort of France, UN Doc A/CONF.2/SR.22 at 15, July 16, 1951; emphasis added; cited in Hathaway, *The Status of Refugee Law*, 7.

30. Hathaway, *The Status of Refugee Law*.

31. Simon Dalby and Gearóid Ó Tuathail, "The Critical Geopolitics Constellation: Problematizing Fusions of Geographical Knowledge and Power," *Political Geography* 15, nos. 6/7 (1996): 451–456; see 452 in particular.

32. Hathaway, *The Status of Refugee Law*, 93.

33. Cited in ibid., 18.

34. Ibid., 18–19; emphasis added.

35. Roxanne Lynn Doty discusses the implicit ordering and hierarchy of sovereignties in *Imperial Encounters* (Minneapolis: University of Minnesota Press, 1996). Through a sustained critique of the international relations (IR) discourse as it pertains to the positioning of the Third World state, she argues that "[o]ne cannot consider the positive sovereignty/negative sovereignty or real state/quasi state oppositions without implicitly resurrecting traces of prior historical oppositions" (155). The designation *Third World* in IR theory almost invariably attributes to regions, like Africa, an inherent lack of local skill and ability for self-goverment. Doty maintains that these superior/inferior classifications reinscribe practices of earlier imperial encounters.

36. As international law, the OAU convention is legally binding and applicable to all signatory states. The OAS definition is based on the Cartegena declaration, which, like the UN Declaration of Human Rights, is not binding. The ten states that signed the Cartegena declaration in 1984 basically agreed to a definition of refugees similar to that enacted by the OAU, though not quite as comprehensive in terms of protection.

37. Hathaway, *The Status of Refugee Law*, 21.

38. The Convention on the Rights of the Child and the Convention against Torture, as well as the Declaration of Human Rights and the two international covenants, are also relevant instruments.

39. Estimates of the number of refugees after the war range from 1.5 to 2 million; Holborn, *Refugees: A Problem of Our Time*; UNHCR, *The State of the World's Refugees: The Challenge of Protection*. In 1970 the figure was 2.5 million; in 1983, 11 million; and in 1993, 18.2 million refugees were counted.

40. UNHCR, *The State of the World's Refugees: In Search of Solutions*, 255.

41. Bill Frelick, "Assistance without Protection: Feed the Hungry, Clothe the Naked, and Watch Them Die," in *World Refugee Survey, 1997* (Washington D.C.: Immigration and Refugee Service of America, 1997).

42. UNHCR, *The State of the World's Refugees: In Search of Solutions.*

43. By January 1994, Canada had spent nearly Can$1 billion on military operations in the former Yugoslavia alone. This amounted to twenty times the funds allocated for humanitarian assistance. See Paul Koring, "Price of Peacekeeping Dwarfs Aid," *Globe and Mail* (Vancouver), January 4, 1994.

44. Overseas Development Institute (ODI), "The State of the International Humanitarian System," briefing paper, 1998 (1) March, 2; "Background Notes: United Nations 9/97" at U.S. Department of State homepage, <http://www.state.gov/www/background_notes/united_nations_0997_bgn.html>.

45. Rosemary Rogers and Emily Copeland, *Forced Migration: Policy Issues in the Post–Cold War World* (Medford, Mass.: Tufts University Press, 1993).

46. Jennifer Hyndman, "International Responses to Human Displacement: Neo-Liberalism and Post–Cold War Geopolitics," *Refuge* 15, no. 3 (June 1996): 5–9.

47. Bill Frelick, "Preventing Refugee Flows: Protection or Peril," in *World Refugee Survey, 1993* (Washington, D.C.: U.S. Committee for Refugees, 1993).

48. UNHCR, *Report of the UNHCR Working Group on International Protection* (Geneva, July 6, 1992).

49. Senior manager, UNHCR, Geneva, interview, October 24, 1994.

50. Ibid.

51. Ibid.

52. This presents a third teleology; UNHCR assists because it can; it can because it's an assistance organization.

53. UNHCR, *UNHCR's Operational Experience with Internally Displaced Persons* (Geneva, 1994), excerpt from the foreword.

54. In the late 1980s, the legitimacy of changes proposed in UNHCR's mandate was challenged by donor governments. Jean-Pierre Hocké became high commissioner for refugees in January 1986; during his tenure he repositioned the agency to exploit the end of the Cold War and openly challenged the conventional approach to protection. Hocké argued that the 1951 convention was outdated and that the vast majority of contemporary refugees do not correspond to the convention definition. Instead, he maintained that these displaced persons were victims of violence, belonging to wider categories of people affected by armed conflict or other more generalized forms of violence or danger. Hocké contended that protection was

not a "legalistic, doctrinaire or static approach" and that it required comprehensive approaches and solutions to refugee crises, the best of which was voluntary repatriation. In making this claim, he was accused of downgrading protection and gambling with the protection of refugees: "It was definitely not a gamble with the protection function of the UNHCR. I can understand, even if I disagree, that some feel that way—those who look statically at the mandate, convention and definition. I came in and said that, if we do that, we become a museum. There were risks in moving people back, but those risks were carefully identified and taken into account." Hocké was forced to resign in 1989. See Lawyers Committee for Human Rights, *The UNHCR at Forty: Refugee Protection at the Crossroads* (New York: Lawyers Committee for Human Rights, 1991), 90, 54.

55. Barbara Demick, "Thousands of Refugees Evacuate Srebrenica after Bosnian Serbs Invade," *Philadelphia Inquirer,* July 11, 1995.

56. Neil Smith and Cindy Katz, "Grounding Metaphor: Towards a Spatialized Politics," in *Place and Politics of Identity,* ed. M. Keith and S. Pile (London: Routledge, 1993), 67–83, at 75.

57. Dalby and Ó Tuathail, "The Critical Geopolitics Constellation," 452.

58. UNHCR, *Note on International Protection,* EXCOM 45th session, A/AC.96/830, 1994, para. 64, p. 29; emphasis in original.

59. As one might expect, not all prima facie refugees stay in the camps. This creates the issue of an illegal refugee population in the urban areas of Nairobi and Mombasa.

60. John Rogge, "The Challenges of Changing Dimensions among the South's Refugees: Illustrations from Somalia," *International Journal of Refugee Law* 5, no. 1 (1993): 12–30, at 24.

61. Ibid.

62. UNHCR, *Country Operations Plan: Kenya* (Nairobi, 1994), 1.

63. The concept of imperial encounter is used in the sense of Roxanne Lynn Doty's book of the same name; see Doty, *Imperial Encounters.*

64. Interview with senior NGO official, January 1995.

65. Gloria Anzaldúa, *Borderlands: The New Mestiza* (San Francisco: Spinsters/Aunt Lute Press, 1987); Angelika Bammer, "Introduction," in *Displacements: Cultural Identities in Question,* ed. A. Bammer (Bloomington and Indianapolis: Indiana University Press, 1994), xi–xx; Caren Kaplan, "The Politics of Location," in *Scattered Hegemonies: Postmodernity and Transnational Feminist Practices,* ed. I. Grewal and C. Kaplan (Minneapolis: University of Minnesota Press, 1994), 137–152; Trinh T. Minh-ha, "Other Than Myself/My Other Self," in *Travellers' Tales: Narratives of Home and Displacement,* ed. G. Robertson, M. Mash, L. Tickner, J. Bird, B. Curtis, and T. Putnam (New York and London: Routledge, 1994), 9–26.

2. BORDER CROSSINGS

1. Donna Haraway, "Cyborgs and Symbionts: Living Toge[...]
New World Order," foreword to *The Cyborg Handbook*, ed. Chris [...]
Gray (New York and London: Routledge, 1995), xi–xx.

2. Doreen Massey, "Power-Geometry and a Progressive Sense of Place,"
in *Mapping the Futures: Local Cultures, Global Change,* ed. J. Bird, B. Curtis, T. Putnam, G. Robertson, and L. Tickner (New York: Routledge, 1993),
59–69, at 61.

3. Stuart Corbridge and Nigel Thrift, "Money, Power, and Space: Introduction and Overview,"in *Money, Power, Space,* ed. S. Corbridge, R. Martin, and N. Thrift (Oxford and Cambridge, Mass.: Blackwell, 1994), 1–26.

4. Ibid.

5. Caren Kaplan, "The Politics of Location," in *Scattered Hegemonies: Postmodernity and Transnational Feminist Practices,* ed. I. Grewal and
C. Kaplan (Minneapolis: University of Minnesota Press, 1994), 137–152,
at 148.

6. Caren Kaplan, "A World without Boundaries," *Social Text* 43 (Fall
1995): 45–66, at 45.

7. UNHCR, *The State of the World's Refugees: In Search of Solutions*
(New York and Oxford: Oxford University Press, 1995).

8. James Clifford, "Diasporas," *Cultural Anthropology* 9, no. 3 (1994):
302–338; "Travelling Cultures," in *Cultural Studies,* ed. L. Grossberg,
C. Nelson, and P. Treichler (New York: Routledge, 1992), 96–116; *The
Predicament of Culture* (Cambridge, Mass.: Harvard University Press,
1988); "Partial Truths," in *Writing Culture: The Poetics and Politics of
Ethnography,* ed. J. Clifford and G. E. Marcus (Berkeley and Los Angeles:
University of California Press, 1986), 1–26. See also Arjun Appadurai,
"Sovereignty without Territoriality: Notes for a Postnational Geography,"
in *Geography of Identity,* ed. P. Yaeger (Ann Arbor: University of Michigan
Press, 1996), 40–58; "Global Ethnoscapes," in *Recapturing Anthropology,*
ed. R. G. Fox (Sante Fe, N.M.: School for American Research, 1991),
191–211.

9. Appadurai, "Global Ethnoscapes," 192.

10. Appadurai, "Sovereignty without Territoriality," 48–49.

11. Clifford, "Partial Truths," 22.

12. Clifford, "Diasporas," 304.

13. David Scott, "Colonial Governmentality," *Social Text* 43 (Fall
1995): 191–220, at 193; emphasis in original.

14. Trinh T. Minh-ha, "Other Than Myself/My Other Self," in *Travellers' Tales: Narratives of Home and Displacement,* ed. G. Robertson,
M. Mash, L. Tickner, J. Bird, B. Curtis, and T. Putnam (New York and London: Routledge, 1994), 9–26, at 23.

15. Ibid., 12.

16. Trinh T. Minh-ha, "Cotton and Iron," in *Out There: Marginalization and Contemporary Cultures,* ed. R. Ferguson, M. Gever, Trinh T. Minh-ha, and C. West (New York: New Museum of Contemporary Art, 1990), 327–336, at 333.

17. Caren Kaplan, *Questions of Travel: Postmodern Discourses of Displacement* (Durham, N.C.: Duke University Press, 1996).

18. Ibid., 105.

19. Ibid., 99.

20. Katharyne Mitchell, "Multiculturalism, or the United Colors of Capitalism?" *Antipode* 25 (1993): 263–294. Caren Kaplan takes on transnational economic relations and cultural politics together in her discussion of Body Shop's marketing approach; see Kaplan, "A World without Boundaries."

21. Rob Wilson and Wimal Dissanayake, "Introduction: Tracking the Global/Local," in *Global/Local: Cultural Production and the Transnational Imaginary,* ed. Rob Wilson and Wimal Dissanayake (Durham, N.C.: Duke University Press, 1996), 1–18; emphasis in original. The authors make the important point that regional identities and "region-states" are increasingly overriding national borders and conventional territorial forms "to create special economic zones of uneven development and transcultural hybridity" (2).

22. UNHCR, *State of the World's Refugees: In Search of Solutions.* "Persons of concern," in this context, include internally displaced persons and people living in refugee-like conditions but who have no official status.

23. This is not to say that refugees should simply be encouraged to leave to resettle elsewhere. It should be noted, however, that many refugees pinned hopes of a better life on the prospect of moving to another country, particularly in the United States, Canada, or Australia.

24. Nigel Thrift, "On the Social and Cultural Determinants of International Financial Centres: The Case of the City of London," in *Money, Power, Space,* ed. S. Corbridge, R. Martin, and N. Thrift (Oxford and Cambridge, Mass.: Blackwell, 1994), 327–355.

25. U.S. Committee for Refugees, *World Refugee Survey, 1995* (Washington, D.C.: Immigration and Refugee Service of America, 1995).

26. Lila Sarick, "Swiss Banks to Assist Holocaust Heirs," *Globe and Mail* (Vancouver), December 30, 1995.

27. See "Tons of Gold from Nazis Go to Fund for Survivors," *New York Times,* July 1, 1998. The *New York Times* published the list of those whose accounts have been dormant since World War II, including the names of those holding power of attorney over some of the accounts. The list was also posted at <http://www.dormantaccounts.ch>.

28. Reuters, "Tons of Gold from Nazis Go to Fund for Survivors," *New*

York Times, July 1, 1998; David Sanger, "Swiss Banks Make Offer on Nazi Loot," *New York Times,* June 20, 1998; and Ernst Abegg, "Swiss Banks Offer to Settle Claims," *Arizona Republic,* June 20, 1998.

29. Joseph Fried, "Swiss Banks Agree to Pay Holocaust Survivors $1.25 Billion," *New York Times,* August 13, 1998.

30. Benedict Anderson, *Imagined Communities: Reflections on the Origin and Spread of Nationalism,* 2d ed. (London and New York: Verso, 1991).

31. Abdi Samatar provides an overview of precolonial (precapitalist) Somali society, its pastoral economy, and the significance of geography in social organization. Clan elders mediated conflicts within and between clans and organized work among clan members for subsistence production. Samatar points out that the clan forum was exclusively male; see Abdi Samatar, "Structural Adjustment as Development Strategy: Bananas, Boom, and Poverty in Somalia," *Economic Geography* 69, no. 1 (1993): 25–43.

32. Otunnu Ogenga, "Factors Affecting the Treatment of Kenyan-Somalis and Somali Refugees in Kenya: A Historical Overview," *Refuge* 12, no. 5 (December 1992): 21–25.

33. African Rights, "Humanitarianism Unbound? Current Dilemmas Facing Multi-Mandate Relief Operations in Political Emergencies" (discussion paper no. 5, London, 1993).

34. Samuel Makinda, *Seeking Peace from Chaos: Humanitarian Intervention in Somalia* (Boulder, Colo., and London: Lynne Rienner, 1993).

35. African Rights, "Humanitarianism Unbound?"

36. IRBD (Immigration and Refugee Board Documentation Centre), Ottawa; response to information request no. KEN 3679, February 1, 1990.

37. Ogenga, "Factors Affecting the Treatment of Kenyan-Somalis and Somali Refugees in Kenya."

38. Charles Njonjo, cited in ibid.

39. Ogenga, "Factors Affecting the Treatment of Kenyan-Somalis and Somali Refugees in Kenya."

40. Makinda, *Seeking Peace from Chaos,* 57.

41. Ibid., 23.

42. Lawyers Committee for Human Rights, *The UNHCR at Forty: Refugee Protection at the Crossroads* (New York: Lawyers Committee for Human Rights, 1991).

43. Arif Dirlik interrogates the notion of "postcolonial" by asking, "[W]hen exactly . . . does the 'postcolonial' begin?" He argues that "postcolonial" has replaced "Third World," abolishing the spatial distinctions of core and periphery. This change also removes the locational markers of the Third World designation, rendering "postcolonial" discursive and not structural. This cultural emphasis of postcolonial, he contends, obfuscates the material relations of global capitalism. Like Dirlik, Ella Shohat and Robert

Stam argue against the use of the term "postcolonial" and for the concept of "postindependence." Their criticism of "postcolonial" is based upon the claim that it depoliticizes the contemporary project of decolonization in postindependence states through deterritorialization, the absence of a politics of location, and the implication that colonial relationships have been extinguished: "While 'colonialism' and 'neocolonialism' imply both oppression and the possibility of resistance, 'postcolonial' posits no clear domination and calls for no clear opposition" (39). While I agree that the politics of decolonization are on-going, I part company with the authors' dismissal of postcolonial theory and criticism as a "fragile instrument for critiquing the unequal distribution of global power and resources" in using such tools in this essay. Rather than arguing either/or, a transnational geopolitics of mobility that incorporates postcolonial theory and its bearing on material, historical relations of power across space enhances their analysis. See Arif Dirlik, "The Postcolonial Aura: Third World Criticism in the Age of Global Capitalism," *Critical Inquiry* 20 (Winter 1994): 328–356; and Ella Shohat and Robert Stam, *Unthinking Eurocentrism: Multiculturalism and the Media* (New York and London: Routledge, 1994). For a more cogent analysis of the postcolonial moment, see Bruce Willems-Braun, "Buried Epistemologies: The Politics of Nature in (Post)colonial British Columbia," *Annals of the Association of American Geographers* 87 no. 1 (1997): 3–31.

44. Colonialism in Kenya transformed patterns of land ownership, particularly in the Rift Valley. Precolonial land tenure in the area was dominated mainly by Masai and Kalenjin peoples, who were subsequently dispossessed of their land when British settlers took to homesteading in the colony. In this region, the British hired mostly Gikuyu people as workers, excluding the previous inhabitants from jobs as well as land. When colonialism formally ended, most of the settlers sold their land to Gikuyus. Though this thumbnail sketch is hardly an analysis of land ownership, it does point to some of the simmering cultural politics and conflict among the Gikuyu, Kalenjin, and Masai groups today.

45. Associated Press, November 13, 1989 (source: UNHCR Refinfo database).

46. *Washington Post,* December 27, 1989 (source: UNHCR Refinfo database).

47. Africa Watch, New York, November 17, 1989 (source: UNHCR Refinfo database).

48. Ibid., 10–11.

49. Ogenga, "Factors Affecting the Treatment of Kenyan-Somalis and Somali Refugees in Kenya."

50. *Africa Events* (London, September 1992) (source UNHCR Refinfo database), 8.

51. Rosemary Rogers and Emily Copeland, *Forced Migration: Policy Issues in the Post–Cold War World* (Medford, Mass.: Tufts University Press, 1993).

52. Netherlands Development Corporation, *Humanitarian Aid to Somalia, Evaluation Report 1994* (The Hague, 1994); U.S. Committee for Refugees, *World Refugee Survey, 1998* (Washington, D.C.: Immigration and Refugee Service of America, 1998), 73.

53. Netherlands Development Corporation, "Humanitarian Aid to Somalia, Evaluation Report 1994."

54. Moi has made such ultimatums on a regular basis; the most recent was in September 1997, when he ordered UNHCR to remove all refugees by the end of the month; see U.S. Committee for Refugees, *World Refugee Survey, 1998* (Washington, D.C.: Immigration and Refugee Service of America, 1998), 73.

55. Ibid.

56. UNHCR, *The State of the World's Refugees: The Challenge of Protection* (Toronto: Penguin, 1993).

57. Makinda, *Seeking Peace from Chaos.*

58. Shohat and Stam, *Unthinking Eurocentrism*, 16.

59. UNHCR, *The State of the World's Refugees: The Challenge of Protection.*

60. This office was located within the U.S. embassy, which was bombed on August 7, 1998.

61. Interview with officer in charge, INS, Nairobi, January 1995.

62. UNHCR, *The State of the World's Refugees: In Search of Solutions.*

63. Chantal Mouffe, "Post-Marxism: Democracy and Identity," *Environment and Planning D: Society and Space* 13 (1995): 259–265; "For a Politics of Nomadic Identity" in *Travellers' Tales: Narratives of Home and Displacement*, ed. G. Robertson, M. Mash, L. Tickner, J. Bird, B. Curtis, and T. Putnam (New York and London: Routledge, 1994), 105–113.

64. Haraway, "Cyborgs and Symbionts," xix.

3. MANAGING DIFFERENCE

1. Alison Crosby, Wenona Giles, and Maja Korac, "Women in Conflict Zones Network" (discussion paper no. 1, draft, York University, June 18, 1996), 3.

2. UNHCR, *The State of the World's Refugees: The Challenge of Protection* (Toronto: Penguin, 1993), 22.

3. Marianne Marchand and Jane Parpart, "Exploding the Canon: An Introduction/Conclusion," in *Feminism/Postmodernism/Development*, ed. M. Marchand and J. Parpart (New York and London: Routledge, 1995), 1–22; Arturo Escobar, *Encountering Development: The Making and Unmaking of the Third World* (Princeton: Princeton University Press, 1995).

4. Liisa Malkki, "National Geographic: The Rooting of Peoples and the Territorialization of National Identity among Scholars and Refugees," *Cultural Anthropology* 7, no. 1 (February 1992): 24–43, at 42.

5. Homi Bhabha, cited in Malkki, "National Geographic," 60; emphasis in original.

6. Bell hooks, "Representing Whiteness in the Black Imagination," in *Cultural Studies*, ed. L. Grossberg, C. Nelson, and P. Treichler (New York and London: Routledge, 1992), 338–346, at 339.

7. Cynthia Cockburn, "Research on Women in Conflict Zones: Questions of Method" (paper presented at the Women in Conflict Zones Network Meeting, Toronto, November 16, 1996).

8. Cynthia Cockburn, *The Space between Us: Negotiating Gender and National Identities in Conflict* (London: Zed Books, 1998).

9. Matthew Sparke, *Negotiating Nation-States: North American Geographies of Culture and Capitalism* (Minneapolis: University of Minnesota Press, forthcoming).

10. Derek Gregory, "Humanistic Geography," in *The Dictionary of Human Geography*, 3rd ed., ed. R. J. Johnston, D. Gregory, and D. M. Smith (Oxford: Blackwell, 1994), 263–266, at 265.

11. Escobar, *Encountering Development*.

12. Robert Young, *Colonial Desire: Hybridity in Theory, Culture, and Race* (New York and London: Routledge, 1995), 54.

13. The first instance of the word "miscegenation" listed in the Oxford English Dictionary is dated 1864. It alluded to the polygenist position of distinct races and the value of racial purity in contrast to mixed race; see Young, *Colonial Desire*.

14. Young, *Colonial Desire*, 54.

15. Cited in Donna Haraway, "Remodeling the Human Way of Life," in *Primate Visions* (New York and London: Routledge, 1989), 186–206, at 198.

16. Ibid., 199.

17. Ibid., 201.

18. Margaret Galey, "Women Find a Place," in *Women, Politics, and the United Nations*, ed. A. Winslow (Westport, Conn.: Greenwood Press, 1995), 11–27; Virginia Allan, Margaret Galey, and Mildred Persinger, "World Conference of International Women's Year," in *Women, Politics, and the United Nations*, ed. Winslow, 29–44.

19. Anne Winslow, "Specialized Agencies and the World Bank," in

Women, Politics, and the United Nations, ed. Winslow; Hilkka Pietilä and Jeanne Vickers, *Making Women Matter: The Role of the United Nations* (London and Atlantic Highlands, N.J.: Zed Books, 1996).

20. Haraway, *Primate Visions,* 286.

21. Pietilä and Vickers, *Making Women Matter.*

22. For a comprehensive review of UNHCR policy, Executive Committee conclusions, and legal protocols regarding women, see *Refugee Survey Quarterly,* "Special Issue on Refugee Women," vol. 14 (Summer 1995), published by UNHCR, Geneva.

23. UNHCR, *Note on Certain Aspects of Sexual Violence against Refugee Women,* Executive Committee, A/AC.96/822 (October 12, 1993); *Making the Linkages: Protection and Assistance Policy and Programming to Benefit Refugee Women,* Joint Meeting of Sub-Committees of Administration and Financial Matters and of the Whole on International Protection. Document EC/1993/SC.2/crp.16 (May, 1993).

24. In 1993, the UN Relief and Rehabilitation Programme for Somalia outlined specific objectives as well as "funding requests by sector" to finance the initiative. The sectors requiring funding noted in table 2 of the document include, among others, civil administration, food security, logistics, potable water, education, health and nutrition, and *Somali women.* While it is true that the document was partly designed to appeal to potential funders, the separation of women from the other activities noted here also contradicts UNHCR's mainstreaming policy; see UN General Assembly, *United Nations Relief and Rehabilitation Programme for Somalia: Covering the Period 1 March–31 December 1993* (March 11, 1993).

25. UNHCR, *Country Operations Plan: Kenya* (Nairobi, October 1994); Mary Anderson, Ann Brazeau, and Catherine Overholt, *A Framework for People-Oriented Planning in Refugee Situations Taking Account of Women, Men, and Children: A Practical Planning Tool for Refugee Workers* (Geneva, UNHCR, December 1992). See also UNHCR, *Guidelines on the Protection of Refugee Women* (Geneva, July 1991).

26. Personal interview with senior NGO staff member, October 28, 1994.

27. My own feminist politics focus on the unequal relations of power across relations of culture, sexuality, nationality, class, and other differences as well as gender and emphasize the *construction* of subordinate categories and identities. They are also attentive to cultural location and material inequalities. The difference between my position and that of UNHCR is that UNHCR policy applies across cultures unproblematically. Cultural difference is subsumed within a single framework of emergency planning.

28. Anderson, Brazeau, and Overholt, *A Framework for People-Oriented Planning*; see also UNHCR, *Guidelines on the Protection of Refugee Women.*

29. UNHCR, *The State of the World's Refugees: The Challenge of Protection*.

30. Marchand and Parpart, "Exploding the Canon."

31. Jane Parpart, "Post-Modernism, Gender, and Development," in *Power of Development*, ed. J. Crush (London: Routledge, 1995), 253–265.

32. Escobar, *Encountering Development*, 106.

33. Mitu Hirshman, "Women and Development: A Critique," in *Feminism/Postmodernism/Development*, ed. M. Marchand and J. Parpart (New York and London: Routledge, 1995), 42–55, at 44.

34. Escobar, *Encountering Development*, 108.

35. Smith, cited in Escobar, *Encountering Development*, 109.

36. Dorothy Smith, *Texts, Facts, and Femininity: Exploring the Relations of Ruling* (New York and London: Routledge, 1993), 12.

37. Saskia Sassen, *Losing Control? Sovereignty in an Age of Globalization* (New York: Columbia University Press, 1996).

38. Inderpal Grewal, "Autobiographical Subjects, Diasporic Locations," in *Scattered Hegemonies*, ed. Grewal and Kaplan, 231–254; see 243–244.

39. See Ella Shohat and Robert Stam, *Unthinking Eurocentrism: Multiculturalism and the Media* (New York and London: Routledge, 1994).

40. Norman Long, "From Paradigm Lost to Paradigm Regained? The Case for Actor-Oriented Sociology of Development," in *Battlefields of Knowledge: The Interlocking of Theory and Practice in Social Research and Development*, ed. N. Long and A. Long (London and New York: Routledge, 1992), 16–43, at 35.

41. UNHCR, *Refugee Women Victims of Violence: A Special Project by UNHCR* (proposal) (Nairobi, October 1993).

42. Interview, UNHCR senior staff member, October 25, 1994; UNHCR, *UNHCR Policy on Refugee Women*.

43. Parpart, "Post-Modernism, Gender, and Development," 254.

44. I borrow here from Teresa de Lauretis's notion of the body as the site of material inscription of power; Teresa de Lauretis, "Eccentric Subjects: Feminist Theory and Historical Consciousness," *Feminist Studies* 16, no. 1 (1990): 115–150.

45. Maria Lugones, cited in Caren Kaplan, "The Politics of Location as Transnational Feminist Critical Practice," in *Scattered Hegemonies*, ed. Grewal and Kaplan, 137–152, at 150.

46. The financing of the WVV project raises other political questions. The initial estimated cost for WVV, as a three-month project, was U.S.$1,119,401, of which more than half was to be spent on improving the security of the camps. Police escorts during refugees' firewood collection, extensive fencing around residential sections of the camp to prevent bandit access, and assistance to Kenyan police by providing communication equip-

ment and vehicle maintenance were among the measures proposed to achieve this goal; see UNHCR, *Refugee Women Victims of Violence*; The Canadian International Development Agency (CIDA), a major funder of the project, issued a mission report assessing the project's achievements late in 1994; see CIDA, *Mission Report on UNHCR Project WVV in Kenya* (International Humanitarian Assistance Division, August 28– September 5, 1994). Canada alone had contributed Can$3.25 million, which represented 36 percent of project funds. Though the project was assessed as having "an important impact," the mission report observed that its funds were used to fill major gaps in general program budgets. The CIDA report noted that major project expenditures did not appear to be specific to women. One of the main WVV budget items was the construction of "live fencing." Live thorn bushes are transplanted around the perimeter of camp compounds as a means of keeping bandits and potential assailants out. As of September 1994, forty-three kilometers of fencing had been completed; another fifty-four kilometers remained to be constructed; see UNHCR, *Kenya, Southern Somalia* (information bulletin, Nairobi, September 1994). Economically, the WVV project has had a number of positive spin-off effects for refugee laborers, contract construction workers, traders, and police officers. Some findings suggest that some WVV funds have been misdirected and used to pay for items that are not part of the project's mandate. Sadly, based on the CIDA audit and its criticisms, it appears that the WVV project proved more useful for UN administrators and local police, for whom new vehicles were provided, than for the refugees affected by violence in the camps.

47. Interview, UNHCR junior staff member, Geneva, October 25, 1994.

48. Nancy Fraser, *Unruly Practices* (Minneapolis: University of Minnesota Press, 1989), 157.

49. Interview, lawyer from FIDA, Dadaab, November 22, 1994.

50. UNHCR, *Voluntary Repatriation: International Protection* (handbook; Geneva, 1996).

51. Inderpal Grewal and Caren Kaplan, "Introduction: Transnational Feminist Practices and Questions of Postmodernity," in *Scattered Hegemonies,* ed. Grewal and Kaplan, 1–33.

52. Seteney Shami, "Transnationalism and Refugee Studies: Rethinking Forced Migration and Identity in the Middle East," *Journal of Refugee Studies* 9, no. 1 (1996): 3–26.

53. Chandra Talpade Mohanty, "Under Western Eyes," in *Third World Women and the Politics of Feminism,* ed. Chandra Talpade Mohanty, Ann Russo, and Lourdes Torres (Bloomington and Indianapolis: University of Indiana Press, 1991); Chantal Mouffe, "Post-Marxism: Democracy and Identity," *Environment and Planning D: Society and Space* 13 (1995):

259–265, and "Feminism, Citizenship, and Radical Democratic Politics," in *Feminists Theorize the Political,* ed. J. Butler and J. Scott (New York and London: Routledge, 1992), 369–384.

54. Katharyne Mitchell, "Different Diasporas and the Hype of Hybridity," *Environment and Planning D: Society and Space* 15, no. 5 (1997): 533–554.

55. UNHCR, *The State of the World's Refugees: A Humanitarian Agenda* (Oxford and New York: Oxford University Press, 1997), 67.

4. IN THE FIELD

1. The Kenyan government maintains a hostile policy toward almost all refugees, who are required to live in camps and thus prohibited from living in urban areas. The location of the camps in border areas is decided by the Kenyan government, not UNHCR.

2. U.S. Committee for Refugees, *World Refugee Survey, 1995* (Washington, D.C.: Immigration and Refugee Service of America, 1995), 61.

3. Netherlands Development Corporation, *Humanitarian Aid to Somalia, Evaluation Report 1994* (The Hague, 1994).

4. See Akhil Gupta and James Ferguson, "Beyond 'Culture': Space, Identity, and the Politics of Difference" *Cultural Anthropology* 7, no. 1 (February 1992): 6–23.

5. Henrietta L. Moore, *A Passion for Difference* (Bloomington and Indianapolis: Indiana University Press, 1994), 106.

6. Gillian Rose, *Feminism and Geography: The Limits of Geographical Knowledge* (Minneapolis: University of Minnesota Press, 1993).

7. Cindy Katz, "Playing the Field: Questions of Fieldwork in Geography," *Professional Geographer* 46, no. 1 (February 1994): 67–72, at 72.

8. Ibid., 68.

9. Gillian Rose, *Feminism and Geography;* Linda McDowell, "Multiple Voices: Speaking from Inside and Outside the Project," *Antipode* 24, no. 1 (1992): 218–237.

10. Caren Kaplan, "'A World without Boundaries': The Body Shop's Trans/national Geographics," *Social Text* 43 (Fall 1995): 45–66.

11. Moore, *A Passion for Difference.* Moore's distinction between local and supralocal is useful in drawing out some of these different locations from which connections can be made. At the same time, it risks reinscribing the binary logic of inside/outside positioning. As long as local and supralocal discourses are multiple in their connections and contexts, the global/local opposition can be avoided.

12. Tejaswini Niranjana, *Siting Translation: History, Post-Structuralism,*

and the Colonial Context (Berkeley and Los Angeles: University of California Press, 1992).

13. Sherene Razack, "The Perils of Storytelling for Refugee Women," in *Development and Diaspora: The Gender Relations of Refugee Experience,* ed. W. Giles, H. Moussa, and P. Van Esterik (Dundas, Ontario: Artemis, 1996), 271–289.

14. See Donna Haraway, *Simians, Cyborgs, and Women: The Reinvention of Nature* (New York: Routledge, 1991).

15. Helene Moussa, *Storm and Sanctuary: The Journey of Ethiopian and Eritrean Refugee Women* (Dundas, Ontario: Artemis, 1993). Helene Moussa's research with Eritrean and Ethiopian refugees addresses the "politics of research" and provided important background for my interviews with refugees. Her positioning as a researcher, however, differs significantly from my own. Her project of tracing the journeys of sixteen Eritrean and Ethiopian women from their homes in the Horn of Africa to Canada focuses on the experience of the women as refugees rather than on UNHCR's strategies to manage refugee populations.

16. The exception to this may be Al-Haramein, whose staff members speak Arabic, from which many Somali words are derived. However, only a few (male) elders and educated Somalis are conversant in Arabic.

17. Norma Alarcón, "Traddutora, Traditora: A Paradigmatic Figure of Chicana Feminism," in *Scattered Hegemonies: Postmodernity and Transnational Feminist Practices,* ed. I. Grewal and C. Kaplan (Minneapolis: University of Minnesota Press, 1994), 113.

18. The articles included in *Scattered Hegemonies,* ed. Grewal and Kaplan, were the primary source of provocation at that time. The work of Niranjana's *Siting Translation* is also helpful here.

19. Mikhail Bakhtin, *The Dialogical Imagination: Four Essays,* trans. Caryl Emerson and Michael Holquist, ed. Michael Holquist (Austin: University of Texas Press, 1981), 293–294; cited in Alarcón, "Traddutora, Traditora," 119.

20. Caren Kaplan, "A World without Boundaries," 61.

21. UNHCR, *Guidelines on the Protection of Refugee Women* (Geneva, July 1991), 47.

22. Ibid., 48.

23. Ibid., 19.

24. Caren Kaplan, "A World without Boundaries," 60; emphasis in original.

25. These maps are adapted directly from the blueprints of UNHCR plans of the three camps; their suggestion of a neat orderliness is not completely accurate. They are simple reproductions, neither endorsing nor critically representing the camps.

26. Interview, UNHCR staff member, Nairobi, November 16, 1994.

27. The implication of permanent buildings is that these camps will be adminstered at this location for some time to come.

28. Interview, UNHCR staff member, Nairobi, November 16, 1994.

29. Robert Cowen and Stephen Odundo Nyangoma, *Refugee Survey Analysis*, CARE Kenya Refugee Assistance Programme (Nairobi, July 1994).

30. Systems of security are also culturally coded, as earlier examples have attempted to illustrate. Nonetheless, UNHCR, with the support of the Kenyan police in the camps, has the authority to practice security with more force than the refugees. One UNHCR field officer, who wears military garb on the days he works in the refugee camps, said, "I have to strike a balance between planning and *nomadisme sauvage* [wild nomadism]."

31. As noted, more than 40 percent of families in the camps were recorded as "female-headed." This designation is potentially misleading because one man may have more than one wife and support more than one household without always being present. My interviews and meetings with refugees in the camps were largely held at their homes. Rarely did I encounter men at home during the day.

32. UNHCR, *The State of the World's Refugees: In Search of Solutions* (Oxford and New York: Oxford University Press, 1995), 60.

33. Isabel Dyck, "Space, Time, and Renegotiating Motherhood: An Exploration of the Domestic Workplace," *Environment and Planning D: Society and Space* 8 (1990). See also Suzanne Mackenzie, "Restructuring the Relations of Work and Life: Women as Environmental Actors, Feminism as Geographical Analysis," in *Remaking Human Geography*, ed. A. Kobayashi and S. Mackenzie (London: Unwin Hyman, 1989), 40–61, and Geraldine Pratt and Susan Hanson, "Women and Work across the Life Course: Moving beyond Essentialism," in *Full Circles: Geographies of Women over the Life Course*, ed. C. Katz and J. Monk (New York: Routledge, 1993), 27–54. Doreen Massey's work on the politics of mobility also serves as corrective to any assumption of absolute space or equality of movement among people; see her "Power-Geometry and a Progressive Sense of Place," in *Mapping the Futures: Local Cultures, Global Change*, ed. J. Bird, B. Curtis, T. Putnam, G. Robertson, and L. Tickner (New York: Routledge, 1993), 59–69.

34. Trinh T. Minh-ha, *Woman, Native, Other* (Bloomington and Indianapolis: Indiana University Press, 1989), 28.

35. To calculate the amount of credit made available on a rotating basis, one might make the following assumptions: each of the five women has a family of five. Each person is allotted 0.5 kg of grain per day, so that a fifteen-day distribution would include 7.5 kg per person and 37.5 kg per family. If each woman contributed one-fifth of her total grain allocation (7.5 kg), the amount collected would equal 37.5 kg. The price of wheat

flour, the most common grain staple, ranged from 3 to 5 Kenyan shillings (KSh) per kilo. This represents a total credit each time of between KSh 112.5 and KSh 187.5, the equivalent of U.S.$2 to U.S.$3.40.

36. Private correspondence from UNHCR staff in Nairobi and Dadaab, June 7, 1996.

37. UNHCR, *The State of the World's Refugees: In Search of Solutions.*

38. In Malawi, the wood consumed by refugees was considerable: some 20,000 hectares of forest per year. In Nepal, Bhutanese refugees used 400 kilos per capita of fuelwood per year. UNHCR provided kerosene stoves and fuel in this case; see UNHCR, *The State of the World's Refugees: In Search of Solutions.* Though relatively expensive fuel alternatives have been employed, major changes in the refugee food basket—which is a significant source of the problem—have not been entertained. UNHCR has a number of nutritionists on staff to ensure that foodstuffs provide sufficient nourishment, but the agency relies on the UN World Food Program (WFP) to collect donations for the camps.

39. Kamala Visweswaran, *Fictions of Feminist Ethnography* (London: Routledge, 1993), 81.

40. UNHCR, *Guidelines on the Protection of Refugee Women,* 48.

41. Meridel Le Sueur, "The Ancient People and the Newly Come," cited in Jane Smiley, *A Thousand Acres* (New York: Fawcett Columbine, 1991).

42. This debate is introduced by Bill Ashcroft, Gareth Griffiths, and Helen Tiffin, eds., *The Post-Colonial Studies Reader* (London and New York: Routledge, 1995), 9.

43. Robert Young, *White Mythologies: Writing History and the West* (New York: Routledge, 1990), 144.

44. Handsets do fall into the hands of bandits and other unauthorized users. One UNHCR handset was stolen during my stay, and was used (I believe) to track a UNHCR vehicle, which was then hijacked and stolen early one morning. UNHCR vehicles are especially valuable, as they contain two sets of radios: one to communicate with people in close proximity on handsets (10 kilometers is roughly their limit), and another to communicate over longer distances on established radio frequencies between Nairobi and other camps.

45. Edward Said, *Culture and Imperialism* (New York: Knopf, 1993), 64.

46. Trinh T. Minh-ha, *Woman, Native, Other,* 54. Here I have not named the women I have interviewed. For reasons of confidentiality and trust, I did not ask them to disclose their names.

47. Caren Kaplan, "A World without Boundaries," 48.

48. Roxanne Lynn Doty analyzes the separation of Europeans and Africans in Kenya during the period of British colonialism: "The separation

of Africans and white settlers was also important in producing and maintaining the respective identities of these subjects, especially the latter"; *Imperial Encounters* (Minneapolis: University of Minnesota Press, 1996), 59. The historical traces of these practices are, of course, relevant to the politics between cultures of North and South in Kenyan refugee camps today.

49. Haraway, *Simians, Cyborgs, and Women,* 201.

50. Ibid.; emphasis in original.

5. ORDERING DISORDER

1. Equally, in the realm of discourse, there are no neutral, uncontaminated concepts that organize humanitarian aid. James Clifford's discussion of the cultural bias in travel terms aptly illustrates this point; James Clifford, *Routes: Travel and Translation in the Late Twentieth Century* (London and Cambridge, Mass.: Harvard University Press, 1997), 39.

2. UNHCR, *The State of the World's Refugees: A Humanitarian Agenda* (Oxford: Oxford University Press, 1997), 45.

3. Nicholas Thomas, *Colonialism's Culture: Anthropology, Travel, and Government* (Princeton: Princeton University Press, 1994), 7.

4. Bruce Willems-Braun, "Buried Epistemologies: The Politics of Nature in (Post)colonial British Columbia," *Annals of the Association of American Geographers* 87, no. 1 (1997): 3–31, at 4.

5. Rajeswari Sunder Rajan, *Real and Imagined Women: Gender, Culture and Postcolonialism* (London and New York: Routledge, 1993).

6. Gayatri Chakravorty Spivak, "Can the Subaltern Speak?" in *Marxism and the Interpretation of Culture,* ed. C. Nelson and L. Grossberg (Urbana: University of Illinois Press, 1988).

7. Spivak, "Can the Subaltern Speak?" 306.

8. Liisa Malkki, "Refugees and Exile: From 'Refugee Studies' to the National Order of Things," *Annual Review of Anthropology* 24 (1995): 495–523, at 498.

9. Liisa Malkki, "National Geographic: The Rooting of Peoples and the Territorialization of National Identity among Scholars and Refugees," *Cultural Anthropology* 7, no. 1 (February 1992): 24–43, at 34.

10. Thomas, *Colonialism's Culture,* 41.

11. Arturo Escobar, *Encountering Development: The Making and Unmaking of the Third World* (Princeton: Princeton University Press, 1995), 107.

12. Barbara Harrell-Bond, *Imposing Aid: Emergency Assistance to Refugees* (Oxford, New York, and Nairobi: Oxford University Press, 1986), 11.

13. Patricia Stamp, "Pastoral Power: Foucault and the New Imperial

Order," *Arena,* no. 3 (1994): 20. Academics are by no means ⌐
these processes of transposing the field into text and image. ⌐
analyses and interventions differ.

14. Miller and Rose, cited in Thomas, *Colonialism's Culture,* ⌐

15. UNHCR, *Country Operations Plan: Kenya* (Nairobi, 199⌐

16. Michel Foucault, "Governmentality," in *The Foucault Effect: Studies in Governmentality,* ed. G. Burchell, C. Gordon, and P. Miller (Chicago: University of Chicago Press, 1991), 87–104, at 102–103.

17. Michel Foucault, *Discipline and Punish: The Birth of the Prison* (New York: Vintage Books, 1977).

18. Lynn Stewart, "Let the Cross Take Possession of the Earth: Geographies of Missionary Power in Eighteenth-Century British Columbia," Ph.D. diss., Department of Geography, University of British Columbia, September 1997, 192; emphasis in original.

19. John Law, *Organizing Modernity* (New York and London: Routledge, 1994), 104; emphasis in original.

20. Benedict Anderson, *Imagined Communities: Reflections on the Origin and Spread of Nationalism,* 2d ed. (London and New York: Verso, 1991).

21. Timothy Mitchell, *Colonising Egypt,* paperback ed. (Berkeley and Los Angeles: University of California Press, 1991).

22. Pramoedya Ananta Toer, cited in Anderson, *Imagined Communities,* 184–185. The irony of Toer's depiction of ex-prisoners is that this census process was perfected only *after* independence in Indonesia. Today all adult citizens in that country must carry their number.

23. Aerial photos offered to me by UNHCR's physical planner/regional registration coordinator later became unavailable. They were to be used as a resource tool for a registration workshop in which participants would count the number of huts within a particular area and estimate the refugee population accordingly.

24. Interview, UNHCR senior manager, Nairobi, November 10, 1994.

25. UNHCR, *Registration: A Practical Guide for Field Staff* (Geneva, May 1994).

26. There are parallels between counting practices in refugee camps and those used to calculate welfare recipients in Canada. The aim of administrators in both situations is to prevent "double-dipping," that is, receiving more than one payment.

27. Interview, UNHCR senior manager, Nairobi, November 10, 1994.

28. Interview, UNHCR staff member, Nairobi, December 7, 1994.

29. UNHCR, *Registration: A Practical Guide for Field Staff,* see 4.9 and annex D (2) in particular.

30. Interview, UNHCR staff member, Nairobi, December 7, 1994.

31. The mail pouch from UNHCR in Nairobi travels first to the UN headquarters in New York and then to UNHCR headquarters in Geneva, a process that generally takes two weeks. This seemingly imperial circulation of information respects organizational hierarchy more than efficiency. This arrangement may change with the new UN reforms and their strong emphasis on efficiency.

32. I would like to thank Carol Faubert and Panos Moumztis at the UNHCR branch office in Nairobi, who kindly provided several sitreps to me for the purposes of this analysis.

33. Michael Shapiro, *Violent Cartographies: Mapping Cultures of War* (Minneapolis: University of Minnesota Press, 1997). Shapiro's reference to "grids of intelligibility" comes from Jacques Derrida, who warns of the dangers of controlling and standardizing discourses and practices to a centralized grid of intelligibility (see citation on page 194). My adoption of the term here embraces similar warnings, but the processes of standardization I speak of are less metanarratives than the construction of official narratives of humanitarian activity.

34. Marlee Kline, "Child Welfare Policy, Public/Private Ideology, and the Leaner (and Meaner) Canadian State," in *Challenging the Public/Private Divide: Feminism, Law, and Public Policy,* ed. Susan B. Boyd (Toronto and Buffalo: University of Toronto Press, 1997).

35. Steve Redding, Paul Sitnam, and Graham Wood, *The Refugee Assistance Project of CARE: Kenya, 1991–1993,* CARE International in Kenya (Nairobi, 1994), 3.

36. Ibid., 5.

37. UNHCR, *Country Operations Plan: Kenya.*

38. Mary Hope Schwoebel and Mohamed Hassan Haji, *Report on Community Consultation,* CARE International Refugee Assistance Project (October 1994), 2.

39. Ibid., 50.

40. Ibid., 12; emphasis added.

41. Ibid., 12.

42. Ibid., 44.

43. Ibid., 42–43.

44. Ibid., 43.

45. Iris Marion Young, "The Ideal of Community and the Politics of Difference," in *Feminism/Postmodernism,* ed. Linda Nicholson (New York and London: Routledge, 1990), 300–323, at 318.

46. In a discussion about the viability of Refugee Self-Management, a UNHCR Kenyan Somali staff member told me that the project would not work for cultural reasons. "Somalis are individuals; they do not think communally." He was convinced that it would not work because whatever struc-

tures might be established, Somalis would still only follow the elders of their own clan (conversation, 27 November 1994, Dadaab).

47. Interview, senior UNHCR officer, Dadaab, November 23, 1994.

48. Field officer, UNHCR Sub-Office Dadaab, November 23, 1994.

49. See Gaim Kibreab, "The Myth of Dependency among Camp Refugees in Somalia 1979–1989," *Journal of Refugee Studies* 6, no. 4 (1993): 321–349.

50. UNHCR, *The State of the World's Refugees: In Search of Solutions* (Oxford and New York: Oxford University Press, 1995), 235.

51. Young, "The Ideal of Community and the Politics of Difference."

52. Trinh Minh-ha, "Cotton and Iron," in *Out There: Marginalization and Contemporary Cultures,* ed. R. Ferguson, M. Gever, Trinh T. Minh-ha, and C. West (New York: New Museum of Contemporary Art, 1990), 327–336, at 331.

53. The UNHCR registration guide outlines options for census taking that do not involve coercion but only refugee cooperation. Door-to-door surveys of individual households constitute one suggested strategy; see UNHCR, *Registration: A Practical Guide for Field Staff.*

54. Anthony Giddens, *A Contemporary Critique of Historical Materialism* (London: Macmillan, 1981).

55. John Tomlinson, *Cultural Imperialism* (Baltimore: Johns Hopkins University Press, 1991).

56. For a more sustained critique of contemporary international development discourses, see Escobar, *Encountering Development.*

57. UNHCR, *Country Operations Plan: Kenya,* 15.

58. Interview, UNHCR senior manager, Nairobi, November 8, 1994.

6. CROSSING BORDERS IN THEORY AND PRACTICE

1. Jennifer Hyndman and Bo Viktor Nylund, "UNHCR and the Status of Refugees in Kenya," *International Journal of Refugee Law* 10, no. 1 (1998): 21–48.

2. Roger Winter, "The Year in Review," in *World Refugee Survey, 1993* (Washington, D.C.: American Council for Nationalities Service, 1993), 2–4, at 2.

3. Samuel Makinda, *Seeking Peace from Chaos: Humanitarian Intervention in Somalia* (Boulder, Colo., and London: Lynne Rienner, 1993), 13.

4. Aristide Zolberg and Agnes Callamard, "Displacement-Generating Conflicts and International Assistance in the Horn of Africa," in *Aid in Place of Migration?* ed. W. R. Böhning and M. L. Schroeder-Paredes (Geneva: International Labour Organization, 1994), 107–117.

5. Makinda, *Seeking Peace from Chaos.*

6. "Somali Fighting Escalates," *Globe and Mail* (Vancouver), April 6, 1996. Reuters reported that seventy-five people were dead after two consecutive days of fighting in Mogadishu. See also Mark Dodd, "Mogadishu's Kesaney Hospital: Solace for all Somalis," May 25, 1996, Reuters, who reports that daily casualties are being admitted to the hospital as a result of fighting in south Mogadishu (source: e.news@clarinet). See also, Moyiga Nduru, "Somalia: UN Expresses Concern over Renewed Fighting," IPS, April 1, 1998.

7. U.S. Committee for Refugees, *World Refugee Survey, 1997* (Washington, D.C.: Immigration and Refugee Service of America, 1997).

8. U.S. Committee for Refugees, *World Refugee Survey, 1998* (Washington, D.C.: Immigration and Refugee Service of America, 1998), 93.

9. "Five Killed as Somali Clan War Resumes," *Daily Nation* (Nairobi), January 30, 1995, 8. Also "Clans Clash in Somalia," *Globe and Mail* (Vancouver), May 6, 1995, A9. It should be noted that once the flow of displaced persons across an international border is deemed legitimate by authorized organizations, in this case UNHCR, the path is accessible not only to those fleeing the direct threats and consequences of conflict. This window of opportunity to move is also made available to those looking for stability, jobs, and a better life. In the face of such adverse conditions in Somalia, it is my assumption that many people have taken advantage of this opportunity.

10. U.S. Committee for Refugees, *World Refugee Survey, 1998,* 74. More than 5,000 Somalis entered Kenya in 1997 seeking refugee assistance due to drought in Somalia.

11. Interview with senior UNHCR manager, Nairobi, November 10, 1994.

12. Interview with UNHCR staff, Mombasa, January 17, 1995.

13. Because ethnic Somalis from the Ogadeni clan comprise a large percentage of the Ethiopian population, many Somalis are seeking citizenship there. Since November 1994, 50,000 Somalis have reportedly sought asylum in Ethiopia; UNHCR, *Informal EXCOM* (January 17, 1995).

14. Interview and correspondence, senior staff member, Australian High Commission, Nairobi, January 24, 1995.

15. Conversation, UNHCR staff member at the branch office in Nairobi, January 26, 1995.

16. Interview with UNHCR field staff, January 17, 1995.

17. U.S. Committee for Refugees, *World Refugee Survey, 1998,* 74.

18. Barbara Harlow, "Sites of Struggle: Immigration, Deportation, Prison, and Exile," in *Reconfigured Spheres: Feminist Explorations of Literary Space,* ed. M. R. Higonnet and J. Templeton (Amherst: University of Massachusetts Press, 1994), 108–124, at 113.

19. Interview with International Federation of the Red Cross (IFRC) delegate, Mombasa, January 20, 1995.

20. Interview with UNHCR field staff, Mombasa, January 17, 1995.

21. Interview with IFRC delegate, Mombasa, January 20, 1995.

22. Edward Said, *The World, the Text, and the Critic* (Cambridge, Mass.: Harvard University Press, 1983).

23. Interview with IFRC delegate, Mombasa, January 20, 1995.

24. Trinh T. Minh-ha, "Cotton and Iron," in *Out There: Marginalization and Contemporary Cultures,* ed. R. Ferguson, M. Gever, Trinh T. Minh-ha, and C. West (New York: New Museum of Contemporary Art, 1990), 327–336, at 333.

25. This figure is a general estimate (from an interview with a UNHCR field staff member in Dadaab, February, 5, 1995) among many, all of which are difficult to substantiate empirically. Some refugee advocates argue that those being served who are not refugees need assistance anyway, given recent drought and the relative poverty of the area.

26. Discussion with two Somali refugee leaders at Utange camp, January 18, 1995.

27. Discussion with two UNHCR staff, Nairobi, January 15, 1995.

28. Interview, refugee woman, zone G, Utange camp, January 18, 1995.

29. Interview, IFRC delegate, Mombasa, January 20, 1995.

30. Wenona Giles, "Aid Recipients or Citizens? Canada's Role in Managing the Gender Relations of Forced Migration," in *Development and Diaspora: The Gender Relations of Refugee Experience,* ed. W. Giles, H. Moussa, and P. Van Esterik (Dundas, Ontario: Artemis, 1996), 44–59.

31. James Hathaway, "Reconceiving Refugee Law as Human Rights Protection," *Journal of Refugee Studies* 4, no. 2 (1991): 113–131, at 128.

32. Interview, psychiatrist, February 5, 1995, UNHCR Office, Dadaab, Kenya.

33. Interviews, UNHCR field staff, Mombasa, January 17, 1995.

34. *Standard on Sunday,* November 6, 1994, 13. Emphasis added.

35. Michael Wakabi, "Somali Refugees Say No to Camp Transfer," *East African,* January 16–22, 1995.

36. Benedict Anderson, *Imagined Communities* (New York: Verso, 1991).

37. Rob Wilson and Wimal Dissanayake, "Introduction: Tracking the Global/Local," in *Global/Local: Cultural Production and Transnational Imaginary,* ed. R. Wilson and W. Dissanayake (Durham, N.C.: Duke University Press, 1996), 1–18, at 2.

38. A considerable literature theorizing nomadic identities and other spatial imaginaries can be found in the work of Gilles Deleuze and Félix Guattari, who explore such concepts as deterritorialization, nomadology,

and smooth and striated space. Their cartographies are open-ended; "a map has multiple entryways"; G. Deleuze and F. Guattari, *A Thousand Plateaus: Capitalism and Schizophrenia* (London: Athlone Press, 1987), 12. Geographer Jane M. Jacobs suitably introduces their work: "The geophilosophy of Deleuze and Guattari propels us toward the 'irreducibility of contingency' and launches us forth from a point, long dear to geographers, where 'milieu' always matters. . . . As geographers have long advocated, to speak of the specificity of place is not to propose a conception of territory as a static or bounded thing"; "Speaking Always as Geographers," *Environment and Planning D: Society and Space* 14 (1996): 379–394, at 380. I detour around this important literature in part because others have engaged it so deftly; see especially the articles by Cindi Katz, Brian Massumi, and Marcus Doel in *Environment and Planning D: Society and Space* 14 [1996], which is an issue devoted to debates and discussions of minor theory and other Deleuzian tales) and in part because it detracts from the central arguments of the chapter.

39. Caren Kaplan, *Questions of Travel: Postmodern Discourses of Displacement* (Durham, N.C.: Duke University Press, 1996).

40. Matthew Sparke, *Negotiating Nation-States: North American Geographies of Culture and Capitalism* (Minneapolis: University of Minnesota Press, forthcoming). Sparke's book addresses, in particular, the radical politics of political theorist Chantal Mouffe and questions the assumed venue of identity politics, namely, the state.

41. Homi K. Bhabha, *The Location of Culture* (New York and London: Routledge, 1994), 164; emphasis added.

42. Kaplan, *Questions of Travel*, 105.

43. Seteney Shami, "Transnationalism and Refugee Studies: Rethinking Forced Migration and Identity in the Middle East," *Journal of Refugee Studies* 9, no. 1 (1996): 3–26; Roger Rouse, "Thinking through Transnationalism: Notes on the Cultural Politics of Class Relations in the Contemporary United States," *Public Culture* 7, no. 2 (1995): 353–402.

44. I thank Julie Murphy Erfani for this insight.

45. Néstor García Canclini, *Hybrid Cultures* (Minneapolis: University of Minnesota Press, 1995).

46. Liisa Malkki, "Refugees and Exile: From 'Refugee Studies' to the National Order of Things," *Annual Review of Anthropology* 24 (1995): 495–523; Shami, "Transnationalism and Refugee Studies."

47. Linda Basch, Nina Glick Schiller, and Cristina Szanton Blanc, *Nations Unbound: Transnational Projects, Postcolonial Predicaments, and Deterritorialized Nation-States* (Amsterdam: Gordon and Breach, 1994).

48. Michael Kearney, "The Local and the Global: The Anthropology of

Globalization and Transnationalism," *Annual Review of Anthropology* 24 (1995): 547–565, at 548.

49. Michael Watts, "Mapping Identities: Place, Space, and Community in an African City," in *Geography of Identity*, ed. P. Yaeger (Ann Arbor: University of Michigan Press, 1996), 59–97.

50. Luin Goldring, "Blurring Borders: Constructing Transnational Community in the Process of Mexico-U.S. Migration," *Research in Community Psychology* 6 (1996): 69–104; Basch, Schiller, and Blanc, *Nations Unbound.*

51. Goldring, "Blurring Borders." James Clifford makes a distinction between paradigms of diaspora and of transnational border crossings. He notes that borderlands and the marginal histories of cultures crossing are distinct from analyses of diaspora in that "they presuppose a territory defined by a geo-political line: two sides arbitrarily separated and policed, but also joined by legal and illegal practices of crossing and communication. . . . It is worth holding onto the historical and geographical specificity of the two paradigms, while recognizing that the concrete predicaments denoted by the terms *border* and *diaspora* bleed into one another"; James Clifford, "Diasporas," *Cultural Anthropology* 9, no. 3 (1994): 302–338, at 304.

52. Inderpal Grewal and Caren Kaplan, "Introduction: Transnational Feminist Practices and Questions of Postmodernity," in *Scattered Hegemonies: Postmodernity and Transnational Feminist Practices,* ed. I. Grewal and C. Kaplan (Minneapolis: University of Minnesota Press, 1994), 1–33, at 7.

53. Basch, Schiller, and Blanc, *Nations Unbound.*

54. For example, see Deborah Sontag and Celia W. Dugger, "The New Immigrant Tide: A Shuttle between Worlds," *New York Times,* July 19, 1998, in which the lives of transmigrants are traced.

7. BEYOND THE STATUS QUO

1. John Eriksson, *The International Response to Conflict and Genocide: Lessons from the Rwanda Experience* (Published by the Steering Committee of the Joint Evaluation of Emergency Assistance to Rwanda, March 1996); Sue Lautze and John Hammond, "Coping with Crisis, Coping with Aid: Capacity Building, Coping Mechanisms, and Dependency, Linking Relief and Development" (report prepared for the UN Department of Humanitarian Affairs [DHA], December 1996); Mark Frohardt, "Reintegration and Human Rights in Post-Genocide Rwanda" (report issued by the U.S. Committee for Refugees, November 1997); Joanna Macrae and Mark Bradbury, "Aid in the Twilight Zone: A Critical Analysis of Humanitarian-

Development Aid Linkages in Situations of Chronic Instability" (report for UNICEF, February 10, 1998); and Sue Lautze, Bruce Jones, and Mark Duffield, *Strategic Humanitarian Coordination in the Great Lakes Region, 1996–97: An Independent Study for the Inter-Agency Standing Committee* (New York: Office for the Coordination of Humanitarian Affairs, 1998).

2. In August 1998, the *Financial Times* reported that UNHCR was cutting its post of mediator, held by Anne-Marie Demmer, who acted as ombudsman for the agency. Demmer has published several analyses highly critical of the organization's management. See Andrew Edgecliffe-Johnson, "UN Refugee Agency Scraps Mediator Post," *Financial Times,* August 17, 1998.

3. Médecins sans Frontières/Doctors without Borders, eds. *World in Crisis: The Politics of Survival at the End of the Twentieth Century* (New York and London: Routledge, 1997).

4. I would like to thank Kerry Demusz for her assessment of coordination and professionalization issues in the field. Leanne Macmillan also provided important insights regarding the role of human rights organizations and objective standards of voluntary return in relation to international refugee law.

5. Lautze, Jones, and Duffield, *Strategic Humanitarian Coordination in the Great Lakes Region, 1996–97,* 2.

6. Ibid.

7. Karin Landgren, "Reconciliation: Forgiveness in the Time of Repatriation," in *World Refugee Survey, 1998* (Washington, D.C.: Immigration and Refugee Service of America, 1998), 20–26.

8. James C. Hathaway and R. Alexander Neve, "Toward the Reformulation of International Refugee Law: A Model for Collectivized and Solution-Oriented Protection" (discussion paper prepared by the Refugee Law Research Unit of the Centre for Refugee Studies, York University, Toronto, Canada, September 1996); Susan Martin and Andy Schoenholtz, "Fixing Temporary Protection in the United States," in *World Refugee Survey, 1998* (Washington, D.C.: Immigration and Refugee Service of America, 1998), 40–47.

9. Lautze, Jones, and Duffield, *Strategic Humanitarian Coordination in the Great Lakes Region, 1996–97,* 1–2.

10. In December 1996, the Canadian government responded to this conundrum by introducing the "refugees-from-abroad class" (RAC). This initiative can be applauded for its recognition that not all refugees fall under the convention definition; however, to the extent that there is no increase in government sponsorship for refugees nor a commitment to renewing this provision after one year, the introduction of the RAC signals a reduction of numbers in the convention refugee class. See U.S. Committee for Refugees,

World Refugee Survey, 1997 (Washington, D.C.: Immigration and Refugee Service of America, 1997).

11. Arjun Appadurai, "Sovereignty without Territory: Notes for a Postnational Cartography," in *Geography of Identity,* ed. Patricia Yaeger (Ann Arbor: University of Michigan Press, 1996), 40–58, at 52.

12. Jennifer Hyndman, "International Responses to Human Displacement: Neo-Liberalism and Post–Cold War Geopolitics," *Refuge* 15, no. 3 (June 1996): 5–9.

13. James C. Hathaway, "Introduction to the Law of Refugee Status" (lecture presented at the Centre for Refugee Studies, York University, June 23, 1994).

14. Francis M. Deng, "The International Protection of the Internally Displaced," *International Journal of Refugee Law,* special issue (Summer 1995): 74–86; and UNHCR, *UNHCR's Operational Experience with Internally Displaced Persons* (Geneva, September 1994). See also Roberta Cohen, "International Protection for Internally Displaced Persons: Next Steps" (focus paper no. 2, Refugee Policy Group, Washington, D.C., January 1994); and Bill Frelick, "Aliens in Their Own Land: Protection and Durable Solutions for Internally Displaced Persons," in *World Refugee Survey, 1998* (Washington, D.C.: Immigration and Refugee Service of America, 1998), 30–39.

15. UNHCR, *State of the World's Refugees: In Search of Solutions* (Oxford and New York: Oxford University Press, 1995), 115.

16. UNHCR, *The State of the World's Refugees: The Challenge of Protection* (Toronto: Penguin, 1993), 169.

17. Office of UNHCR, "Issues and Challenges in International Protection in Africa," *International Journal of Refugee Law,* special issue (Summer 1995): 55–73, at 67.

18. Appadurai, "Sovereignty without Territoriality," 56.

19. Lila Abu-Lughod, "Writing against Culture," in *Recapturing Anthropology,* ed. R. G. Fox (Sante Fe, N.M.: School for American Research, 1991), 137–162, at 158.

20. Nira Yuval-Davis, "Identity Politics and Women's Ethnicity," in *Identity Politics and Women: Cultural Reassertions and Feminisms in International Perspective,* ed. V. Moghadam (Boulder, Colo., San Francisco, and Oxford: Westview Press, 1994).

21. Frelick, "Aliens in Their Own Land," 30.

22. Quick impact projects (QIPs) provide a good example of how UNHCR has traversed the so-called relief-to-development continuum. The rehabilitation of social and physical infrastructure and small-scale community projects that attend to the needs of the population have proven useful, if not perfect, strategies of assisting refugees returning to their homes.

23. UNHCR, *UNHCR's Operational Experience with Internally Displaced Persons,* excerpt from the foreword by former director of the Division of International Protection.

24. Caren Kaplan, "The Politics of Location," in *Scattered Hegemonies: Postmodernity and Transnational Feminist Practices,* ed. I. Grewal and C. Kaplan (Minneapolis: University of Minnesota Press, 1994), 137–152, at 139.

25. Senior manager, UNHCR, Geneva, October 18, 1994.

26. Zygmunt Bauman, *Postmodern Ethics* (Oxford and Cambridge, Mass.: Blackwell, 1993), 243; emphasis in original.

27. For an incisive discussion of a postmodern "politics of needs interpretation," see Nancy Fraser, "Women, Welfare, and Politics," in *Unruly Practices* (Minneapolis: University of Minnesota Press, 1989).

28. David Rhode, "Turner Pledges $1 Billion for UN," reprinted from the *New York Times* in *Arizona Republic,* September 19, 1997. See also, Adam Cohen, "Putting His Money . . ." in *Time,* September 29, 1997.

29. See Wenona Giles, "Aid Recipients or Citizens? Canada's Role in Managing the Gender Relations of Forced Migration," in *Development and Diaspora: The Gender Relations of Refugee Experience,* ed. W. Giles, H. Moussa, and P. Van Esterik (Dundas, Ontario: Artemis, 1996); and Alexa Cartwright, "Unmaking Progress: The Impact of Structural Adjustment Programs on Women in Managua, Nicaragua," M.A. thesis, Department of Geography, Simon Fraser University, Vancouver, 1993.

30. M. Hayes, *The New Right in Britain* (London and Boulder, Colo.: Pluto Press, 1994). Hayes maintains that neoliberalism and neoconservatism are identifiably separate trends, representing "two analytically distinct social images, contained within a unified but flexible ideological canopy," namely, the New Right (31).

31. UNHCR, *State of the World's Refugees: In Search of Solutions.*

32. Daniel Warner and James Hathaway, "Refugee Law and Human Rights: Warner and Hathaway in Debate," *Journal of Refugee Studies* 5, no. 2 (1992): 162–171; Hathaway and Neve, "Toward the Reformulation of International Refugee Law."

33. In 1995, UNHCR counted more than 3.5 million persons of concern, excluding those assisted as returnees, refugees, and IDPs. See UNHCR, *State of the World's Refugees: In Search of Solutions,* 247.

34. U.S. Committee for Refugees, *World Refugee Survey, 1995* (Washington, D.C.: Immigration and Refugee Service of America, 1995). There are no persons of concern determination offices outside Bangkok. The four to six weeks that most Burmese applicants have to wait to get an interview with UNHCR creates financial hardship for many would-be refugees, who

have already financed their own travel and subsistence from the border to the capital (personal correspondence, Burmese-Canadian immigrant in Vancouver, July 30, 1997).

35. Donna Haraway, "Cyborgs and Symbionts: Living Together in the New World Order," foreword to *The Cyborg Handbook,* ed. Chris Hables Gray (New York and London: Routledge, 1995), xi–xx, at xix.

Bibliography

Abegg, E. "Swiss Banks Offer to Settle Claims," *Arizona Republic,* June 20, 1998.

Abu-Lughod, L. "Writing against Culture." In *Recapturing Anthropology,* edited by R. G. Fox, 137–162. Sante Fe, N.M.: School for American Research, 1991.

Achebe, C. *Things Fall Apart.* New York: Astor-Honor, 1959.

Africa Events. London, September 1992. Source: UNHCR REFINFO database, Center for Documentation of Refugees, Geneva.

Africa Watch. New York, November 17, 1989. Source: UNHCR REFINFO database, Center for Documentation of Refugees, Geneva.

African Rights. "Humanitarianism Unbound? Current Dilemmas Facing Multi-Mandate Relief Operations in Political Emergencies." Discussion paper no. 5. London, 1993.

Alarcón, N. "Traddutora, Traditora: A Paradigmatic Figure of Chicana Feminism." In *Scattered Hegemonies,* edited by I. Grewal and C. Kaplan, 110–133. Minneapolis: University of Minnesota Press, 1994.

Allan, V., M. Galey, and M. Persinger. "World Conference of International Women's Year." In *Women, Politics, and the United Nations,* edited by A. Winslow, 29–44. Westport, Conn., and London: Greenwood Press, 1995.

Anderson, B. *Imagined Communities: Reflections on the Origin and Spread of Nationalism,* 2d ed. London and New York: Verso, 1991.

Anderson, M. B., A. M. Brazeau, and C. Overholt. *A Framework for People-Oriented Planning in Refugee Situations Taking Account of Women,*

Men, and Children: A Practical Planning Tool for Refugee Workers. Geneva, UNHCR, December 1992.

Anyang' Nyongó, P., and J. Abonyo Nyang'aya. "Comprehensive Solutions to Refugee Problems in Africa." *International Journal of Refugee Law,* special issue (Summer 1995): 164–171.

Anzaldúa, G. *Borderlands: The New Mestiza.* San Francisco: Spinsters/Aunt Lute Press, 1987.

Appadurai, A. "Sovereignty without Territoriality: Notes for a Postnational Geography." In *Geography of Identity,* edited by P. Yaeger, 40–58. Ann Arbor: University of Michigan Press, 1996.

————. "Global Ethnoscapes." In *Recapturing Anthropology,* edited by R. G. Fox, 191–211. Sante Fe, N.M.: School for American Research, 1991.

Arendt, H. *The Origins of Totalitarianism.* Cleveland and New York: Meridian, 1958.

Ashcroft, B., G. Griffiths, and H. Tiffin, eds. *The Post-Colonial Studies Reader.* London and New York: Routledge, 1995.

Associated Press. November 13, 1989. Source: UNHCR REFINFO database, Center for Documentation of Refugees, Geneva.

Atwood, M. *The Handmaid's Tale.* Toronto: Seal Books, 1985.

Bammer, A. "Introduction." In *Displacements: Cultural Identities in Question,* edited by A. Bammer, xi–xx. Bloomington and Indianapolis: Indiana University Press, 1994.

Barlow, T. "Theorizing Woman: *Funü, Guojia, Jiating* (Chinese Women, Chinese State, Chinese Family)." In *Scattered Hegemonies: Postmodernity and Transnational Feminist Practices,* edited by I. Grewal and C. Kaplan, 173–196. Minneapolis: University of Minnesota Press, 1994.

Barthes, R. *Mythologies.* London: Paladin, 1973.

Basch, L., N. Glick Schiller, and C. Szanton Blanc. *Nations Unbound: Transnational Projects, Postcolonial Predicaments, and Deterritorialized Nation-States.* Langhorne, Pa.: Gordon and Breach, 1994.

Bauman, Z. *Postmodern Ethics.* Oxford and Cambridge, Mass.: Blackwell, 1993.

Bell, C., and H. Newby. "Community, Communion, Class, and Community Action: The Social Sources of the New Urban Politics." In *Social Areas in Cities: Processes, Patterns, and Problems,* edited by D. T. Herbert and R. J. Johnston, 283–302. Chichester, England: John Wiley, 1978.

Bhabha, H. *The Location of Culture.* London and New York: Routledge, 1994.

Black, R. "Geography and Refugees: Current Issues." In *Geography and Refugees: Patterns and Processes of Change,* edited by R. Black and V. Robinson, 3–13. London and New York: Belhaven Press, 1993.

Black, R., and V. Robinson, eds. *Geography and Refugees: Patterns and Processes of Change.* London and New York: Belhaven Press, 1993.

Blomley, N., and J. C. Bakan. "Spacing Out: Towards a Critical Geography of Law." *The Osgoode Hall Law Journal* 30, no. 3 (1992): 661–690.

Bondi, L., and M. Domosh. "Other Figures in Other Places: On Feminism, Postmodernism, and Geography." In *Environment and Planning D: Society and Space* 10, no. 2 (1992): 199–213.

Butler, J. P. *Bodies That Matter: On the Discursive Limits of "Sex."* New York: Routledge, 1993.

Canadian Council for Refugees. *Resolutions.* Montreal, June 1, 1996.

Canclini, N. G. *Hybrid Cultures: Strategies for Entering and Leaving Modernity.* Minneapolis: University of Minnesota Press, 1995.

Caputo, J., and M. Yount. "Institutions, Normalization, Power." In *Foucault and the Critique of Institutions,* edited by J. Caputo and M. Yount, 3–23. University Park: Pennsylvania State University, 1993.

Chimni, B. S. "The Meaning of Words and the Role of UNHCR in Voluntary Repatriation." *International Journal of Refugee Law* 5, no. 3 (1993): 442–459.

CIDA. *Mission Report on UNHCR Project WVV in Kenya.* International Humanitarian Assistance Division, August 28–September 5, 1994.

"Clans Clash in Somalia," *Globe and Mail* (Vancouver). May 6, 1995.

Clifford, J. "Diasporas." *Cultural Anthropology* 9, no. 3 (1994): 302–338.

———. "Travelling Cultures." In *Cultural Studies,* edited by L. Grossberg, C. Nelson, and P. Treichler, 96–116. New York: Routledge, 1992.

———. *The Predicament of Culture.* Cambridge, Mass.: Harvard University Press, 1988.

———. "Partial Truths." In *Writing Culture: The Poetics and Politics of Ethnography,* edited by J. Clifford and G. E. Marcus, 1–26. Berkeley and Los Angeles: University of California Press, 1986.

Cockburn, C. *The Space between Us: Negotiating Gender and National Identities in Conflict.* London: Zed Books, 1998.

———. "Research on Women in Conflict Zones: Questions of Method." Paper presented at the Women in Conflict Zones Network Meeting, Toronto, November 16, 1996.

Cohen, A. "Putting His Money . . ." *Time,* September 29, 1997.

Cohen, R. "International Protection for Internally Displaced Persons—Next Steps." Focus paper no. 2, Refugee Policy Group, Washington, D.C., January 1994.

Corbridge, S., R. Martin, and N. Thrift, eds. *Money, Power, Space.* Oxford and Cambridge: Blackwell, 1994.

Corbridge, S., and N. Thrift. "Money, Power, and Space: Introduction and

Overview." In *Money, Power, Space,* edited by S. Corbridge, R. Martin, and N. Thrift, 1–26. Oxford and Cambridge, Mass.: Blackwell, 1994.

Cowen, R., and S. Odundo Nyangoma. *Refugee Survey Analysis.* CARE Kenya Refugee Assistance Programme. Nairobi, July 1994.

Crosby, A., W. Giles, and M. Korac. "Women in Conflict Zones Network." Discussion paper no. 1, draft, York University, June 18, 1996.

Crush, J., ed. *Power of Development.* New York and London: Routledge, 1995.

Crush, J., and W. James. *Crossing Boundaries: Mine Migrancy in a Democratic South Africa.* Cape Town: Institute for Democracy in South Africa, and Ottawa: International Development Research Centre, 1995.

Daley, P. "From Kipande to Kibali: The Incorporation of Refugees and Labour Migrants in Western Tanzania, 1900–1987." In *Geography and Refugees: Patterns and Processes of Change,* edited by R. Black and V. Robinson, 17–32. London: Belhaven Press, 1993.

Davis, M. "Fortress Los Angeles: The Militarization of Urban Space." In *Variations on a Theme Park: The New American City and the End of Public Space,* edited by M. Sorkin, 154–180. New York: Noonday Press, 1992.

de Lauretis, T. "Eccentric Subjects: Feminist Theory and Historical Consciousness." *Feminist Studies* 16, no. 1 (1990): 115–150.

Deleuze, G., and F. Guattari. *A Thousand Plateaus: Capitalism and Schizophrenia.* London: Athlone Press, 1987.

Demick, Barbara. "Thousands of Refugees Evacuate Srebrenica after Bosnian Serbs Invade." *Philadelphia Inquirer,* July 11, 1995.

Deng, F. M. "The International Protection of the Internally Displaced." *International Journal of Refugee Law,* special issue (Summer 1995): 74–86.

Dhareshwar, V. "The Predicament of Theory." In *Theory between the Disciplines: Authority, Vision, Politics,* edited by M. Kreiswirth and M. A. Cheetham, 231–251. Ann Arbor: University of Michigan Press, 1990.

Dirlik, A. "The Postcolonial Aura: Third World Criticism in the Age of Global Capitalism." *Critical Inquiry* 20 (Winter 1994): 328–356.

Dodd, M. "Mogadishu's Kesaney hospital: Solace for All Somalis," May 25, 1996, Reuters. Source: e.news@clarinet.

Driver, F. "Discipline without Frontiers? Representations of the Mettray Reformatory Colony in Britain, 1840–1880." *Journal of Historical Sociology* 3, no. 3 (September 1990): 272–293.

Drumtra, J. "Life after Death: Suspicion and Reintegration in Post-Genocide Rwanda." In *World Refugee Survey, 1998,* 27–29. Washington, D.C.: Immigration and Refugee Service of America, 1998.

Dyck, I. "Space, Time, and Renegotiating Motherhood: An Exploration of the Domestic Workplace." *Environment and Planning D: Society and Space* 8, no. 4 (1990): 459–484.

Eriksson, J. *The International Response to Conflict and Genocide: Lessons from the Rwanda Experience.* Published by the Steering Committee of the Joint Evaluation of Emergency Assistance to Rwanda, March 1996.

Escobar, A. *Encountering Development: The Making and Unmaking of the Third World.* Princeton: Princeton University Press, 1995.

Findlay, A. "End of the Cold War: End of Afghan Relief Aid?" In *Geography and Refugees: Patterns and Processes of Change,* edited by R. Black and V. Robinson, 185–197. London and New York: Belhaven Press, 1993.

"Five Killed as Somali Clan War Resumes." *Daily Nation* (Nairobi), January 30, 1995.

Foucault, M. "Governmentality." In *The Foucault Effect: Studies in Governmentality,* edited by G. Burchell, C. Gordon, and P. Miller, 87–104. Chicago: University of Chicago Press, 1991.

———. *Power/Knowledge: Selected Interviews and Other Writings, 1972–1977.* Edited by Colin Gordon. New York: Pantheon, 1980.

———. "Social Security." In *Politics, Philosophy, Culture: Interviews and Other Writings, 1977–1984,* edited by L. D. Kritzman, trans. Alan Sheridan, 159–177. New York: Routledge, 1988.

———. *Discipline and Punish: The Birth of the Prison.* New York: Vintage Books, 1977.

———. *The Order of Things: An Archaeology of the Human Sciences.* New York: Vintage, 1970.

Fraser, N. *Justice Interruptus: Critical Reflections on the "Postsocialist" Condition.* New York : Routlege, 1997.

———. "Women, Welfare, and Politics." In *Unruly Practices.* Minneapolis: University of Minnesota Press, 1989.

Frelick, B. "Aliens in Their Own Land: Protection and Durable Solutions for Internally Displaced Persons." In *World Refugee Survey, 1998,* 30–39. Washington, D.C.: Immigration and Refugee Service of America, 1998.

———. "Preventing Refugee Flows: Protection or Peril." In *World Refugee Survey, 1993.* (Washington, D.C.: American Council for Nationalities Service, 1993).

———. "Call Them What They Are: Refugees." In *World Refugee Survey, 1992.* Washington, D.C.: American Council for Nationalities Service, 1992.

Frohardt, M. "Reintegration and Human Rights in Post-Genocide Rwanda." Report issued by the U.S. Committee for Refugees, November 1997.

Galey, M. "Women Find a Place." In *Women, Politics, and the United*

Nations, edited by A. Winslow, 11–27. Westport, Conn., and London: Greenwood Press, 1995.

Gersony, R. "Why Somalis Flee: A Synthesis of Conflict Experience in Northern Somalia by Somali Refugees, Displaced Persons, and Others." *International Journal of Refugee Law* 2, no. 1 (1990): 4–55.

"Get Out, Maybe." *Economist.* Reprinted in *Globe and Mail* (Vancouver), February 20, 1996.

Giddens, A. *A Contemporary Critique of Historical Materialism.* London: Macmillan, 1981.

Giles, W. "Aid Recipients or Citizens? Canada's Role in Managing the Gender Relations of Forced Migration." In *Development and Diaspora: The Gender Relations of Refugee Experience,* edited by W. Giles, H. Moussa, and P. Van Esterik, 44–59. Dundas, Ontario: Artemis, 1996.

Goldring, L. "Blurring Borders: Constructing Transnational Community in the Process of Mexico-U.S. Migration." *Research in Community Psychology* 6 (1996): 69–104.

———. "The Power of Status in Transnational Social Fields." *Comparative Urban and Community Research* 6 (1996): 165–195.

Goodwin-Gill, G. S. "United Nations Reform and the Future of Refugee Protection." Commentary on the UN "Reflections" paper, posted on forced migration listserve, June 4, 1997.

———. "The Language of Protection." *International Journal of Refugee Law* 1, no. 1 (1989): 6–19.

Gourevitch, P. "The Genocide Fax." *The New Yorker,* May 11, 1998, 42–46.

Gregory, D. *Geographical Imaginations.* Oxford: Blackwell, 1994.

———. "Humanistic Geography." In *The Dictionary of Human Geography,* 3rd ed., edited by R. J. Johnston, D. Gregory, and D. M. Smith, 263–266. Oxford: Blackwell, 1994.

Grewal, I. "Autobiographical Subjects, Diasporic Locations." In *Scattered Hegemonies: Postmodernity and Transnational Feminist Practices,* edited by I. Grewal and C. Kaplan, 231–254. Minneapolis: University of Minnesota Press, 1994.

Grewal, I., and C. Kaplan. "Introduction: Transnational Feminist Practices and Questions of Postmodernity." In *Scattered Hegemonies: Postmodernity and Transnational Feminist Practices,* edited by I. Grewal and C. Kaplan, 1–33. Minneapolis: University of Minnesota Press, 1994.

Gupta, A., and J. Ferguson. "Beyond 'Culture': Space, Identity, and the Politics of Difference." *Cultural Anthropology* 7, no. 1 (February 1992): 6–23.

Hanson, S., and G. Pratt. *Gender, Work, and Space.* New York and London: Routledge, 1995.

Haraway, D. "Cyborgs and Symbionts: Living Together in the New World Order." Foreword to *The Cyborg Handbook,* edited by Chris Hables Gray, xi–xx. New York and London: Routledge, 1995.

———. "The Bio-Politics of a Multicultural Field." In *The Racial Economy of Science,* edited by S. Harding, 377–397. Bloomington and Indianapolis: Indiana University Press, 1993.

———. "The Promises of Monsters: A Regenerative Politics for Inappropriate/d Others." In *Cultural Studies,* edited by L. Grossberg, C. Nelson, and P. Treichler, 295–337. New York: Routledge, 1992.

———. "Situated Knowledges." In *Simians, Cyborgs, and Women: The Reinvention of Nature,* 183–201. New York and London: Routledge, 1991.

———. "Remodeling the Human Way of Life." In *Primate Visions,* 186–206. New York and London: Routledge, 1989.

———. "Women's Place Is in the Jungle." In *Primate Visions,* 279–303. New York and London: Routledge, 1989.

Harlow, B. "Sites of Struggle: Immigration, Deportation, Prison, and Exile." In *Reconfigured Spheres: Feminist Explorations of Literary Space,* edited by M. R. Higonnet and J. Templeton, 108–124. Amherst: University of Massachussets Press, 1994.

Harrell-Bond, B. *Imposing Aid: Emergency Assistance to Refugees.* Oxford, New York, and Nairobi: Oxford University Press, 1986.

Harvey, D. "From Space to Place and Back Again: Reflections on the Condition of Postmodernity." In *Mapping the Futures: Local Cultures, Global Change,* edited by J. Bird, B. Curtis, T. Putnam, G. Robertson, and L. Tickner, 3–29. New York and London: Routledge, 1993.

Hathaway, J. C. "Deflecting Refugees from Canada." *Globe and Mail* (Vancouver), December 5, 1995.

———. "Introduction to the Law of Refugee Status." Lecture presented at the Centre for Refugee Studies, York University, June 23, 1994.

———. "Reconceiving Refugee Law as Human Rights Protection." *Journal of Refugee Studies* 4, no. 2 (1991): 113–131.

———. *The Status of Refugee Law.* Markham and Vancouver: Butterworths, 1991.

Hayes, M. *The New Right in Britain.* London and Boulder: Pluto Press, 1994.

Hiebert, D. "Canadian Immigration: Policy, Politics, Geography." In *Canadian Geographer* 38, no. 3 (1994): 254–258.

Hirshman, M. "Women and Development: A Critique." In *Feminism/Postmodernism/Development,* edited by M. Marchand and J. Parpart, 42–55. New York and London: Routledge, 1995.

Holborn, L. *Refugees: A Problem of Our Time. The Work of UNHCR 1951–72.* 2 vols. Metuchen, N.J.: Scarecrow Press, 1975.

hooks, b. "Representing Whiteness in the Black Imagination." In *Cultural Studies*, edited by L. Grossberg, C. Nelson, and P. Treichler, 338–346. New York and London: Routledge, 1992.

———. "Marginality as Site of Resistance." In *Out There: Marginalization and Contemporary Cultures*, edited by R. Ferguson, M. Gever, Trinh T. Minh-ha, and C. West, 341–343. New York: New Museum of Contemporary Art, 1990.

———. "Talking Back." In *Out There: Marginalization and Contemporary Cultures*, edited by R. Ferguson, M. Gever, Trinh T. Minh-ha, and C. West, 337–340. New York: New Museum of Contemporary Art, 1990.

Hope Schwoebel, M., and Mohamed Hassan Haji. *Report on Community Consultation*. CARE International Refugee Assistance Project. October 1994.

Hyndman, J. "Border Crossings." *Antipode* 29, no. 2 (1997): 149–176.

———. "Refugee Self-Management and the Question of Governance." *Refuge* 16, no. 2 (June 1997): 149–176.

———. "International Responses to Human Displacement: Neo-Liberalism and Post–Cold War Geopolitics." *Refuge* 15, no. 3 (June 1996): 5–9.

Hyndman, J., and B. V. Nylund. "UNHCR and the Status of Refugees in Kenya." *International Journal of Refugee Law* 10, no. 1 (1998): 21–48.

Ignatieff, M. "Alone with the Secretary-General." *The New Yorker*, August 14, 1995.

———. *Blood and Belonging: Journeys into the New Nationalism*. New York: Farrar, Straus, and Giroux, 1993.

———. *The Needs of Strangers*. New York and London: Penguin, 1984.

Indra, D. "Ethnic Human Rights and Feminist Theory: Gender Implications for Refugee Studies and Practice." *Journal for Refugee Studies* 2, no. 2 (1989): 221–241.

IRBD (Immigration and Refugee Board Documentation Centre). Response to information request no. KEN 3679. Ottawa, February 1, 1990.

Jackson, P. J. *Dictionary of Human Geography,* 3rd ed. Edited by R. J. Johnston, D. Gregory, and David M. Smith. Oxford and Cambridge, Mass.: Blackwell, 1994.

Jacobs, J. M. "Speaking Always as Geographers." *Environment and Planning D: Society and Space* 14, no. 4 (1996): 379–383.

Kaplan, C. *Questions of Travel: Postmodern Discourses of Displacement*. Durham, N.C.: Duke University Press, 1996.

———. "'A World without Boundaries': The Body Shop's Trans/national Geographics." *Social Text* 43 (Fall 1995): 45–66.

———. "The Politics of Location." In *Scattered Hegemonies: Postmodernity and Transnational Feminist Practices*, edited by I. Grewal and C. Kaplan, 137–152. Minneapolis: University of Minnesota Press, 1994.

Katz, C. "Playing the Field: Questions of Fieldwork in Geography." *Professional Geographer* 46, no. 1 (February 1994): 67–72.

Kearney, M. "The Local and the Global: The Anthropology of Globalization and Transnationalism." *Annual Review of Anthropology* 24 (1995): 547–565.

Kibreab, G. "The Myth of Dependency among Camp Refugees in Somalia, 1979–1989." *Journal of Refugee Studies* 6, no. 4 (1993): 321–349.

Kline, M. "Blue Meanies in Alberta: Tory Tactics and the Privatization of Child Welfare." In *Challenging the Public/Private Divide: Feminism, Law, and Public Policy,* edited by Susan B. Boyd, 330–359. Toronto and Buffalo: University of Toronto Press, 1997.

Koptiuch, K. "'Cultural Defense' and Criminological Displacements: Gender, Race, and (Trans)Nation in the Legal Surveillance of U.S. Diaspora Asians." In *Displacement, Diaspora, and Geographies of Identity,* edited by S. Lavie and T. Swedenburg, 215–233. Durham, N.C.: Duke University Press, 1996.

Koring, P. "Price of Peacekeeping Dwarfs Aid." *Globe and Mail* (Vancouver), January 4, 1994.

Kuhlman, T. *Asylum or Aid? The Economic Integration of Ethiopian and Eritrean Refugees in the Sudan.* Aldershot, England: Avebury Publications, 1994.

———. *Burden or Boom? Eritrean Refugees in the Sudan.* London: Zed Books, 1990.

Landgren, K. "Reconciliation: Forgiveness in the Time of Repatriation." *World Refugee Survey, 1998,* 20–26. Washington, D.C.: Immigration and Refugee Service of America, 1998.

Lautze, S., and J. Hammond. "Coping with Crisis, Coping with Aid: Capacity Building, Coping Mechanisms, and Dependency, Linking Relief and Development." Report prepared for the UN Department of Humanitarian Affairs (DHA), December 1996.

Lautze, S., B. Jones, and M.Duffield. *Strategic Humanitarian Coordination in the Great Lakes Region, 1996–97: An Independent Study for the Inter-Agency Standing Committee.* New York: Office for the Coordination of Humanitarian Affairs, 1998.

Law, J. *Organizing Modernity.* Oxford: Blackwell, 1994.

Lawyers Committee for Human Rights. *The UNHCR at Forty: Refugee Protection at the Crossroads.* New York: Lawyers Committee for Human Rights, 1991.

Loescher, G. *Beyond Charity: International Cooperation and the Global Refugee Crisis.* New York: Oxford University Press, 1993.

Long, N. "From Paradigm Lost to Paradigm Regained? The Case for Actor-Oriented Sociology of Development." In *Battlefields of Knowledge: The*

Interlocking of Theory and Practice in Social Research and Development, edited by N. Long and A. Long, 16–43. London and New York: Routledge, 1992.

Mackenzie, S. "Restructuring the Relations of Work and Life: Women as Environmental Actors, Feminism as Geographical Analysis." In *Remaking Human Geography,* edited by A. Kobayashi and S. Mackenzie, 40–61. London: Unwin Hyman, 1989.

Macrae, J., and M. Bradbury. "Aid in the Twilight Zone: A Critical Analysis of Humanitarian-Development Aid Linkages in Situations of Chronic Instability." Report for UNICEF, February 10, 1998.

Makinda, S. M. *Seeking Peace from Chaos: Humanitarian Intervention in Somalia.* Boulder, Colo., and London: Lynne Rienner, 1993.

———. "Kenya's Role in the Somali-Ethiopian Conflict." Working paper no. 55, Australia National University, Strategic and Defence Studies Centre, 1982.

Malkki, L. H. "Refugees and Exile: From 'Refugee Studies' to the National Order of Things." *Annual Review of Anthropology* 24 (1995): 495–523.

———. "National Geographic: The Rooting of Peoples and the Territorialization of National Identity among Scholars and Refugees." *Cultural Anthropology* 7, no. 1 (February 1992): 24–43.

Mani, L. "Cultural Theory, Colonial Texts: Reading Eyewitness Accounts of Widow Burning." In *Cultural Studies,* edited by L. Grossberg, C. Nelson, and P. Treichler, 392–408. New York and London: Routledge, 1992.

Marchand, M. H., and J. L. Parpart. "Expolding the Canon: An Introduction/Conclusion." In *Feminism/Postmodernism/Development,* edited by M. H. Marchand and J. L. Parpart, 1–22. New York and London: Routledge, 1995.

Martin, S., and A. Schoenholtz. "Fixing Temporary Protection in the United States." In *World Refugee Survey, 1998,* 40–47. Washington, D.C.: Immigration and Refugee Service of America, 1998.

Massey, D. "Power-Geometry and a Progressive Sense of Place." In *Mapping the Futures: Local Cultures, Global Change,* edited by J. Bird, B. Curtis, T. Putnam, G. Robertson, and L. Tickner, 59–69. New York: Routledge, 1993.

———. "A Global Sense of Place." *Marxism Today,* June 1991: 24–29.

McDowell, L. "Multiple Voices: Speaking from Inside and Outside the Project." *Antipode* 24, no. 1 (1992): 218–237.

Mitchell, K. "Transnational Discourse: Bringing the Geography Back In." *Antipode* 29, no. 2 (1997): 101–114.

———. "Different Diasporas and the Hype of Hybridity." *Environment and Planning D: Society and Space* 15, no. 5 (1997): 533–554.

———. "Multiculturalism, or the United Colors of Capitalism?" *Antipode* 25, no. 4 (1993): 263–294.

Mitchell, T. *Colonising Egypt,* paperback ed. Berkeley and Los Angeles: University of California Press, 1991.

Mohanty, C. T. "Under Western Eyes." In *Third World Women and the Politics of Feminism,* edited by Chandra Talpade Mohanty, Ann Russo, and Lourdes Torres. Bloomington and Indianapolis: University of Indiana Press, 1991.

Moore, H. L. *A Passion for Difference.* Bloomington and Indianapolis: Indiana University Press, 1994.

Moss Kanter, R. *The Change Masters.* New York: Simon and Schuster, 1983.

Mouffe, C. "Post-Marxism: Democracy and Identity." *Environment and Planning D: Society and Space* 13 (1995): 259–265.

———. "For a Politics of Nomadic Identity." In *Travellers' Tales: Narratives of Home and Displacement,* edited by G. Robertson, M. Mash, L. Tickner, J. Bird, B. Curtis, and T. Putnam, 105–113. New York and London: Routledge, 1994.

———. "Feminism, Citizenship, and Radical Democratic Politics." In *Feminists Theorize the Political,* edited by J. Butler and J. Scott, 369–384. New York and London: Routledge, 1992.

Moussa, H. *Storm and Sanctuary: The Journey of Ethiopian and Eritrean Refugee Women.* Dundas, Ontario: Artemis, 1993.

Murphy Erfani, Julie. "Globalizing Tenochtitlán? Feminist Geopolitics: Mexico City as Borderland." In *The U.S.-Mexico Border: Transcending Divisions, Contesting Identities,* ed. David Spener and Kathy Standt, 143–168. Boulder, Colo.: Lynne Rienner, 1998.

Nduru, M. "Somalia: UN Expresses Concern over Renewed Fighting." IPS. April 1, 1998.

Netherlands Development Corporation. *Humanitarian Aid to Somalia, Evaluation Report 1994.* The Hague, 1994.

Niranjana, T. *Siting Translation: History, Post-Structuralism, and the Colonial Context.* Berkeley and Los Angeles: University of California Press, 1992.

Nixon, R. "Refugees and Homecomings: Bessie Head and the End of Exile." In *Travellers' Tales: Narratives of Home and Displacement,* edited by G. Robertson, M. Mash, L. Tickner, J. Bird, B. Curtis, and T. Putnam, 114–128. New York and London: Routledge, 1994.

Ó Tuathail, G. *Critical Geopolitics: The Politics of Writing Global Space.* Minneapolis: University of Minnesota Press, 1996.

———. "An Anti-Geo-Political Eye: Maggie O'Kane in Bosnia, 1992–93." *Gender, Place, and Culture* 3, no. 2 (1996): 171–185.

Ogenga, O. "Factors Affecting the Treatment of Kenyan-Somalis and Somali Refugees in Kenya: A Historical Overview." *Refuge* 12, no. 5 (December, 1992): 21–25.

Parpart, J. "Post-Modernism, Gender, and Development." In *Power of Development,* edited by J. Crush, 253–265. London and New York: Routledge, 1995.

Pettman, J. J. *Worlding Women: A Feminist International Politics.* London and New York: Routledge, 1996.

Philo, C. "Foucault's Geography." *Environment and Planning D: Society and Space* 10, no. 2 (1992): 137–161.

Pietilä, H., and J. Vickers. *Making Women Matter: The Role of the United Nations.* London: Zed Books, 1996.

Pratt, G. "Travelling Metaphors in Feminist Theory." Manuscript, University of British Columbia, September 1993.

———. "Debates and Reports: Reflections on Poststructuralism and Feminist Empirics, Theory, and Practice." *Antipode* 25, no. 1 (1993): 51–63.

———. "Commentary." *Environment and Planning D: Society and Space* 10, no. 3 (1992): 241–244.

Pratt, G., and S. Hanson. "Women and Work across the Life Course: Moving beyond Essentialism." In *Full Circles: Geographies of Women over the Life Course,* edited by C. Katz and J. Monk, 27–54. New York and London: Routledge, 1993.

Pratt, M. L. *Imperial Eyes: Travel Writing and Transculturation.* New York and London: Routledge, 1992.

———. "Fieldwork in Common Places." In *Writing Culture: The Poetics and Politics of Ethnography,* edited by J. Clifford and G. E. Marcus, 27–50. Berkeley and Los Angeles: University of California Press, 1986.

Pred, A., and M. Watts. *Reworking Modernity.* New Brunswick, N.J.: Rutgers University Press, 1992.

Rajan, Rajeswari Sunder. *Real and Imagined Women: Gender, Culture and Postcolonialism.* London and New York: Routledge, 1993.

Razack, S. "The Perils of Storytelling for Refugee Women." In *Development and Diaspora: The Gender Relations of Refugee Experience,* edited by W. Giles, H. Moussa, and P. Van Esterik, 271–289. Dundas, Ontario: Artemis, 1996.

Redding, S., P. Sitnam, and G. Wood. *The Refugee Assistance Project of CARE: Kenya, 1991–1993.* CARE International in Kenya. Nairobi, 1994.

Reuters. "Tons of Gold from Nazis Go to Fund for Survivors," *New York Times,* July 1, 1998.

Rhode, D. " Turner Pledges $1 Billion for UN." Reprinted from the *New York Times* in *Arizona Republic,* September 19, 1997.

Rizvi, Z. "The Protection of Refugees." Paper presented to the International Symposium Assistance to Refugees: Alternative Viewpoints, Oxford, 1984.

Rogers, R., and E. Copeland. *Forced Migration: Policy Issues in the Post–Cold War World*. Medford, Mass.: Tufts University Press, 1993.

Rogge, J. "The Challenges of Changing Dimensions among the South's Refugees: Illustrations from Somalia." *International Journal of Refugee Law* 5, no. 1 (1993): 12–30.

———, ed. *Refugees: A Third World Dilemma*. Totowa, N.J.: Rowman and Allanheld, 1987.

———. *Too Many, Too Long: Sudan's Twenty-Year Refugee Dilemma*. Totowa, N.J.: Rowman and Allanheld, 1985.

Rose, G. *Feminism and Geography: The Limits of Geographical Knowledge*. Minneapolis: University of Minnesota Press, 1993.

Rouse, R. "Thinking Through Transnationalism: Notes on the Cultural Politics of Class Relations in the Contemporary United States." *Public Culture* 7, no. 2 (1995): 353–402.

Sahnoun, M. *Somalia: The Missed Opportunities*. Washington, D.C.: U.S. Institute of Peace Press, 1994.

Said, E. *Culture and Imperialism*. New York: Knopf, 1993.

———. "Reflections on Exile." In *Out There: Marginalization and Contemporary Cultures*, edited by R. Ferguson, M. Gever, Trinh T. Minh-ha, and C. West, 357–366. New York: New Museum of Contemporary Art, 1990.

———. *The World, the Text, and the Critic*. Cambridge, Mass.: Harvard University Press, 1983.

———. *Orientalism*. New York: Pantheon, 1978.

Samatar, A. "Structural Adjustment as Development Strategy: Bananas, Boom, and Poverty in Somalia." *Economic Geography* 69, no. 1 (1993): 25–43.

Sanger, D. "Swiss Banks Make Offer on Nazi Loot." *New York Times*, June 20, 1998.

Sarick, L. "Swiss Banks to Assist Holocaust Heirs." *Globe and Mail* (Vancouver), December 30, 1995.

Sassen, S. *Losing Control? Sovereignty in an Age of Globalization*. New York: Columbia University Press, 1996.

Schenkenberg van Mierop, E. "Protection of Civilians in Conflict" In *World in Crisis: The Politics of Survival at the End of the Twentieth Century*, edited by Médecins sans Frontières/Doctors without Borders, 1–15. New York and London: Routledge, 1997.

Scott, D. "Colonial Governmentality." *Social Text* 43 (Fall 1995): 191–220.

Shami, S. "Transnationalism and Refugee Studies: Rethinking Forced

Migration and Identity in the Middle East." *Journal of Refugee Studies* 9, no. 1 (1996): 3–26.

Shapiro, M. *Violent Cartographies: Mapping Cultures of War*. Minneapolis: University of Minnesota Press, 1997.

Shohat, E., and R. Stam. *Unthinking Eurocentrism: Multiculturalism and the Media*. New York and London: Routledge, 1994.

Shrestha, N. "Becoming a Development Category." In *Power of Development*, edited by J. Crush, 266–277. New York and London: Routledge, 1995.

Smelser, W. R. *Refugees: Extended Exile*. Washington, D.C.: Center for Strategic and International Studies, 1987.

Smiley, J. *A Thousand Acres*. New York: Fawcett Columbine, 1991.

Smith, D. E. *Texts, Facts, and Femininity: Exploring the Relations of Ruling*. New York and London: Routledge, 1993.

Smith, G. *The Dictionary of Human Geography*, 3rd ed. Edited by R. J. Johnston, D. Gregory, and D. M. Smith. Oxford: Blackwell, 1994.

Smith, N., and C. Katz. "Grounding Metaphor: Towards a Spatialized Politics." In *Place and Politics of Identity*, edited by M. Keith and S. Pile, 67–83. London and New York: Routledge, 1993.

"Somali Fighting Escalates." *Globe and Mail* (Vancouver). April 6, 1996.

Sontag, S., and C. W. Dugger, "The New Immigrant Tide: A Shuttle between Worlds." *New York Times*, July 19, 1998.

Soper, K. *Humanism and Anti-Humanism*. London: Hutchinson, 1986.

Sparke, M. *Negotiating Nation-States: North American Geographies of Culture and Capitalism*. Minneapolis: University of Minnesota Press, forthcoming.

———. "Writing on Patriarchal Missiles: The Chauvinism of the 'Gulf War' and the Limits of Critique." *Environment and Planning A* 26, no. 7 (1994): 1061–1089.

Spivak, G. C. "Explanation and Culture: Marginalia." In *Out There: Marginalization and Contemporary Cultures*, edited by R. Ferguson, M. Gever, Trinh T. Minh-ha, and C. West, 377–394. New York: New Museum of Contemporary Art, 1990.

———. "Can the Subaltern Speak?" In *Marxism and the Interpretation of Culture*, edited by C. Nelson and L. Grossberg, 271–313. Urbana: University of Illinois Press, 1988.

Stamp, P. "Pastoral Power: Foucault and the New Imperial Order." *Arena*, no. 3 (1994): 11–22.

Standard on Sunday (Nairobi), November 6, 1994.

Stevenson, J. "Hope Restored in Somalia?" *Foriegn Policy*, no. 91 (Summer 1993): 138–154.

Stewart, L. "Let the Cross Take Possession of the Earth: Geographies of

Missionary Power in Eighteenth-Century British Columbia." Ph.D. diss., Department of Geography, University of British Columbia, September 1997.

Strange, S. "From Bretton Woods to the Casino Economy." In *Money, Power, Space,* edited by S. Corbridge, R. Martin, and N. Thrift, 49–62. Oxford and Cambridge: Blackwell, 1994.

Suhrke, A. "Towards a Comprehensive Refugee Policy: Conflict and Refugees in the Post–Cold War World." In *Aid in Place of Migration?* edited by W. R. Böhning and M.-L. Schloeter-Paredes, 13–38. Geneva: International Labour Organization, 1994.

Thomas, N. *Colonialism Culture: Anthropology, Travel, and Government.* Princeton: Princeton University Press, 1994.

Thrift, N. "On the Social and Cultural Determinants of International Financial Centres: The Case of the City of London." In *Money, Power, Space,* edited by S. Corbridge, R. Martin, and N. Thrift, 327–355. Oxford and Cambridge, Mass.: Blackwell, 1994.

Tomlinson, J. *Cultural Imperialism.* Baltimore: Johns Hopkins University Press, 1991.

Trinh T. Minh-ha, "Other Than Myself/My Other Self." In *Travellers' Tales: Narratives of Home and Displacement,* edited by G. Robertson, M. Mash, L. Tickner, J. Bird, B. Curtis, and T. Putnam, 9–26. New York and London: Routledge, 1994.

———. "Cotton and Iron." In *Out There: Marginalization and Contemporary Cultures,* edited by R. Ferguson, M. Gever, Trinh T. Minh-ha, and C. West, 327–336. New York: New Museum of Contemporary Art, 1990.

———. *Woman, Native, Other: Writing Postcoloniality and Feminism.* Bloomington and Indianapolis: Indiana University Press, 1989.

UN General Assembly. *Renewing the United Nations: A Programme for Reform,* A/51/950. July 14, 1997. Submitted by Secretary-General Kofi Annan.

———. UN reform website at <http://www.un.org/reform/>.

———. *United Nations Relief and Rehabilitation Programme for Somalia: Covering the Period 1 March–31 December 1993.* March 11, 1993.

"UN Reform Plan Disappoints US." *Washington Post.* Reprinted in *Vancouver Sun,* July 17, 1997.

UNHCR. *Resettlement Handbook, Update: April 1998.* Division of International Protection. Geneva, April 1998.

———. *The State of the World's Refugees: A Humanitarian Agenda.* Oxford and New York: Oxford University Press, 1997.

———. *Refugee Survey Quarterly,* special issue on refugee women (Summer 1995). Geneva, Centre for Documentation on Refugees.

———. *The State of the World's Refugees: In Search of Solutions.* Oxford and New York: Oxford University Press, 1995.

———. *Informal EXCOM.* January 17, 1995.

———. *Note on International Protection,* EXCOM 45th session, A/AC.96/830. 1994.

———. *Country Operations Plan: Kenya.* Nairobi, October 1994.

———. *UNHCR's Operational Experience with Internally Displaced Persons.* Geneva, September 1994.

———. *Note on Human Resource Management.* EC/1994/SC.2/CRP.20. Geneva, June 7, 1994.

———. *Registration: A Practical Guide for Field Staff.* Geneva, May 1994.

———. *The State of the World's Refugees: The Challenge of Protection.* Toronto: Penguin, 1993.

———. *Note on Certain Aspects of Sexual Violence against Refugee Women.* Executive Committee, A/AC.96/822. October 12, 1993.

———. *Refugee Women Victims of Violence: A Special Project by UNHCR.* Proposal. Nairobi, October 1993.

———. *UNHCR-BO Kenya: Protection, Repatriation, and Resettlement Section.* Workshop document, August 1993.

———. Speech by Sadako Ogata to the Centre for the Study of Global Governance, London School of Economics, May 1993.

———. *Making the Linkages: Protection and Assistance Policy and Programming to Benefit Refugee Women.* Joint Meeting of Sub-Committees of Administration and Financial Matters and of the Whole on International Protection. Document EC/1993/SC.2/crp.16. May 1993.

———. Statement by High Commissioner Sadako Ogata, UNHCR, at the Roundtable on Refugees: Challenge to Solidarity. New York, March 9, 1993. Source: UNHCR REFINFO database, Center for Documentation of Refugees, Geneva.

———. Speech by Sadako Ogata to the New School of Social Research, New York, November 1992. Source: UNHCR REFINFO database, Center for Documentation of Refugees, Geneva.

———. *Report of the UNHCR Working Group on International Protection.* Geneva, July 6, 1992.

———. *Guidelines on the Protection of Refugee Women.* Geneva, July 1991.

———. *UNHCR Policy on Refugee Women.* Geneva, August 1990.

U.S. Committee for Refugees. *World Refugee Survey, 1998.* Washington, D.C.: Immigration and Refugee Service of America, 1998.

———. *World Refugee Survey, 1997.* Washington, D.C.: Immigration and Refugee Service of America, 1997.

———. *World Refugee Survey, 1996.* Washington, D.C.: Immigration and Refugee Service of America, 1996.

————. *World Refugee Survey, 1995.* Washington, D.C.: Immigration and Refugee Service of America, 1995.

————. *World Refugee Survey, 1994.* Washington, D.C.: Immigration and Refugee Service of America, 1994.

————. *World Refugee Survey, 1993.* Washington, D.C.: American Council for Nationalities Service, 1993.

————. *World Refugee Survey, 1992.* Washington, D.C.: American Council for Nationalities Service, 1992.

U.S. Department of State, Department of Justice and Department of Health and Human Services. "Report to the Congress on Proposed Refugee Admissions for Fiscal Year 1996." July 1995.

————. "Report to the Congress on Proposed Refugee Admissions for Fiscal Year 1995." September 1994.

U.S. Department of State, Office of the Inspector General. "Report of Audit: Refugee Admissions Program, 6-CI-008." January 1996.

Visweswaran, K. *Fictions of Feminist Ethnography.* London and New York: Routledge, 1993.

Wakabi, M. "Somali Refugees Say No to Camp Transfer." *East African,* January 16–22, 1995.

Warner, D., and J. Hathaway. "Refugee Law and Human Rights: Warner and Hathaway in Debate." *Journal of Refugee Studies* 5, no. 2 (1992): 162–171.

Washington Post. December 27, 1989. Source: UNHCR REFINFO database, Center for Documentation of Refugees, Geneva.

Watts, M. *Silent Violence: Food, Famine, and Peasantry in Northern Nigeria.* Berkeley and Los Angeles: University of California Press, 1983.

Weiss, T. G., and L. Minear. *Humanitarianism across Borders: Sustaining Civilians in Times of War.* Boulder, Colo., and London: Lynne Rienner, 1993.

Willems-Braun, B. "Buried Epistemologies: The Politics of Nature in (Post)colonial British Columbia." *Annals of the Association of American Geographers* 87, no. 1 (1997): 3–31.

Winslow, A. "Specialized Agencies and the World Bank." In *Women, Politics, and the United Nations,* edited by A. Winslow, 155–175. Westport, Conn., and London: Greenwood Press, 1995.

Winter, R. "A Year in Review." In *World Refugee Survey, 1998,* 14–19. Washington, D.C.: Immigration and Refugee Service of America, 1998.

————. "The Year in Review." In *World Refugee Survey, 1993.* Washington, D.C.: American Council for Nationalities Service, 1993.

Young, I. M. "The Ideal of Community and the Politics of Difference." In *Feminism/Postmodernism,* edited by L. Nicholson, 300–323. New York and London: Routledge, 1990.

Young, R. *White Mythologies: Writing History and the West.* London: Routledge, 1990.

Yount, M. "The Normalizing Powers of Affirmative Action." In *Foucault and the Critique of Institutions,* edited by J. Caputo and M. Yount, 191–229. University Park: Pennsylvania State University, 1993.

Yuval-Davis, N. "Identity Politics and Women's Ethnicity." In *Identity Politics and Women: Cultural Reassertations and Feminisms in International Perspective,* edited by V. Moghadam, 408–424. Boulder, Colo., San Francisco, and Oxford: Westview, 1994.

Zolberg, A. "Migrants and Refugees: A Historical Perspective." *Refugees* 91 (December 1992): 36–39.

Zolberg, A., and A. Callamard. "Displacement-Generating Conflicts and International Assistance in the Horn of Africa." In *Aid in Place of Migration?* edited by W. R. Böhning and M.-L. Schloeter-Paredes, 101–117. Geneva: International Labour Organization, 1994.

Index

JENNIFER HYNDMAN is assistant professor of geography at Arizona State University West. She has worked in humanitarian operations for the United Nations High Commissioner for Refugees and CARE, assisting both refugees and displaced persons in Kenya and Somalia. Her areas of specialization include humanitarian policy and emergency operations, refugee resettlement in North America, and transnational migration. Her current research examines the efficacy and gender dimensions of safe spaces within war zones in Sri Lanka, Bosnia-Herzegovina, and Somalia.